fine Cooking
Make It Tonight

150 Quick & Delicious Weeknight Meals

Editors and Contributors of *Fine Cooking*

The Taunton Press

The Taunton Press
Inspiration for hands-on living®

The Taunton Press, Inc.
63 South Main Street
PO Box 5506, Newtown, CT 06470-5506
e-mail: tp@taunton.com

Editor: Carolyn Mandarano
Copy editor: Nina Rynd Whitnah
Indexer: Heidi Blough
Cover design: Kimberly Adis
Cover photographer: Scott Phillips, © The Taunton Press, Inc.
Cover food stylist: Adrienne Anderson
Interior design: Kimberly Adis
Layout: David Giammattei
Photographers: Scott Phillips, © The Taunton Press, Inc., except for p. 34, 40,
60, 107, 129, 130, and 212 by Maren Caruso, © The Taunton Press, Inc.; p. 30 and
122 © Pernille Pedersen

Fine Cooking® is a trademark of The Taunton Press, Inc., registered in the U.S.
Patent and Trademark Office.

The following names/manufacturers appearing in *Fine Cooking Make it Tonight*
are trademarks: Dos Equis® Amber, Heinz®, Lee Kum Kee®, Lizano®,
McCormick®, Muir Glen®, Old Bay®, Pernod®, Pyrex®, Sambuco®, Tabasco®,
The Spice Hunter®

Library of Congress Cataloging-in-Publication Data

Fine cooking make it tonight : 150 quick & delicious weeknight recipes / editors
and contributors of Fine cooking.
    p. cm.
  Includes index.
  ISBN 978-1-60085-825-3
1. Dinners and dining. I. Taunton's fine cooking.
  TX737.F54 2012
  641.5'4--dc23
                        2012017401

Printed in the United States of America
10 9 8 7 6 5 4 3 2 1

contents

thai-style stir-fried chicken
and basil
(recipe on p. 12)

chicken, turkey & duck

jerk chicken drumsticks

10 thin scallions, white and tender green parts, coarsely chopped

1 Scotch bonnet or habanero chile, seeded and coarsely chopped

2 Tbs. distilled white-wine vinegar

1 Tbs. fresh thyme leaves

3 medium cloves garlic, chopped

1¼ tsp. ground allspice

1 tsp. kosher salt; more as needed

½ tsp. freshly ground black pepper

10 chicken drumsticks (3½ lb.)

Vegetable oil or cooking spray for the pan

Scotch bonnet chiles are authentic, but they're very hot and can be hard to find; the habanero chile is a good substitute. If you want to tame the heat, use less habanero or Scotch bonnet but don't substitute a less spicy variety.

1. In a food processor, pulse the scallions, chiles, vinegar, thyme, garlic, allspice, salt, and pepper to a thick paste.

2. Transfer the paste to a large bowl, add the chicken, and toss to coat. Let stand for 10 minutes.

3. Position an oven rack in the center of the oven and heat the broiler to high. Line the bottom of a broiler pan with foil and replace the perforated top part of the pan. Oil the pan or coat with cooking spray. Arrange the chicken on the broiler pan. Season generously on all sides with salt.

4. Broil the chicken in the center of the oven, turning once after about 10 minutes, until fully cooked and nicely browned in spots, about 20 minutes total. Transfer to a platter and serve.   *—Lori Longbotham*

PER SERVING: 330 CALORIES | 35G PROTEIN | 3G CARB | 18G TOTAL FAT, 5G SAT FAT | 7G MONO FAT | 4G POLY FAT | 125MG CHOL | 200MG SODIUM | 0G FIBER

lime chicken with poblano sour cream

SERVES 4

- 4 large poblano chiles
- 1 large lime
- ½ cup sour cream or Mexican crema
- 2 Tbs. chopped fresh cilantro, plus a few sprigs for garnish (optional)
- 2 tsp. kosher salt; more to taste
- 1 Tbs. ground coriander
- 1 tsp. ground cumin
- ½ tsp. freshly ground black pepper
- 8 medium (5- to 6-oz.) bone-in, skin-on chicken thighs, trimmed
- 3 Tbs. extra-virgin olive oil

Sour cream and lime juice temper the heat of roasted poblano peppers in this southwestern chicken dish. Cooking both the poblanos and the chicken under the broiler makes it super fast.

1. Position an oven rack 5 to 6 inches from the broiler element and heat the broiler to high. Line the bottom of a broiler pan with foil and replace the perforated top part of the pan. Broil the poblanos, turning 3 times, until blackened, 12 to 15 minutes total. Put the poblanos in a medium bowl, top with a dinner plate, and let stand for 5 minutes.

2. Meanwhile, cut the lime in half. Cut one half into wedges and squeeze the other half to get 2 tsp. juice. Measure the juice into a small bowl and stir in the sour cream or crema and the chopped cilantro.

3. Transfer the poblanos to a cutting board to cool a bit, then peel away the burned skin, discard the stems and seeds, and cut into ½-inch dice. Add to the sour cream mixture and stir to combine. Season to taste with salt.

4. In a small bowl, combine the 2 tsp. salt with the coriander, cumin, and pepper. Coat the chicken with the oil and season on both sides with the spice mixture. Put the chicken skin side down on the broiler pan, and broil until well browned, 7 to 10 minutes. Turn the chicken over with tongs and continue to broil, checking frequently, until the chicken is dark brown and cooked through (an instant-read thermometer should register at least 165°F), 4 to 6 minutes more. If the chicken threatens to burn before it's cooked through, move the pan to a lower rack.

5. Transfer the chicken to serving plates, spoon the poblano sour cream on the side, and garnish with cilantro sprigs, if using, and the lime wedges for squeezing over the chicken. Serve hot.
—Lori Longbotham

PER SERVING: 540 CALORIES | 39G PROTEIN | 4G CARB | 39G TOTAL FAT | 11G SAT FAT | 17G MONO FAT | 6G POLY FAT | 160MG CHOL | 700MG SODIUM | 1G FIBER

buttermilk country fried chicken with cucumber salad

- ¼ cup halved and very thinly sliced red onion
- 1 very small clove garlic
  Kosher salt
- 1 Tbs. canola or vegetable oil, plus 1 to 1¼ cups for frying
- ¾ cup plus 2 Tbs. buttermilk
- 1½ tsp. fresh lemon juice
- 1 Tbs. chopped fresh dill
  Freshly ground black pepper
- ½ English cucumber, halved lengthwise, seeded, and thinly sliced crosswise (about 1 heaping cup sliced)
- ¾ cup unbleached all-purpose flour
- 2 boneless, skinless chicken breast halves (about ¾ lb. total), pounded to an even thickness (about ½ inch thick)

Many buttermilk fried chicken recipes call for marinating the chicken overnight, but not this one. Here, a dip in the buttermilk and a dredge in flour is all you need to get the golden, crunchy coating everyone loves. The bright cucumber salad balances out the meal.

1. Put the onion in a small bowl, cover it with very hot water, and let it sit for 15 minutes. Roughly chop the garlic, sprinkle it with a generous pinch of salt, and mash it into a paste with the side of a chef's knife. In a medium bowl, whisk the mashed garlic, 1 Tbs. oil, 2 Tbs. buttermilk, the lemon juice, dill, ¼ tsp. salt, and a few grinds of pepper. Toss the cucumber in the bowl with the dressing. Drain the onion, toss it with the cucumber salad, and let sit to allow the flavors to meld.

2. Put the flour in a shallow bowl and, in another shallow bowl, mix the remaining ¾ cup buttermilk with 1 tsp. salt. Season the chicken with ¾ tsp. salt and ¼ tsp. pepper. Dip the chicken in the buttermilk and then dredge it in the flour. (You can let the chicken sit in the flour while the oil heats; gently shake off excess flour before cooking.)

3. Choose a skillet (preferably cast iron) that's large enough to fit the chicken. Pour in oil to a depth of ¼ inch (about 1 cup for a 10-inch skillet or 1¼ cups for an 11-inch skillet). Heat over medium-high heat. When the oil is shimmering and the chicken sizzles briskly when a corner is dipped in the oil, cook the chicken until golden brown on both sides, 2 to 3 minutes per side. Transfer the chicken to paper towels and pat lightly to absorb excess oil. Sprinkle the chicken with a pinch of salt and serve it with the cucumber salad. —*Allison Ehri Kreitler*

PER SERVING: 320 CALORIES | 37G PROTEIN | 10G CARB | 14G TOTAL FAT | 2G SAT FAT | 7G MONO FAT | 3.5G POLY FAT | 95MG CHOL | 960MG SODIUM | 1G FIBER

> **Vegetable oil is a broad term for a category of oils pressed from the seeds, nuts, grains, or fruits of plants. For sautéing and frying, you'll do best using an oil with a high smoke point. Your better bets for serious frying include grapeseed, peanut, corn, and safflower oils.**

quick chicken vindaloo

SERVES 4

- **1½ Tbs. curry powder**
- **2 tsp. hot paprika**
- **¾ tsp. freshly ground black pepper; more as needed**
- **1½ lb. boneless, skinless chicken thighs, trimmed and cut into ¾- to 1-inch pieces**
- **8 medium cloves garlic, minced**
- **4 Tbs. red-wine vinegar**
- **1 tsp. kosher salt; more as needed**
- **2 Tbs. canola oil**
- **1 medium yellow onion, thinly sliced**
- **1 Tbs. grated fresh ginger**
- **1 14½-oz. can diced tomatoes, drained; ⅓ cup juice reserved**
- **3 Tbs. chopped fresh cilantro**

Vindaloo is an extremely spicy Indian curry dish; this version has heat but doesn't overwhelm. Serve with jasmine rice and store-bought naan.

1. In a small bowl, stir the curry powder, paprika, and pepper. Put the chicken in a medium nonreactive bowl, sprinkle with 1 Tbs. of the curry powder mixture, about half of the garlic, the vinegar, and ¾ tsp. salt; toss to coat. Set aside at room temperature.

2. Heat the oil in a 10- to 11-inch, straight-sided sauté pan over high heat until shimmering. Add the onion and ¼ tsp. salt and cook, stirring occasionally with a wooden spoon, until it softens and begins to brown around the edges, 4 to 5 minutes. Reduce the heat to medium high, add the ginger, the remaining garlic, and the remaining curry powder mixture and cook, stirring, until fragrant and well combined, about 45 seconds.

3. Add the tomatoes and mix to combine, scraping the bottom of the pan with the spoon. Stir in the chicken, reserved tomato juice, remaining 2 Tbs. vinegar, and ⅔ cup water. Bring to a boil, cover partially, reduce the heat to medium, and simmer, stirring occasionally, until the chicken is tender and cooked through, 15 to 20 minutes. Season to taste with salt and pepper. Serve sprinkled with the cilantro.
—*Dawn Yanagihara*

PER SERVING: 360 CALORIES | 33G PROTEIN | 12G CARB | 20G TOTAL FAT | 4G SAT FAT | 9G MONO FAT | 5G POLY FAT | 110MG CHOL | 670MG SODIUM | 2G FIBER

sesame chicken with ginger and snow peas

SERVES 4

- **1** to 1¼ lb. boneless, skinless chicken breasts (2 to 3), very thinly sliced on the diagonal
- **2** Tbs. soy sauce
- **1** Tbs. Asian sesame oil
- **1** Tbs. plus 1 tsp. rice vinegar
- **2** Tbs. ketchup
- **8** scallions
- **6** oz. snow peas, trimmed (about 1½ cups)
- **2** Tbs. minced fresh ginger
- **3** Tbs. canola oil
- **2** Tbs. lightly toasted sesame seeds

Before cutting the chicken, freeze it for 10 minutes so that it firms up, making it easier to slice thinly.

1. In a large bowl, toss the chicken with 1 Tbs. of the soy sauce, 1½ tsp. of the sesame oil, and 1 tsp. of the rice vinegar.

2. In a 1-cup liquid measuring cup or another bowl, combine ¼ cup water with the ketchup and the remaining 1 Tbs. soy sauce, 1 Tbs. vinegar, and 1½ tsp. sesame oil.

3. Trim the scallions and separate the dark green tops from the light green and white bottoms. Slice the tops into 2-inch pieces and the bottoms into thin rounds. Combine both in a medium bowl with the snow peas and ginger.

4. Heat 1½ Tbs. of the oil in a 12-inch nonstick skillet or large stir-fry pan over medium-high heat until shimmering hot. Add the chicken and cook, stirring occasionally, until it loses most of its raw appearance, 1 to 2 minutes. Transfer to a large plate.

5. Add the remaining 1½ Tbs. oil and the scallions, snow peas, and ginger and cook, stirring occasionally, until the ginger and scallions start to brown, about 2 minutes.

6. Return the chicken to the pan and add the ketchup mixture and half of the sesame seeds. Cook, stirring, until the chicken is cooked through and the snow peas are crisp-tender, 2 to 3 minutes. Transfer to a platter, sprinkle with the remaining sesame seeds, and serve.
—*Tony Rosenfeld*

PER SERVING: 310 CALORIES | 26G PROTEIN | 10G CARB | 19G TOTAL FAT | 2.5G SAT FAT | 9G MONO FAT | 6G POLY FAT | 65MG CHOL | 800MG SODIUM | 2G FIBER

More about Snow Peas

Snow peas are a variety of pea that's eaten pod and all while the pods are still thin and tender. They cook very quickly and take well to blanching, steaming, and, of course, stir-frying. Snow peas pair well with scallions, toasted sesame seeds, ginger, shellfish, and rich nut oils.

Choosing
Choose dark green, dense-looking peas with no signs of drying or cracking.

Prepping
Trim the peas by breaking off the stem end and pulling off the tough "string" that runs across the top of the pod.

grilled rosemary chicken thighs with sweet-and-sour orange dipping sauce

SERVES 4 TO 6

1 Tbs. plus 1 tsp. minced fresh rosemary

2 tsp. dark brown sugar

2 tsp. kosher salt

1 tsp. freshly ground black pepper

1 tsp. crushed red pepper flakes

2 Tbs. vegetable oil; more for the grill

2½ lb. boneless, skinless chicken thighs (about 8 large, 10 medium, or 12 small), trimmed of excess fat

1 cup orange marmalade

¼ cup rice vinegar

Chicken thighs offer all the benefits of boneless, skinless chicken breasts—convenience and fast cooking—without the tendency to turn tasteless and dry, thanks to their slightly higher fat content. The hearty flavor of thighs and their ability to stay juicy on the grill are sure to win over anyone who claims to be dark-meat averse.

1. In a small bowl, mix the 1 Tbs. rosemary with the brown sugar, salt, pepper, and red pepper flakes. In a shallow pan, drizzle the oil over the chicken and toss to coat. Sprinkle the chicken evenly with the rosemary mixture.

2. Warm the marmalade, vinegar, and remaining 1 tsp. rosemary in a small saucepan over low heat until just warm; set aside in a warm spot.

3. Prepare a hot charcoal fire or heat a gas grill with all burners on medium high for 10 minutes. Clean the hot grate with a wire brush and then lubricate it with an oil-soaked paper towel. Put the chicken on the grate and grill (covered on a gas grill or uncovered over a charcoal fire) until one side has dark grill marks, 5 to 6 minutes for large thighs or 4 to 5 minutes for medium and small thighs. Turn and continue to grill until well marked on the other sides and cooked through, 5 to 6 minutes longer for large thighs or 4 to 5 minutes for medium and small thighs.

4. Move the thighs to a platter and let rest for 4 to 5 minutes. Serve hot, warm, or at room temperature with individual bowls of warm marmalade dipping sauce. —*Pam Anderson*

PER SERVING: 380 CALORIES | 34G PROTEIN | 19G CARB | 19G TOTAL FAT | 4.5G SAT FAT | 7G MONO FAT | 5G POLY FAT | 125MG CHOL | 500MG SODIUM | 0G FIBER

More about Rosemary

This classic herb, with its pine needlelike leaves and piney scent, is one of the few that's truly hardy in cold weather, making it the perfect herb for winter cooking. Luckily, its flavor pairs well with other cold-weather foods.

Choosing
Fresh rosemary is now available at most grocery stores. You'll often see it in packages of 4- to 5-inch sprigs or as bundles of long, straight branches. Be sure the leaves look fresh, green, and pliable, not dry, brittle, or blackened.

Storing
Store rosemary in the refrigerator wrapped in a damp dishtowel for up to a week.

thai-style stir-fried chicken and basil

SERVES 2 TO 3

2 Tbs. vegetable oil

4 medium shallots, peeled and thinly sliced

2 medium cloves garlic, thinly sliced

¼ tsp. crushed red pepper flakes

1 lb. chicken breast cutlets (about ¼ inch thick), cut crosswise into 1-inch-wide strips

1 Tbs. fish sauce

1 Tbs. fresh lime juice

2 tsp. packed light brown sugar

1 cup lightly packed fresh basil leaves

If you like, use a mix of fresh cilantro and mint instead of basil. Serve over cooked jasmine rice.

1. Heat the oil in a well-seasoned wok or a 12-inch heavy-duty skillet over medium-high heat until shimmering hot. Add the shallots, garlic, and red pepper flakes; cook, stirring frequently, until the shallots start to soften but not brown, 1 to 2 minutes. Add the chicken and cook, stirring, until it's no longer pink and the shallots are beginning to brown, 2 to 3 minutes.

2. Add the fish sauce, lime juice, sugar, and ¼ cup water. Cook, stirring frequently, until the chicken is just cooked through and the liquid reduces to a saucy consistency, 2 to 3 minutes. (If the sauce reduces before the chicken is cooked through, add water, 1 Tbs. at a time.) Remove from the heat, add the basil, and stir to wilt it.
—Lori Longbotham

PER SERVING: 280 CALORIES | 32G PROTEIN | 8G CARB | 13G TOTAL FAT | 2G SAT FAT | 5G MONO FAT | 5G POLY FAT | 85MG CHOL | 540MG SODIUM | 0G FIBER

More about Fish Sauce

This pungent amber brown liquid is a mainstay in Southeast Asian cooking. Known as nam pla in Thai and nuoc cham in Vietnamese, fish sauce imparts a distinctive salty flavor to many of the region's dishes. Though its aroma is strongly fishy straight from the bottle, cooking mellows it considerably, as does combining it with other assertive ingredients, like lime juice, chile, and garlic.

Fish sauce is made from freshly caught fish that are too small for substantial eating, such as anchovies. The fish are packed between layers of salt in an earthenware vessel. A bamboo mat is placed over the final layer and topped with a weight to keep the fish in place. They are then covered with an airtight top and set in a warm sunny spot where they are left to ferment for 9 months and up to a year. As the fish break down, they produce a brown liquid—the fish sauce—which is drained from a spigot at the bottom of the container.

chicken sauté with lemon, cumin & parsley

SERVES 2 TO 3

- 1 medium lemon
- 3 Tbs. extra-virgin olive oil
- 1 large red onion, thinly sliced
- 1 medium clove garlic, smashed and peeled
- 6 boneless, skinless chicken thighs (1 lb.), trimmed and cut into ½-inch-thick strips
- ¾ tsp. ground cumin
- ½ tsp. kosher salt
- ¼ tsp. freshly ground black pepper
- ¼ cup chopped fresh flat-leaf parsley

Serve this brightly flavored dish over baby spinach, with crusty bread on the side.

1. Finely grate 1 tsp. zest from the lemon and then juice the lemon.

2. Heat the oil in a 12-inch skillet over medium heat until shimmering hot. Add the onion and garlic and cook, stirring frequently, until the onion begins to soften, 3 to 5 minutes. Add the chicken, lemon zest, cumin, salt, and pepper and cook, stirring, until the chicken is just cooked through, 4 to 6 minutes. Remove the skillet from the heat and stir in the parsley and 2 Tbs. of the lemon juice. Discard the garlic if you like. Season to taste with salt and pepper. —*Lori Longbotham*

PER SERVING: 370 CALORIES | 28G PROTEIN | 7G CARB | 25G TOTAL FAT | 5G SAT FAT | 14G MONO FAT | 4G POLY FAT | 100MG CHOL | 280MG SODIUM | 1G FIBER

chicken breasts stuffed with sun-dried tomatoes and green olives

SERVES 4

Pinch of saffron (about 20 threads)

¼ cup extra-virgin olive oil

2½ tsp. fresh lemon juice

1½ tsp. mild honey, such as clover

½ tsp. freshly grated lemon zest

¼ tsp. crushed red pepper flakes

1 large clove garlic, crushed and peeled

1½ tsp. kosher salt

¼ cup drained oil-packed sun-dried tomatoes, very coarsely chopped

¼ cup pitted green olives, such as manzanilla

¼ cup loosely packed fresh flat-leaf parsley leaves, coarsely chopped

4 split skin-on, bone-in chicken breasts (3 to 3 ½ lb.)

½ tsp. freshly ground black pepper

Originally produced in Italy as a way to preserve abundant tomato crops for the winter months, chewy sun-dried tomatoes add deep flavor to this dish.

1. Position a rack in the middle of the oven and heat the oven to 425°F.

2. Soak the saffron in 2 tsp. hot water for 5 minutes. In a food processor, purée the saffron and soaking water with the olive oil, lemon juice, honey, lemon zest, red pepper flakes, garlic, and ½ tsp. salt. Add the sun-dried tomatoes, olives, and parsley. Pulse to form a coarsely chopped stuffing (it should be coarser than pesto).

3. If any of the backbone is still attached to the chicken, cut it off with poultry shears. Trim off the side flap with rib meat and bones. Use your finger to make a small opening between the skin and the flesh of the breasts. Run your finger under the skin to separate it from the breasts, making a pocket and being careful not to detach the edges of the skin. Stuff the tomato mixture into the pocket, distributing it evenly over the chicken. Pat the skin back in place and season with 1 tsp. salt and pepper. Line a heavy-duty, rimmed baking sheet with aluminum foil. Roast the chicken on the baking sheet until the juices run clear and a meat thermometer registers 165°F, about 30 minutes. *—Allison Ehri Kreitler*

PER SERVING: 550 CALORIES | 60G PROTEIN | 5G CARB | 31G TOTAL FAT | 7G SAT FAT | 17G MONO FAT | 5G POLY FAT | 165MG CHOL | 570MG SODIUM | 1G FIBER

More about Saffron

A key ingredient in bouillabaisse and paella, saffron has the reputation of being the most expensive spice by weight in the world. The stigma of a little purple perennial crocus flower, it must be gathered by hand during a harvest that lasts just a couple of weeks in the fall, and there are only three stigmas per blossom. It takes about 75,000 flowers to yield a pound of saffron. Fortunately, a pinch (about 20 threads) is usually all it takes to impart saffron's distinctive yellow color and vaguely metallic, dried alfalfa hay, and bittersweet wildflower-honey flavor.

Buying

When buying saffron, keep two rules in mind. First, buy it in threads only. Powdered saffron can contain other products, and it's difficult to know whether you're buying the pure spice. Second, look for saffron that contains only short, deep red threads; this grade is some-

times called coupé. Lesser grades of saffron include threads with some yellow areas (which is the style part of the flower). The yellow part doesn't have the same coloring and flavoring power as the red stigmas, so the saffron isn't as potent.

Prepping

Liquid helps draw out the flavor and color from saffron, so crumble it directly into broths, sauces, or soups. If using in something less fluid, let it steep in a little hot water for a few minutes first and add the water and saffron to the dish. You can also infuse oil with saffron, but the flavor and color won't come through as well as they do in water.

Storing

Stored in a sealed container in a dark place, saffron should last a couple of years before the flavor starts to diminish.

egg foo yung
with chicken and shiitake

SERVES 4

½ lb. boneless, skinless
chicken breasts, trimmed
and cut crosswise into
¼-inch strips

1 Tbs. plus 1 tsp. soy sauce

1 Tbs. Asian sesame oil

6 large eggs, beaten

¾ tsp. kosher salt

½ tsp. freshly ground black
pepper

1 Tbs. oyster sauce
(preferably Lee Kum Kee®)

1 tsp. white vinegar

¼ cup canola or peanut oil

½ red bell pepper, cored,
seeded, and very thinly
sliced

6 scallions, trimmed and
thinly sliced (white and
1 Tbs. green parts kept
separate)

3½ oz. fresh shiitake mushrooms, stemmed and
thinly sliced

Serve this Chinese-American classic with bok choy sautéed with ginger and garlic.

1. In a large bowl, toss the chicken with 1 tsp. each of the soy sauce and sesame oil. In another large bowl, beat the eggs with ¼ tsp. salt, ½ tsp. pepper, and 1 tsp. of the sesame oil. In a small bowl, whisk the oyster sauce and vinegar with the remaining 1 Tbs. soy sauce and the remaining 1 tsp. sesame oil.

2. Heat 1 Tbs. of the canola oil in a large (12-inch) nonstick skillet over medium-high heat. Add the chicken and cook, stirring, until it loses its raw color, 2 to 3 minutes; transfer to a plate. Add 1 Tbs. of canola oil, the bell pepper, and scallion whites and cook, stirring, until the vegetables begin to brown, about 2 minutes. Add the shiitake, sprinkle with ½ tsp. salt, and cook until softened, about 2 minutes. Add the vegetables and chicken to the egg mixture and stir gently to combine.

3. Wipe out the skillet with paper towels. Heat the remaining 2 Tbs. oil over medium-high heat until shimmering hot. Add the egg mixture, reduce the heat to medium, and cook, running a spatula in short, circular motions along the bottom of the pan, until the eggs begin to set, 2 to 3 minutes. Reduce the heat to low and gently press on the eggs with the spatula to flatten them. Cook until the eggs are just firm to the touch, about 2 minutes. Set a large plate over the pan and flip the eggs onto the plate so the bottom faces up. Drizzle with the oyster sauce mixture, sprinkle with the scallion greens, and serve.

—Tony Rosenfeld

PER SERVING: 350 CALORIES | 22G PROTEIN | 8G CARB | 26G TOTAL FAT | 4G SAT FAT |
14G MONO FAT | 7G POLY FAT | 350MG CHOL | 910MG SODIUM | 1G FIBER

chicken adobo with rice

SERVES 4

- 1½ cups long-grain white rice
- Kosher salt
- 1 Tbs. vegetable oil
- 1½ lb. boneless, skinless chicken thighs, trimmed and cut into 1-inch strips
- Freshly ground black pepper
- 4 large cloves garlic, minced
- ½ cup distilled white vinegar
- ½ cup lower-sodium soy sauce
- 1 dried bay leaf
- 1 tsp. freshly cracked black peppercorns

Based on traditional Filipino chicken adobo, or chicken stewed in vinegar, this is a perfect weeknight dish, as most of the ingredients come from the pantry. Serve with a fresh green salad.

1. Put the rice, a big pinch of salt, and 3 cups of water in a 3-quart saucepan. Bring to a boil, reduce the heat to a simmer, cover, and cook until the water is absorbed and the rice is tender, about 15 minutes. Remove from the heat and set aside with the cover on.

2. Meanwhile, heat the oil in a 12-inch heavy-duty skillet over medium-high heat. Add the chicken, season with ¼ tsp. each salt and pepper, and cook, stirring occasionally, until light golden brown, 4 to 6 minutes. Add the garlic and cook, stirring occasionally, 2 more minutes. Add the vinegar, soy sauce, bay leaf, and peppercorns. Bring to a boil, reduce the heat to medium low, and simmer until the liquid reduces by about one-quarter, 8 to 10 minutes. Discard the bay leaf.

3. Just before serving, uncover the rice and fluff it with a fork. Serve the chicken and sauce over the rice. —*Adeena Sussman*

PER SERVING: 670 CALORIES | 38G PROTEIN | 89G CARB | 7G TOTAL FAT | 4G SAT FAT | 7G MONO FAT | 4.5G POLY FAT | 110MG CHOL | 1270MG SODIUM | 1G FIBER

pan-roasted chicken with olives and lemon

SERVES 4

1 4-lb. chicken, cut into eight pieces

Kosher salt and freshly ground black pepper

1 medium lemon

1 Tbs. unsalted butter; more as needed

1 Tbs. extra-virgin olive oil

5 medium shallots, peeled and quartered lengthwise

¾ cup jarred brined olives, rinsed, pitted, and halved

8 fresh sage leaves

6 small fresh or 3 dried bay leaves

2 sprigs fresh thyme, plus 1 tsp. chopped

This dish is elegant enough for entertaining but simple enough to make anytime.

1. Position a rack in the center of the oven and heat the oven to 425°F.

2. Season the chicken generously on all sides with salt and pepper.

3. Cut the ends off the lemon, stand it on one end, and slice off the peel and the bitter white pith to expose the flesh. Cut the lemon segments from the membranes, letting them drop into a small bowl. Cut each segment crosswise into 4 pieces.

4. Heat the butter and the oil in a 12-inch ovenproof skillet over medium-high heat. Working in batches if necessary, cook the chicken skin side down until golden brown, 5 to 6 minutes. Transfer the chicken to a plate. Pour off all but 2 Tbs. of the fat. Add the shallots, olives, sage, bay leaves, thyme sprigs, and lemon segments, and cook until fragrant, 1 to 2 minutes.

5. Return the chicken to the pan skin side up and transfer to the oven. Roast until an instant-read thermometer inserted into the thickest part of a thigh registers 165°F, 18 to 20 minutes. Serve, sprinkled with the chopped thyme. —*Melissa Pellegrino*

PER SERVING: 630 CALORIES | 60G PROTEIN | 6G CARB | 40G TOTAL FAT | 11G SAT FAT | 18G MONO FAT | 7G POLY FAT | 200MG CHOL | 850MG SODIUM | 1G FIBER

orange and soy–glazed chicken thighs

SERVES 4

Vegetable oil for the broiler pan

8   bone-in, skin-on chicken thighs, trimmed

Kosher salt and freshly ground black pepper

16   small to medium shiitake mushrooms, stemmed

3   medium scallions (green parts only), cut into 3-inch lengths

½   cup soy sauce

⅓   cup granulated sugar

2   Tbs. mirin

½   tsp. finely grated orange zest

2   Tbs. fresh orange juice

1¼   tsp. cornstarch

2   tsp. toasted sesame seeds

There's no better accompaniment to this dish than steamed white rice. Leftover sauce keeps in the refrigerator for up to 3 weeks and is also great on steak or salmon.

1. Position a rack about 7 inches from the broiler and heat the oven to 450°F. Line the bottom of a broiler pan with foil and lightly oil the top of the pan.

2. Season the chicken all over with 1 tsp. salt and ½ tsp. pepper. Arrange the shiitake in 8 pairs, gill sides up, on the prepared broiler pan and season with salt and pepper. Arrange 2 or 3 scallion pieces on top of each mushroom pair, then put a chicken thigh, skin side up, on top. Press with your hand to flatten. Roast until the edges of the chicken begin to brown and an instant-read thermometer inserted in a thick part of the biggest thigh registers 165°F, about 20 minutes. Turn the broiler to high and broil until the skin is crisp and deeply browned, 5 to 6 minutes, rotating the pan once for even browning.

3. While the chicken is cooking, combine the soy sauce, sugar, mirin, and orange zest in a small saucepan. Bring to a simmer over medium heat, stirring to dissolve the sugar.

4. In a small bowl, stir the orange juice and cornstarch; add this mixture to the saucepan. Return to a simmer and cook, stirring constantly, until thickened and glossy, about 1 minute.

5. To serve, transfer the chicken, scallions, and mushrooms to dinner plates, drizzle with the sauce, and sprinkle with the sesame seeds.
—*Dawn Yanagihara*

PER SERVING: 390 CALORIES | 33G PROTEIN | 17G CARB | 21G TOTAL FAT | 6G SAT FAT | 8G MONO FAT | 5G POLY FAT | 115MG CHOL | 960MG SODIUM | 2G FIBER

More about Mirin

Choosing

Mirin is a sweet, golden yellow wine used in Japanese cooking as a sweetener. It's more refined and mellower than table sugar and has a distinctive fragrance. When used in a basting sauce, mirin gives meats and fish an appealing gloss. In a marinade, mirin tenderizes, in addition to providing flavor. If you don't have mirin, substitute 1 Tbs. sake or white wine plus 2 tsp. sugar.

The best mirin may be labeled hon-mirin: honjozo (which means "true mirin: naturally brewed"). Even though this isn't "real" mirin in the artisanal sense, it does retain some of the traditional processing steps. Lower-quality mirin is sold under the name mirin-fu chomiryo ("a kind of mirin") and aji-mirin ("mirin taste"). You'll find the best selection of mirin at a specialty market.

Refrigerated, mirin will keep for 2 months.

sautéed sausages and cabbage with apricot-mango chutney

- **1** cup cider vinegar
- **⅓** cup granulated sugar
- **1** medium serrano chile, seeded and thinly sliced
- **4** tsp. finely grated fresh ginger
- **4** tsp. minced garlic (5 medium cloves)
- Kosher salt
- **3** small fresh apricots, peeled, pitted, and cut into ½-inch pieces (about 1⅓ cups)
- **1** large slightly underripe mango, peeled, pitted, and cut into ½-inch pieces (about 1½ cups)
- **2** Tbs. extra-virgin olive oil
- **4** cooked chicken sausages
- **¾** tsp. fennel seed
- **¾** tsp. coriander seed
- **½** tsp. cumin seed
- **1** small yellow onion, very thinly sliced
- **1** small head green cabbage, cored and very thinly sliced (8 cups)
- Freshly ground black pepper

An Indian flavor profile (coriander, cumin, and ginger) gives this quick one-dish meal an exotic edge. Chicken sausages are available in many flavors at supermarkets; in their place, try sweet or hot Italian-style links.

1. Combine the vinegar, sugar, chile, ginger, garlic, and ¼ tsp. salt in a 2-quart saucepan. Bring to a boil over medium-high heat, stirring occasionally, until the sugar is dissolved, 3 to 4 minutes. Stir in the apricots and mango. Reduce the heat to low and simmer, stirring occasionally, until the fruit is soft and the mixture is thickened, about 25 minutes. Season to taste with salt and let cool to room temperature.

2. Meanwhile, in a 12-inch nonstick skillet, heat 1 Tbs. of the oil over medium-high heat. Add the sausages and cook, turning occasionally, until well browned, 4 to 5 minutes. Transfer to a cutting board and slice each in half on the diagonal.

3. Heat the remaining 1 Tbs. oil in the skillet over medium-high heat. Add the fennel, coriander, and cumin seeds and cook, stirring occa-

sionally, until fragrant, about 1 minute. Add the onion and cook, stirring, until just softened, 2 to 3 minutes. Add the cabbage, 1 tsp. salt, ½ tsp. pepper, and 1 Tbs. water and reduce the heat to medium. Return the sausages to the skillet, burying them in the cabbage mixture. Cover the pan and cook for about 3 minutes. Uncover and continue to cook until the cabbage is just barely tender and the sausages are hot. Season to taste with salt.

4. Serve the chutney with the sausages and cabbage.
—*Samantha Seneviratne*

PER SERVING: 350 CALORIES | 15G PROTEIN | 44G CARB | 12G TOTAL FAT | 2.5G SAT FAT | 5G MONO FAT | 1G POLY FAT | 35MG CHOL | 850MG SODIUM | 7G FIBER

how to cut a mango

Follow these steps to release the flesh from the pit, then cut the flesh into chunks or matchsticks.

Use a very sharp vegetable peeler or a paring knife to remove the skin from the mango; try not to take a lot of the fruit along with it. Cut a slice off the stem end to make a stable base and then stand the mango upright on the base.

Cut the flesh away from each broad side of the fruit. The pit tapers at the top and bottom, so start a little closer to the center and cut down in a slight arc to follow the contour of the pit. Repeat along the two remaining narrow sides, trying to avoid the fibrous edge of the pit

thai-style spicy chicken in lettuce cups

SERVES 4

- 3   Tbs. uncooked jasmine rice
- 3   Tbs. fish sauce
- 1   stalk lemongrass, trimmed, outer layers removed, and inner core minced (1 Tbs.)
- 1   tsp. crushed red pepper flakes
- ½   tsp. packed light brown sugar
- 1¼   lb. ground chicken, preferably dark meat
- 1   medium shallot, minced (⅓ cup)
- 3   Tbs. fresh lime juice
- 3   medium scallions, thinly sliced on the diagonal
- 2   Tbs. coarsely chopped fresh cilantro
- 2   Tbs. coarsely chopped fresh mint
- 1   medium head butter lettuce, for serving

This spicy ground-chicken dish is known as larb in Laos and Thailand. It's often served over lettuce, cabbage, or vegetables, with steamed sticky rice. We like to serve it in lettuce cups for an Asian take on tacos.

1. Toast the rice in an 8-inch skillet over medium-low heat, stirring frequently, until golden, 4 to 5 minutes (the rice will begin to smoke after a couple of minutes). Let the rice cool slightly and then grind in a spice grinder until the largest pieces resemble very coarse cornmeal; the mixture should not be completely powdery.

2. Combine the fish sauce, lemongrass, pepper flakes, brown sugar, and ½ cup water in a 12-inch nonstick skillet and bring to a simmer over high heat. Separate the chicken into large clumps and add to the pan. Cook, breaking up the chicken into small pieces with a wooden spoon, until the meat is no longer pink, 5 to 6 minutes. Sprinkle 1 Tbs. of the ground rice over the chicken and continue to cook, stirring frequently, until the liquid in the pan has thickened, about 2 minutes longer.

3. Remove from the heat. Stir in the shallot. Sprinkle with the lime juice, scallions, cilantro, and mint and stir gently to combine. Transfer to a serving dish and sprinkle with 1 tsp. of the remaining ground rice. Serve with the lettuce leaves on the side to use as cups for the chicken.

—Dawn Yanagihara

PER SERVING: 240 CALORIES | 27G PROTEIN | 8G CARB | 12G TOTAL FAT | 3.5G SAT FAT | 5G MONO FAT | 2G POLY FAT | 120MG CHOL | 1,130MG SODIUM | 1G FIBER

More about Lemongrass

Lemongrass, a stiff grass native to India, is widely used as a herb in Asian cuisine. Evergreen in warm climates, lemongrass is a sharp-bladed, perennial, blue-green grass that grows in 3- to 6-foot-tall cascading clumps.

This citrusy plant plays a starring role in many Southeast-Asian cuisines, adding its unique flavor to everything from curries to cold drinks. Not long ago, it was nearly impossible to find except in Asian markets. But these days, lemongrass is going mainstream, making its way into the produce section of your supermarket.

Choosing

Much of lemongrass's flavor is concentrated in its lower, canelike stalks, which is why most markets sell them already trimmed of their leafy tops, leaving just a few short, spiky blades still attached. Look for firm, pale green stalks with fat, bulbous bottoms and reasonably fresh-looking tops (they may be a little dry but shouldn't be desiccated or yellowed).

Prepping

There are two main ways to cook with lemongrass, and each determines how you handle it. To infuse teas, broths, soups, and braising liquids, trim off the spiky tops and the bases, crush the stalks with the side of a knife to release their aromatic oils, and then cut them into 1- or 2-inch pieces. Remove the pieces before eating (they tend to be woody) or eat around them.

To use lemongrass in marinades, stir-fries, salads, spice rubs, and curry pastes, trim the top and base of the stalks—you want to use only the bottom 4 inches or so. Then peel off any dry or tough outer layers before finely chopping or mincing. Lemongrass holds up to long cooking and gains intensity the longer it's cooked. If you'd like a strong lemongrass flavor, add minced lemongrass at the start of cooking, browning it along with the other aromatics. For a lighter, fresher lemongrass flavor, add it near the end of cooking.

Storing

To store, wrap in plastic and refrigerate for 2 to 3 weeks, or freeze for up to 6 months.

quick chicken parmesan

SERVES 4

Nonstick cooking spray

½ cup unbleached all-purpose flour

Freshly ground black pepper

2 large eggs

1½ cups panko breadcrumbs

4 thin-sliced boneless, skinless chicken breast cutlets (about 14 oz.)

Kosher salt

5 Tbs. olive oil

¼ cup freshly grated Parmigiano- Reggiano (use the small holes on a box grater)

4 oz. fresh mozzarella, thinly sliced

1 small yellow onion, chopped

2 medium cloves garlic, finely chopped

1 14.5-oz. can crushed tomatoes (preferably Muir Glen® fire-roasted crushed tomatoes)

¼ cup packed fresh basil, chopped (½ oz.)

Crisp chicken cutlets are topped with two cheeses and a super-fast tomato sauce in this easy take on an Italian restaurant favorite.

1. Position a rack in the center of the oven and heat the oven to 425°F. Line a large rimmed baking sheet with foil and lightly coat the foil with nonstick cooking spray.

2. Mix the flour and ¼ tsp. pepper in a wide, shallow dish. In a second wide, shallow dish, lightly beat the eggs with 1 Tbs. water. Put the panko in a third wide, shallow dish. Season the chicken with salt and coat each piece in the flour, tapping off the excess, then the egg, and then the panko, pressing the panko to help it adhere.

3. Heat 2 Tbs. of the oil in a 12-inch nonstick skillet over medium-high heat. Working in two batches, cook the chicken, flipping once, until the crumbs are golden and the chicken is almost cooked through, 1 to 2 minutes per side, adding 2 Tbs. more oil for the second batch. Transfer the chicken to the prepared baking sheet. Sprinkle the chicken with the Parmigiano and then top evenly with the mozzarella. Bake until the cheese is melted and the chicken is cooked through, 5 to 7 minutes.

4. Meanwhile, wipe the skillet clean and set over medium heat. Pour in the remaining 1 Tbs. oil and then add the onion and garlic. Cook, stirring often, until the onion is tender and lightly browned, 3 to 4 minutes. Stir in the tomatoes and ¼ tsp. salt. Simmer, stirring occasionally, until thickened, 4 to 5 minutes. Remove from the heat and stir in the basil. Season to taste with salt and pepper. Serve the sauce over the chicken. —*Melissa Gaman*

PER SERVING: 480 CALORIES | 33G PROTEIN | 24G CARB | 28G TOTAL FAT | 8G SAT FAT | 16G MONO FAT | 3G POLY FAT | 160MG CHOL | 610MG SODIUM | 3G FIBER

orange chicken with scallions

SERVES 2 TO 3

- **1** large navel orange
- **1** Tbs. soy sauce
- **1** Tbs. rice vinegar
- **2** tsp. light brown sugar
- **⅛** tsp. crushed red pepper flakes
- **1** lb. boneless, skinless chicken breasts, cut into 1-inch cubes
- **¾** tsp. kosher salt
- **2** large egg whites
- **⅓** cup cornstarch
- **3** to 4 Tbs. canola or peanut oil
- **4** scallions, trimmed and thinly sliced (keep whites and greens separate)

Navel oranges are generally in season from November through May. Choose ones that feel heavy for their size (signaling they're juicy) with a skin that does not feel loose.

1. Using a vegetable peeler, shave the zest from the orange in long, wide strips. If necessary, remove any large patches of bitter white pith from the zest strips with a paring knife. Juice the orange into a small bowl and mix with the soy sauce, rice vinegar, brown sugar, and red pepper flakes.

2. Sprinkle the chicken with ½ tsp. of the salt. In a mini chopper or food processor, process the egg whites, cornstarch, and ¼ tsp. salt until smooth. In a medium bowl, toss the chicken with the cornstarch batter.

3. Heat 2 Tbs. of the oil in a 12-inch nonstick skillet or large stir-fry pan over medium-high heat until shimmering hot. Using tongs, transfer about half the chicken to the pan. Reduce the heat to medium and cook, flipping every minute or so, until the chicken browns and crisps all over and is firm to the touch, 3 to 4 minutes. With clean tongs, transfer to a paper-towel-lined plate. Add the remaining 1 Tbs. oil to the skillet (or 2 Tbs. oil if the pan seems very dry) and repeat the cooking process with the remaining chicken; transfer to the plate.

4. Put the orange zest strips in the skillet and cook, stirring, until they darken in spots, 15 to 30 seconds. Stir the orange juice mixture and add it to the pan. Let it boil for about 10 seconds and then add the chicken and the scallion whites. Cook, stirring often, until the sauce reduces to a glaze and the chicken is just cooked through—check by cutting into a thicker piece—1 to 2 minutes. If the chicken isn't cooked through but the glaze is cooking away, add a couple tablespoons of water and continue cooking. Serve sprinkled with the scallion greens.
—*Tony Rosenfeld*

PER SERVING: 430 CALORIES | 36G PROTEIN | 30G CARB | 18G TOTAL FAT | 2G SAT FAT | 9G MONO FAT | 5G POLY FAT | 85MG CHOL | 830MG SODIUM | 1G FIBER

turkey cutlets and black beans with tangerine-habanero mojo sauce

SERVES 4

- **5** to 6 Tbs. olive oil
- **3** medium cloves garlic, thinly sliced
- **½** plus ⅛ tsp. ground cumin
- **½** cup fresh tangerine juice (from 2 tangerines)
- **2** Tbs. fresh lime juice (from 1 lime)
- **½** tsp. seeded and minced habanero chile
- Kosher salt and freshly ground black pepper
- **1** small red onion, chopped
- **1** 15 ½-oz. can black beans, rinsed and drained
- **2** Tbs. chopped fresh cilantro
- **4** turkey breast cutlets (about 1¼ lb.)

Mojo (pronounced moe-hoe) is a Caribbean and Latin American garlic, chile, and citrus sauce that pairs well with meat, poultry, and seafood. Here, it's made with tangerine and lime, so it's both sweet and tart. If habaneros are scarce, try a Scotch bonnet, jalapeño, or serrano chile instead.

1. In a 10-inch skillet, heat 2 Tbs. of the oil and the garlic over medium heat until the garlic is golden, about 3 minutes. Stir in ⅛ tsp. of the cumin. Add the tangerine juice, lime juice, and habanero. Bring to a simmer and cook for about 3 minutes. Season to taste with salt and pepper; set the mojo sauce aside. (The sauce can be served warm or at room temperature.)

2. Heat 2 Tbs. of the oil in a 12-inch nonstick skillet over medium-high heat. Add the onion and ¼ tsp. salt and cook, stirring occasionally, until softened, 3 to 5 minutes. Add the beans and the remaining ½ tsp. cumin and cook until the beans are heated through, 2 to 3 minutes. Stir in the cilantro and season to taste with salt and pepper. Transfer the beans to a bowl and cover with foil to keep warm.

3. Wash and dry the skillet. Season the turkey cutlets on both sides with salt and pepper. Heat 1 Tbs. of the oil in the skillet over medium-high heat until very hot. Add as many cutlets as will comfortably fit in a single layer and cook until browned on both sides and just cooked through, about 2 minutes per side. Transfer to a plate and tent with foil to keep warm. Repeat with the remaining cutlets, adding the remaining 1 Tbs. oil if needed.

4. Divide the cutlets and black beans among individual plates. Spoon the mojo sauce over and serve.

—*Dawn Yanagihara*

PER SERVING: 410 CALORIES | 39G PROTEIN | 22G CARB | 18G TOTAL FAT | 2.5G SAT FAT | 13G MONO FAT | 2G POLY FAT | 95MG CHOL | 210MG SODIUM | 5G FIBER

pretzel-crusted chicken breasts with mustard-dill dipping sauce

SERVES 4

- ½ cup unbleached all-purpose flour
- 2 large eggs
- ¼ cup plus 1 Tbs. Dijon mustard
- 3 cups pretzels (not low-sodium)
- 3 boneless, skinless chicken breast halves (about 1½ lb.)
- Freshly ground black pepper
- ½ cup mayonnaise
- 2 Tbs. finely chopped fresh dill
- 1 tsp. honey
- ½ cup vegetable oil

Ground pretzels make a great crunchy-salty coating for chicken.

1. Put the flour in a wide, shallow bowl. In another wide, shallow bowl, lightly beat the eggs and 1 Tbs. of the mustard. Process the pretzels in a food processor until a coarse flour forms, about 30 seconds. Transfer the pretzel flour to a third wide, shallow bowl. Line up the flour, egg, and pretzel bowls in that order.

2. Put the chicken on a cutting board, and holding your knife parallel to the board, split each breast in half horizontally. Sprinkle both sides of the chicken lightly with pepper. Dredge both sides of the chicken in the flour, then the egg, and then the pretzel flour, coating well and shaking off the excess. Transfer to a baking sheet and refrigerate for 5 minutes.

3. Meanwhile, in a small bowl, mix the remaining ¼ cup mustard with the mayonnaise, dill, honey, and ⅛ tsp. black pepper; set aside.

4. Heat the oil in a 12-inch skillet over medium-high heat. When the oil is hot but not smoking, add 3 of the chicken breast pieces. Cook until the first side is dark brown, about 2 minutes. Carefully flip and cook until the chicken is cooked through and the second side is golden brown, about 2 minutes more; if the chicken seems to be browning too fast, reduce the heat to medium. Transfer to a clean cutting board and cover to keep warm. Repeat with the remaining chicken.

5. Slice the chicken on the diagonal. Divide the slices among 4 dinner plates and serve with the dipping sauce. —*Dina Cheney*

PER SERVING: 810 CALORIES | 43G PROTEIN | 47G CARB | 50G TOTAL FAT | 8G SAT FAT | 17G MONO FAT | 22G POLY FAT | 210MG CHOL | 1,210MG SODIUM | 2G FIBER

crispy noodle cakes with hoisin chicken

SERVES 2

- ¼ lb. dried rice sticks (vermicelli)
- 1 Tbs. plus 1 tsp. Asian sesame oil
- 2 small boneless, skinless chicken breast halves (about ¾ lb.), cut into ½-inch dice
- 1 tsp. dry sherry
- Kosher salt
- 2 Tbs. hoisin sauce
- 1 Tbs. soy sauce
- 2 tsp. rice vinegar
- 3 Tbs. canola oil
- 3½ oz. shiitake mushrooms, stemmed and thinly sliced (1½ cups)
- 4 oz. baby spinach (4 lightly packed cups)
- Asian chile sauce, like Sriracha (optional)

This recipe calls for dried rice vermicelli, the rice flour version of Italy's classic thin pasta. Here, the cooked vermicelli is formed into cakes, pan-fried until crisp, and topped with a savory mixture of chicken, mushrooms, and spinach.

1. Bring a medium pot of water to a boil. Remove the pot from the heat, add the noodles, and soak them until tender, about 5 minutes. Drain, transfer to a baking sheet lined with paper towels, and pat dry. Toss the noodles with 1 Tbs. of the sesame oil.

2. Toss the chicken with the remaining 1 tsp. sesame oil, the sherry, and ¼ tsp. salt.

3. In a small bowl, mix the hoisin sauce, soy sauce, and vinegar.

4. Heat 1½ Tbs. of the canola oil in a 12-inch nonstick skillet over medium-high heat until shimmering hot. Add the mushrooms and cook, stirring, until softened and lightly browned, about 2 minutes. Add the chicken and cook, stirring, until it just loses its raw color, about 2 minutes. Add the spinach and cook, stirring, until it wilts, about 1 minute. Add the hoisin mixture and cook, stirring, until the chicken is cooked through, about 1 minute. Transfer to a bowl.

5. Wipe out the skillet with a paper towel. Heat the remaining 1½ Tbs. oil over medium heat. Divide the noodles in half and spread them in the pan, forming 2 oblong cakes (if they become entangled, just cut them apart with scissors). Sprinkle lightly with salt and cook until the bottoms are lightly browned and crisp, 4 to 5 minutes. Flip, sprinkle lightly with salt, and cook until the second sides are browned and crisp, about 4 minutes more. Transfer to serving plates, top with the chicken, and serve with chile sauce, if using. —*Tony Rosenfeld*

PER SERVING: 750 CALORIES | 42G PROTEIN | 60G CARB | 35G TOTAL FAT | 4G SAT FAT | 18G MONO FAT | 11G POLY FAT | 95MG CHOL | 1,240MG SODIUM | 4G FIBER

tex-mex chicken with chiles and cheese

SERVES 4

- 1¼ **lb. boneless, skinless chicken breast halves, trimmed and sliced ¼ inch thick**
- 1½ **tsp. chili powder**
- ½ **tsp. ground cumin**
- 1¼ **tsp. kosher salt**
- ½ **tsp. freshly ground black pepper**
- ½ **cup unbleached all-purpose flour**
- 3½ **Tbs. unsalted butter**
- 1½ **cups fresh or thawed frozen corn kernels**
- 1 **medium jalapeño, seeded (if desired) and thinly sliced**
- 1 **large clove garlic, minced**
- 2 **to 3 medium limes, 1 or 2 juiced to yield 3 Tbs. and 1 cut into wedges**
- 1 **Tbs. chopped fresh oregano**
- 1 **cup grated sharp Cheddar**

Serve with rice pilaf, or wrap the chicken in warm corn tortillas.

1. Position a rack about 4 inches from the broiler and heat the broiler to high. Toss the chicken with the chili powder, cumin, ¾ tsp. salt, and the black pepper. Lightly dredge the chicken in the flour and shake off any excess.

2. Melt 2½ Tbs. of the butter in a 12-inch ovenproof skillet (preferably cast iron) over medium-high heat. Add the chicken and cook, stirring occasionally, until browned, about 5 minutes. Transfer to a plate.

3. Add the remaining 1 Tbs. butter, the corn, jalapeño, garlic, and remaining ½ tsp. salt. Cook, stirring, until the corn begins to brown lightly, 2 to 3 minutes. Add the chicken, lime juice, oregano, and ½ cup water. Cook, stirring, until the chicken is just cooked through, about 2 minutes. Sprinkle with the Cheddar and transfer the skillet to the broiler. Broil until the cheese melts and browns on top, about 3 minutes. Serve with lime wedges.   —*Tony Rosenfeld*

PER SERVING: 470 CALORIES | 38G PROTEIN | 28G CARB | 23G TOTAL FAT | 13G SAT FAT | 4G MONO FAT | 1.5G POLY FAT | 130MG CHOL | 610MG SODIUM | 3G FIBER

grilled five-spice chicken thighs with soy-vinegar sauce and cilantro

SERVES 4 TO 6

- 2 **Tbs. Chinese five-spice powder**
- 1 **Tbs. plus 1 tsp. dark brown sugar**
- 1 **tsp. garlic powder**
- ¾ **tsp. kosher salt**
- 2 **Tbs. soy sauce**
- 2 **tsp. rice vinegar**
- 1 **tsp. Asian sesame oil**
- ¼ **tsp. crushed red pepper flakes**
- 2½ **lb. boneless, skinless chicken thighs (about 8 large, 10 medium, or 12 small), trimmed of excess fat**
- 2 **Tbs. vegetable oil; more for the grill**
- 3 **Tbs. chopped fresh cilantro**

Five-spice powder is typically composed of star anise, cloves, fennel seed, cinnamon, and Sichuan peppercorns. Some well-stocked supermarkets carry five-spice powder (McCormick sells a version), or check at an Asian market.

1. Mix the five-spice powder, the 1 Tbs. sugar, the garlic powder, and the salt in a small bowl. In another bowl, mix the soy sauce, vinegar, sesame oil, red pepper flakes, and remaining 1 tsp. sugar.

2. Put the chicken in a shallow pan, drizzle with the vegetable oil, and toss to coat evenly. Sprinkle the spice mixture over the chicken; toss and rub to coat thoroughly.

3. Prepare a hot charcoal fire or heat a gas grill with all burners on medium high for 10 minutes. Clean the hot grate with a wire brush and then lubricate it with an oil-soaked paper towel. Put the chicken on the grate and grill (covered on a gas grill or uncovered over a charcoal fire) until one side has dark grill marks, 5 to 6 minutes for large thighs or 4 to 5 minutes for medium and small thighs. Turn and continue to grill until well marked on the other sides and cooked through, 5 to 6 minutes longer for large thighs or 4 to 5 minutes for medium and small thighs.

4. Move the thighs to a serving dish. Drizzle with about half of the soy mixture, sprinkle with the cilantro, and toss to coat. Let rest for 4 to 5 minutes, tossing once or twice. Serve hot, warm, or at room temperature, with the remaining soy mixture passed at the table.
—*Pam Anderson*

PER SERVING: 340 CALORIES | 35G PROTEIN | 6G CARB | 20G TOTAL FAT | 4.5G SAT FAT | 8G MONO FAT | 6G POLY FAT | 125MG CHOL | 690MG SODIUM | 0G FIBER

Variation

Prepare as kebabs

Trim the thighs and then slice them lengthwise into 1½- to 2-inch-wide strips. Toss with the flavorings; then thread the chicken onto six 8- or 12-inch skewers (soak wood skewers in water for at least 20 minutes first), folding each strip in half as you skewer it. If some strips are very thick, cut them in half crosswise rather than folding them so that all the pieces of chicken are roughly the same size. Grill the kebabs, turning them every 4 to 5 minutes as dark grill marks form, until cooked through, 12 to 15 minutes total.

lemon chicken breasts with capers

SERVES 4

- **4** boneless, skinless chicken breasts (6 oz. each)
- **½** cup freshly grated Parmigiano-Reggiano
- **¼** cup fine, dry breadcrumbs
- **4** Tbs. capers, rinsed, drained, patted dry, and chopped
- **1** lemon, zest finely grated and juiced
- **2** Tbs. chopped fresh flat-leaf parsley
   Kosher salt and freshly ground black pepper
- **3** Tbs. unsalted butter
- **1** Tbs. olive oil
- **2** medium cloves garlic, thinly sliced
- **½** cup lower-salt chicken broth

This sauté takes the traditional flavorings of chicken piccata and turns them outside-in. Boneless chicken breasts are stuffed with capers, lemon zest, and Parmigiano. Breadcrumbs are added to help hold the mixture together.

1. Position a rack in the center of the oven and heat the oven to 425°F. Make a lengthwise horizontal slice almost all the way through each chicken breast and open each up like a book. Flatten the chicken with a meat mallet until it is ¼ inch thick. Put the Parmigiano, breadcrumbs, 3 Tbs. capers, lemon zest, and 1 Tbs. parsley in a mini chopper or food processor and pulse a few times to combine. Sprinkle the mixture on top of the chicken breasts. Fold each breast closed and secure with toothpicks. Sprinkle the breasts with ¾ tsp. salt and ½ tsp. pepper.

2. Heat 1 Tbs. butter and the oil in a large (12-inch), heavy-duty, oven-proof skillet over medium-high heat until the butter melts and starts to foam, about 2 minutes. Add the chicken and cook, without touching, until it browns and easily releases from the pan, about 2 minutes. Turn the chicken and cook the other side until browned, about 2 more minutes.

3. Add the garlic and the remaining tablespoon capers to the skillet, transfer the pan to the oven, and roast uncovered until the chicken cooks through (an instant-read thermometer inserted into the thickest part should register 165°F), about 8 minutes. Transfer the chicken to a serving platter and tent with foil.

4. Set the skillet over medium-high heat. Add the chicken broth and cook, scraping the bottom of the pan with a wooden spoon to loosen any browned bits, until it reduces by about half, about 2 minutes. Remove from the heat and whisk in 2 Tbs. of the lemon juice and the remaining 2 Tbs. butter. Taste and add more lemon juice, salt, and pepper if needed. Serve the chicken drizzled with the butter sauce and sprinkled with the remaining tablespoon parsley.

—Tony Rosenfeld

CHICKEN, TURKEY & DUCK **35**

quick tandoori chicken thighs

SERVES 4 TO 6

- **1** cup plain low-fat yogurt
- **2** Tbs. fresh lemon juice
- **1** Tbs. minced fresh ginger
- **2** tsp. minced garlic
- **1** tsp. ground turmeric
- **½** tsp. ground coriander
- **½** tsp. ground cumin
- **½** tsp. garam masala

  Kosher salt and freshly ground black pepper

- **8** skin-on, bone-in chicken thighs

  Vegetable oil for the grill

The yogurt in this spicy marinade helps tenderize the chicken and brings lots of tangy flavor to the dish.

1. In a large bowl, whisk the yogurt, lemon juice, ginger, garlic, turmeric, coriander, cumin, garam masala, ½ tsp. salt, and several grinds of black pepper. Add the chicken thighs to the marinade and turn to coat them thoroughly. Cover and refrigerate while you heat the grill.

2. Prepare a medium gas or charcoal grill fire. If you are using a charcoal grill, spread the hot coals across two-thirds of the bottom grate and leave the remaining portion clear. If you are using gas, turn one of the burners to low to create a cooler zone. Scrub the grill grate with a wire brush and then use a paper towel to wipe it with oil.

3. Remove the chicken thighs from the marinade and wipe off the excess (don't worry if some remains). Put the chicken, skin side down, directly over the hot part of the grill and grill, covered, until the skin is browned, 3 to 4 minutes (don't leave the grill at this point because flare-ups may occur; if they do, move the chicken away from the flame).

4. Flip the chicken and grill until well browned on the second side, 3 to 4 minutes. Move the thighs to the cooler part of the grill and continue to grill, covered, until their internal temperature registers 165°F on an instant-read thermometer, 10 to 15 minutes more.

—*Domenica Marchetti*

PER SERVING: 210 CALORIES | 21G PROTEIN | 1G CARB | 13G TOTAL FAT | 3.5G SAT FAT | 5G MONO FAT | 3G POLY FAT | 80MG CHOL | 105MG SODIUM | 0G FIBER

plum-glazed duck breasts

2   boneless, skin-on duck breast halves (about 1 lb. each)

Kosher salt and freshly ground black pepper

½   cup plum preserves

1   Tbs. reduced-sodium soy sauce

¼   tsp. five-spice powder

Pinch crushed red pepper flakes

3   scallions, thinly sliced

> Duck breasts are best served medium rare so they stay juicy and tender, but feel free to adjust the cooking time to achieve your preferred doneness.

The elegance of this dish belies its simplicity. The secret is the sweet spiced glaze, made with plum preserves and Asian seasonings. If you can't find plum preserves, cherry or currant preserves make good substitutes.

1. Position a rack in the center of the oven and heat the oven to 425°F. Trim any excess skin and fat from the duck and score the remaining skin and fat underneath in a 1-inch diamond pattern, taking care not to cut the flesh. Pat the duck dry and season generously with salt and pepper.

2. Heat a 12-inch heavy-duty skillet over medium-high heat. Put the duck in the skillet skin side down, reduce the heat to medium low, and render the fat until only a thin, crisp layer of skin remains, about 8 minutes.

3. Meanwhile, in a small bowl, combine the preserves, soy sauce, five-spice powder, and red pepper flakes.

4. Turn the duck over, carefully spoon off most of the fat from the skillet, and brush the preserves mixture over the breasts.

5. Transfer the skillet to the oven and roast until an instant-read thermometer inserted into the thickest part of a breast registers 135°F for medium rare, 8 to 10 minutes. Transfer the duck to a cutting board and let rest for 5 minutes.

6. Meanwhile, tilt the skillet and spoon off as much fat from the pan juice as possible. Slice the duck diagonally into ¼-inch slices. Arrange on plates and spoon the pan juice over. Sprinkle with the scallions and serve. —*Joanna Pruess*

PER SERVING: 300 CALORIES | 24G PROTEIN | 27G CARB | 11G TOTAL FAT | 3G SAT FAT | 5G MONO FAT | 1.5G POLY FAT | 135MG CHOL | 500MG SODIUM | 0G FIBER

pan-seared chicken thighs with beer and grainy mustard sauce

SERVES 4

8 small bone-in, skin-on chicken thighs (4 to 5 oz. each), trimmed of excess skin and fat

Kosher salt and freshly ground black pepper

2 tsp. vegetable oil

2 medium shallots, minced

1½ tsp. unbleached all-purpose flour

1 cup amber lager, such as Dos Equis® Amber

½ cup lower-salt chicken broth

1½ Tbs. pure maple syrup

½ tsp. chopped fresh thyme; more for garnish

1 Tbs. whole-grain mustard

1 oz. (2 Tbs.) unsalted butter

Maple syrup adds a hint of sweetness that rounds out the mustard's bite in this quick pan sauce. Not in the mood for chicken? Try it with pork chops instead.

1. Position a rack in the lower third of the oven, set a large rimmed baking sheet on the rack, and heat the oven to 475°F. Season the chicken thighs all over with salt and pepper.

2. Heat the oil in a 12-inch, heavy-duty, ovenproof skillet over medium-high heat until shimmering hot. Swirl to coat the pan bottom. Arrange the chicken in the pan skin side down in a single layer (it will likely be a snug fit), cover with an ovenproof splatter screen (if you have one), and cook until the skin is deep golden brown, about 7 minutes. Turn the thighs and transfer the skillet and splatter screen, if using, to the oven. Roast until an instant-read thermometer inserted into the thickest part of a thigh registers 170°F, 5 to 8 minutes. Transfer to a plate.

3. Pour off all but 1 Tbs. fat from the skillet. Add the shallots and sauté over medium heat until softened, about 2 minutes. Stir in the flour until combined. Stir in the beer, chicken broth, maple syrup, and thyme. Increase the heat to high and bring to a boil, scraping up any browned bits from the skillet with a wooden spoon. Simmer vigorously until reduced to about 1 cup, about 3 minutes. Remove from the heat and whisk in the mustard, then the butter. Season the sauce to taste with salt and pepper.

4. To serve, dip each chicken thigh in the sauce and turn to coat. Arrange 2 thighs on each of 4 plates, spoon additional sauce over them, and garnish with the thyme. Serve immediately.
—*Dawn Yanagihara*

PER SERVING: 420 CALORIES | 32G PROTEIN | 9G CARB | 27G TOTAL FAT | 9G SAT FAT | 10G MONO FAT | 5G POLY FAT | 125MG CHOL | 480MG SODIUM | 1G FIBER

poblanos stuffed with cheddar and chicken

SERVES 4

- **4** large poblano chiles
- **2** medium tomatoes, chopped
- **½** medium white onion, chopped
- **1** large clove garlic, chopped
- **1** tsp. dried oregano, crumbled
- **1** tsp. ground cumin
- Generous pinch ground cinnamon
- Kosher salt
- **1** Tbs. olive oil
- **2** cups shredded cooked chicken, preferably dark meat
- **1½** cups cooked brown or white rice
- **2** cups grated sharp or extra-sharp white Cheddar (about 7 oz.)
- **¼** cup chopped fresh cilantro (including some tender stems)
- **1** Tbs. fresh lime juice

Traditional chile rellenos are stuffed, coated in an egg batter, and fried. This stuffed pepper variation has no breading, making it a lighter meal. Removing the seeds and white inner membrane of the pepper ensures they won't be too hot; substitute black beans for the chicken to create a vegetarian variation of the dish.

1. Position an oven rack about 4 inches from the broiler and heat the broiler on high. Line a large rimmed baking sheet with foil.

2. Slit the chiles from stem to tip and set on the baking sheet. Broil, turning every few minutes, until blackened all over, 5 to 8 minutes. Let cool slightly, peel off the skins, and cut out the seed cores, leaving the stems on. Turn the chiles inside out, flick out any remaining seeds, and turn right side out. Return the poblanos to the baking sheet.

3. Purée the tomatoes, onion, garlic, oregano, cumin, cinnamon, and ½ tsp. salt in a food processor. Heat the oil in a 12-inch skillet over medium heat. Add the purée and cook, stirring frequently, until the liquid has evaporated and the mixture looks thick and pulpy, 8 to 11 minutes. Remove the pan from the heat. Stir in the chicken and rice, and then 1 cup of the cheese, the cilantro, and the lime juice. Season to taste with salt. Divide the filling among the peppers, wrapping the sides of the peppers up and around the filling, some of which will still be exposed.

4. Broil the peppers until the cheese is melting and the tops begin to brown, about 4 minutes. Top with the remaining 1 cup cheese and broil until the cheese is completely melted, about 2 minutes.
—Allison Ehri Kreitler

sirloin steaks with garlicky
swiss chard
(recipe on p. 53)

beef, pork & lamb

spicy beef with peanuts and chiles

SERVES 4

- **1 lb. flank steak, thinly sliced on the diagonal against the grain**
- **2 Tbs. soy sauce**
- **2 tsp. fish sauce**
- **¼ tsp. kosher salt; more to taste**
- **2 Tbs. fresh lime juice**
- **1 Tbs. light brown sugar**
- **¼ cup salted peanuts**
- **2 large shallots, coarsely chopped**
- **2 Thai or serrano chiles, stemmed and coarsely chopped (don't seed)**
- **3 Tbs. canola or peanut oil**
- **⅓ cup coarsely chopped fresh cilantro**
- **3 Tbs. chopped fresh basil**

Flank steak isn't really a steak at all, but actually an entire cut of meat. The flank is a lean cut with a visible longitudinal grain that absorbs marinades well. It's known for its beefy flavor and firm texture.

1. Toss the steak with 1 Tbs. of the soy sauce, 1 tsp. of the fish sauce, and the salt. Combine the remaining 1 Tbs. soy sauce and 1 tsp. fish sauce with 1 Tbs. of the lime juice and the brown sugar and set aside.

2. Pulse the peanuts, shallots, and chiles in a food processor until finely chopped. Transfer to a small bowl.

3. Set a 12-inch skillet over medium-high heat until hot, about 1 minute. Add 1½ Tbs. of the oil and once it's shimmering, add the beef. Cook, stirring, until the beef just loses its raw appearance, about 2 minutes. Transfer to a plate.

4. Reduce the heat to medium, add the remaining 1½ Tbs. oil and the shallot mixture, sprinkle with salt, and cook, stirring, until the shallots are soft, about 2 minutes.

5. Return the beef to the pan. Stir the soy mixture and add it, along with half of the cilantro and basil, and cook, stirring to let the flavors meld, 2 minutes. Season to taste with salt and serve sprinkled with the remaining lime juice, cilantro, and basil. —*Tony Rosenfeld*

PER SERVING: 350 CALORIES | 27G PROTEIN | 8G CARB | 23G TOTAL FAT | 5G SAT FAT | 12G MONO FAT | 5G POLY FAT | 45MG CHOL | 1,040G SODIUM | 1G FIBER

More about Serrano Chiles

Very hot chiles that are smaller and hotter than jalapeños, serranos are most often sold green, when they lend a tangy, herbal, vegetal flavor. In late summer, you may see fully ripe, red serrano chiles. If your market doesn't have serranos, substitute another small, hot chile, such as the Thai bird chile.

Choose chiles that are shiny and firm with strong, uniform color. They should feel dense and heavy for their size. Avoid chiles that are flaccid, wrinkled, bruised, blemished, or discolored.

pecan-crusted skirt steak

SERVES 4

½ Tbs. olive oil

1½ lb. skirt steak, trimmed

2 tsp. kosher salt

½ tsp. freshly ground black pepper

¾ cup pecan pieces

2 Tbs. cold butter, cut into small pieces

2 tsp. honey

1½ tsp. roughly chopped fresh rosemary

This main course is just right with coleslaw or with steamed broccoli served with a few lemon wedges on the side.

1. Position an oven rack about 6 inches from the broiler and heat the broiler on high.

2. Line a large, rimmed, baking sheet with foil and grease the foil with the oil. If necessary, cut the steak crosswise into pieces 8 to 10 inches long. Arrange the steak on the baking sheet in a single layer and season with 1 tsp. salt and ¼ tsp. pepper. Put the pecans, butter, honey, rosemary, 1 tsp. salt, and ¼ tsp. pepper in a food processor and pulse until well combined and the pecans are finely chopped.

3. Broil the steak until lightly browned, 3 to 4 minutes. Flip it and broil until it's cooked nearly to your liking, about 3 minutes more for medium rare. Spread the pecan mixture over the steak, patting the mixture with the back of a spoon to help it adhere. Continue broiling until the pecan coating is toasted and fragrant, 1 to 2 minutes. Set the steak aside to rest for 5 minutes.

4. Thinly slice the steak against the grain and transfer to plates. If the pecan coating falls off the steak as you're slicing it, spoon it over the top. —*Liz Pearson*

PER SERVING: 510 CALORIES | 36G PROTEIN | 6G CARB | 39G TOTAL FAT | 11G SAT FAT | 20G MONO FAT | 6G POLY FAT | 100MG CHOL | 680MG SODIUM | 2G FIBER

quick beef enchiladas with salsa verde

SERVES 4

Kosher salt

- **1** lb. tomatillos (about 15 medium), husked and rinsed
- **3** jalapeños, stemmed and halved lengthwise (seeded, if you like)
- **1** large yellow onion, half cut into 4 wedges, half chopped
- **⅔** cup roughly chopped fresh cilantro
- **1½** Tbs. canola oil
- **1** lb. lean ground beef
- **2** tsp. ground cumin
- **¼** tsp. freshly ground black pepper
- **8** 6-inch corn tortillas
- **1½** cups shredded Monterey Jack

An easy, homemade salsa verde adds a tangy kick to these hearty enchiladas.

1. Bring a medium pot of salted water to a boil. Add the tomatillos, jalapeños, and onion wedges; cover and simmer until tender, about 10 minutes. Drain well and transfer to a blender along with ⅓ cup of the cilantro. Purée until just slightly chunky and season to taste with salt.

2. Meanwhile, heat 1 Tbs. of the oil in a large skillet over medium-high heat. Add the beef, chopped onion, cumin, 1 tsp. salt, and the pepper and cook, stirring occasionally to break up the meat, until cooked through, about 5 minutes. Stir ½ cup of the salsa verde into the beef.

3. Position a rack about 6 inches from the broiler and heat the broiler to high. Grease a 9x13-inch metal or ceramic baking dish with the remaining ½ Tbs. oil.

4. Wrap the tortillas in a few slightly damp paper towels and microwave on high until warm, 30 to 45 seconds. Working with one tortilla at a time, spoon some of the beef mixture down the center of the tortilla and sprinkle with 1 Tbs. of the cheese. Roll up snugly and transfer to the prepared baking dish, seam side down. Repeat with the remaining tortillas and beef mixture. Pour the remaining salsa verde over the enchiladas and sprinkle with the remaining cheese. Broil until golden brown and bubbly, 3 to 5 minutes. Garnish with the remaining cilantro and serve. —*Liz Pearson*

PER SERVING: 580 CALORIES | 36G PROTEIN | 40G CARB | 31G TOTAL FAT | 12G SAT FAT | 12G MONO FAT | 3.5G POLY FAT | 110MG CHOL | 790MG SODIUM | 6G FIBER

thai-style steak with red curry sauce and spicy carrot salad

SERVES 4

1½ lb. sirloin steak

1½ tsp. kosher salt

¼ tsp. freshly ground black pepper

2 Tbs. canola oil

3 Tbs. fresh lime juice

2 Tbs. fish sauce

2 tsp. light brown sugar

6 medium carrots, peeled and grated

¼ cup tightly packed fresh cilantro, roughly chopped

1 to 2 jalapeño or serrano chiles, stemmed, seeded, and finely chopped

⅔ cup canned unsweetened coconut milk

1 Tbs. Thai red curry paste

You can find Thai red curry paste in the Asian section of your supermarket, or try an Asian market, which might have more brand options. Be sure to shake the coconut milk vigorously before you open the can.

1. Season the steak all over with the salt and pepper. Heat 1 Tbs. of the oil in a large heavy-duty skillet over medium-high heat. Cook the steak, flipping once, until it's well browned on the outside and medium rare on the inside, 10 to 12 minutes total.

2. Meanwhile, put the remaining 1 Tbs. oil, 2 Tbs. of the lime juice, 1½ Tbs. of the fish sauce, and 1 tsp. of the sugar in a large bowl and whisk to combine and dissolve the sugar. Add the carrots, cilantro, and chiles and toss well to coat.

3. When the steak is done, transfer to a large plate, loosely cover with foil, and keep warm. Return the skillet to the stovetop over medium-low heat. Add ⅓ cup water and bring to a boil, scraping with a wooden spoon to release any brown bits. Add the coconut milk, curry paste, and the remaining 1 Tbs. lime juice, ½ Tbs. fish sauce, and 1 tsp. sugar; cook, whisking constantly, until thickened and fragrant, 4 to 5 minutes. Season to taste with salt and pepper.

4. Thinly slice the steak across the grain and transfer to plates. Spoon the sauce over the top and serve with the carrot salad on the side.
—*Liz Pearson*

PER SERVING: 400 CALORIES | 30G PROTEIN | 15G CARB | 25G TOTAL FAT | 11G SAT FAT | 9G MONO FAT | 2.5G POLY FAT | 75MG CHOL | 1,300MG SODIUM | 3G FIBER

beef ragù over spaghetti squash with garlic bread

SERVES 4

¼ **baguette, halved lengthwise**

1½ **Tbs. unsalted butter, melted**

6 **medium cloves garlic**

Kosher salt and freshly ground black pepper

1 **small (2½-lb.) spaghetti squash, halved lengthwise and seeded**

1 **Tbs. extra-virgin olive oil**

1 **lb. lean ground beef**

1 **small yellow onion, finely chopped**

1 **15-oz. can crushed tomatoes**

¼ **cup coarsely chopped fresh basil**

¼ **cup freshly grated Parmigiano-Reggiano**

Spaghetti squash is used like pasta to delicious effect, and a quick garlic bread rounds out the meal.

1. Heat the oven to 375°F. Arrange the bread cut side up on a foil-lined baking sheet. Brush it with the butter. Peel and chop the garlic. Divide the garlic in half and sprinkle one-half with a generous pinch of salt. Using the flat side of a chef's knife, mince and mash the garlic and salt together to form a smooth paste. Spread each piece of bread evenly with garlic paste and season with salt and pepper. Bake until light golden brown and crisp, 12 to 14 minutes. Cut each piece in half to make 4 pieces total, and cover with foil to keep warm.

2. Meanwhile, arrange the spaghetti squash in a single layer in the bottom of a large, wide pot. (Don't worry if the squash halves don't lie completely flat in the pot.) Add ½ inch of water, cover the pot, and bring to a boil. Reduce to a simmer and cook until the squash is tender enough to shred when raked with a fork but still somewhat crisp, 15 to 20 minutes. Transfer the squash to a plate and set aside until cool enough to handle.

3. While the squash cooks, heat the oil in a 12-inch skillet over medium-high heat. Add the beef, the remaining chopped garlic, onion, ½ tsp. salt, and ¼ tsp. pepper; cook, stirring to break up the meat, until just cooked through, 5 to 6 minutes. Drain and discard the fat if necessary. Add the tomatoes, basil, and ¼ cup water; stir well and bring to a boil. Reduce the heat to medium low and simmer for 10 minutes. Season to taste with salt and pepper.

4. With a fork, rake the squash flesh into strands, transfer to plates, and season to taste with salt. Ladle the beef ragù over the squash and garnish with the Parmigiano. Serve with the garlic bread. —*Liz Pearson*

PER SERVING: 370 CALORIES | 26G PROTEIN | 27G CARB | 19G TOTAL FAT | 8G SAT FAT | 8G MONO FAT | 1.5G POLY FAT | 80MG CHOL | 410MG SODIUM | 6G FIBER

smoky rib-eye steaks with loaded mashed potatoes

SERVES 4

- **2 lb. Yukon Gold potatoes, scrubbed and cut into 1-inch chunks**
- **4 slices thick-cut bacon**
- **2 boneless beef rib-eye steaks (about 2 lb. total)**
- **1½ tsp. sweet smoked paprika**
- **Kosher salt and freshly ground black pepper**
- **½ cup whole milk**
- **2 Tbs. unsalted butter**
- **3 oz. (¾ cup) grated sharp Cheddar**
- **½ cup sour cream**
- **2 medium scallions, thinly sliced**

All the ingredients in a loaded baked potato—bacon, scallions, cheese, and sour cream—are added to mashed potatoes in this hearty meal.

1. Arrange a steamer basket in a large pot with 1 inch of water in the bottom. Spread the potatoes in the basket in an even layer, cover, and bring to a boil. Reduce the heat to medium low and steam until the potatoes are tender, about 15 minutes.

2. Meanwhile, cook the bacon in a large cast-iron skillet over medium heat, turning once, until crisp, 7 to 8 minutes total. Transfer the bacon to a paper-towel-lined plate; discard all but 1 Tbs. of the fat from the skillet.

3. Season the steaks all over with the paprika, 1½ tsp. salt, and ½ tsp. pepper. Heat the skillet with the reserved bacon fat over medium-high heat. Arrange the steaks in the skillet in a single layer. Cook, flipping once, until deep golden brown outside and medium rare inside, 10 to 12 minutes total. Transfer the steaks to a cutting board and let rest for 5 minutes.

4. Meanwhile, transfer the hot potatoes to a large bowl. Stir in the milk and butter and mash with a potato masher until just combined. Stir in the cheese, sour cream, scallions, and salt and pepper to taste.

5. Slice the steaks across the grain and transfer to dinner plates. Serve the potatoes on the side with the bacon crumbled on top.
—*Liz Pearson*

PER SERVING: 870 CALORIES | 59G PROTEIN | 41G CARB | 52G TOTAL FAT | 25G SAT FAT | 19G MONO FAT | 2G POLY FAT | 170MG CHOL | 910MG SODIUM | 4G FIBER

More about Yukon Golds

Developed in Canada, Yukon Golds are a cross between a North American white potato and a wild South American yellow-fleshed one. Their golden flesh is richly flavored and fairly firm and moist, with medium starch content. A perfect compromise between dry, fluffy russet potatoes and moist, waxy varieties, Yukon Golds are incredibly versatile. They're superb for mashing and in soups and chowders, and they're great for roasting and sautéing, too.

Choose Yukon Golds that feel heavy and firm. Avoid those that are soft, wrinkled, or blemished. And try not to buy potatoes in plastic bags since it's hard to evaluate them. Small, immature Yukon Golds are often sold as "baby Yukon Golds." They're good for roasting and are a substitute for fingerlings or new potatoes. Refuse to buy potatoes that show even a hint of green. They've been "lightstruck." The green indicates the presence of solanine, which is produced when potatoes are exposed to light, either in the field or after harvest. This mildly poisonous alkaloid has a bitter flavor that can cause an upset stomach. If your potatoes turn green after you get them home, peel off all traces of the colored flesh before cooking.

Prepping

Wash well and remove any blemishes with a paring knife. Peel or not as your recipe advises. Potatoes cooked in their skins will be more flavorful, hold their shape better, and absorb less water. Also, the skins come off much easier once the potatoes have been cooked.

Storing

Store potatoes away from light in a place that's cool (but not cold) and dry. Any potato that's stored too long at a low temperature will take on an unpleasant sweetness as the starch converts to sugar. Potatoes and onions release gases that interact and make each spoil more quickly, so store them separately.

cube steak with lime mojo

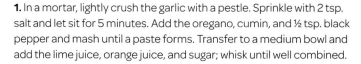

SERVES 4

- 8 medium cloves garlic, peeled

  Kosher salt

- 1½ tsp. finely chopped fresh oregano

- 1 tsp. ground cumin

  Freshly ground black pepper

- ¾ cup fresh lime juice (from about 4 medium limes)

- ½ cup fresh orange juice (from about 1 large orange)

- 1 tsp. granulated sugar

- 4 beef cube steaks (1¼ to 1½ lb. total)

- 1 Tbs. canola oil

- ½ large white onion, thinly sliced

- ½ large red bell pepper, cored and thinly sliced

Mojo is a garlicky citrus sauce that's popular throughout Latin America and the Caribbean. This lime-heavy version (most mojo is made with sour oranges, a tropical fruit) is a perfect marinade for cube steak, a quick-cooking cut of beef round. Serve with rice and beans or rice pilaf.

1. In a mortar, lightly crush the garlic with a pestle. Sprinkle with 2 tsp. salt and let sit for 5 minutes. Add the oregano, cumin, and ½ tsp. black pepper and mash until a paste forms. Transfer to a medium bowl and add the lime juice, orange juice, and sugar; whisk until well combined.

2. Lay the steaks in a 9x13-inch glass or ceramic dish and pour the garlic mixture (the mojo) over them. Let the steaks marinate for no more than 10 minutes.

3. Meanwhile, heat the oil in a 12-inch skillet over high heat. Add the onions and peppers and cook, stirring constantly, until they begin to soften, about 2 minutes. Transfer to a bowl.

4. Add the steaks to the pan along with 2 Tbs. of the mojo (discard the rest). Cook for 2 minutes, flip, add the onions and peppers, cover, and cook for 1 minute more. Uncover and continue cooking until the meat is just cooked through, about 2 minutes more.

5. Serve the steaks topped with the onions, peppers, and a drizzle of the cooked mojo. —*Julissa Roberts*

PER SERVING: 230 CALORIES | 27G PROTEIN | 6G CARB | 10G TOTAL FAT | 2.5G SAT FAT | 4.5G MONO FAT | 1.5G POLY FAT | 60MG CHOL | 200MG SODIUM | 1G FIBER

> Room-temperature limes are easier to juice than cold ones. Let the fruit sit out of the refrigerator for an hour or two; then just before juicing, roll it on the counter, pressing down hard on the lime with your palm. This softens and breaks open the cells inside, letting the lime yield more of its juice.

sirloin steaks with garlicky swiss chard

SERVES 4

- 2 lb. sirloin steak, 1 inch thick
- 1½ tsp. dried rosemary, coarsely chopped
- Kosher salt and freshly ground black pepper
- ¼ cup extra-virgin olive oil
- ¾ cup dry red wine, such as merlot
- 4 large cloves garlic, minced
- 2 Tbs. red-wine vinegar
- 1 tsp. granulated sugar
- ½ tsp. Dijon mustard
- 2 large bunches Swiss chard (about 1½ lb. total), stems very thinly sliced and leaves roughly chopped
- 2 oz. (1 cup) pecorino romano, thinly shaved with a vegetable peeler (optional)

Sear the steak, and then finish it in the oven while you cook the chard. Serve with roasted potatoes or rice pilaf.

1. Position a rack in the center of the oven and heat the oven to 400°F. Trim and cut the steak into 4 portions. Season the steaks all over with the rosemary, 2 tsp. salt, and ½ tsp. pepper.

2. Heat 1 Tbs. of the oil in a large (12-inch) skillet over medium-high heat. Working in 2 batches if necessary, arrange the steaks in the skillet in a single layer and cook, turning once, until nicely browned, 3 to 4 minutes per side. Remove the skillet from the heat, transfer the steaks to a rimmed baking sheet, and roast until medium rare (130°F to 135°F), 4 to 6 minutes more. Set the steaks aside to rest.

3. Meanwhile, return the skillet to medium-high heat. Carefully add the wine and cook, scraping up any browned bits with a wooden spoon, until reduced by about half, 3 to 4 minutes.

4. Add the garlic to the skillet and cook until fragrant, about 10 seconds. Whisk in the vinegar, sugar, mustard, ¼ tsp. salt, and ⅛ tsp. pepper. Drizzle in the remaining 3 Tbs. oil while whisking constantly.

5. Add the chard stems and cook, stirring occasionally, until beginning to soften, 5 minutes. Add the chard leaves in batches and cook, tossing, until the leaves are wilted enough to fit comfortably in the skillet, about 2 minutes. Cover the skillet and cook, tossing once or twice, until just tender, about 5 minutes.

6. Transfer the steaks to plates and top with the chard. Sprinkle with the pecorino romano, if using, and serve. —*Liz Pearson*

PER SERVING: 530 CALORIES | 43G PROTEIN | 10G CARB | 31G TOTAL FAT | 10G SAT FAT | 15G MONO FAT | 2G POLY FAT | 110MG CHOL | 1,320MG SODIUM | 3G FIBER

More about Swiss Chard

Swiss chard has a thick, flat central stem and glossy green, slightly crinkled leaves. Colorful rainbow chard is the tastiest chard variety, because each color has a slightly different flavor. It has the familiar mineral quality of spinach, slightly exaggerated toward the flavor of beets (the red leaves even more so), with a mild sea-salty dimension as well. Chard can be used much like spinach in braises, gratins, and the like, though unlike spinach it's a bit too tough to serve raw. At the market, look for bunches with perky leaves and no decay on the stems.

Prepping

Though the thick stems are good to eat, they take longer to cook than the leaves, so you'll need to remove them and cook them separately (or start them before you add the leaves). To remove the stems, simply lay each leaf flat and run a sharp knife down both sides of the stem.

skirt steak tacos with spicy sour cream

SERVES 4

- ½ cup sour cream
- ¼ tsp. ground chipotle chile
- Kosher salt
- 1 Tbs. extra-virgin olive oil
- 1 tsp. ground cumin
- Freshly ground pepper
- 1 lb. skirt steak (¾ inch thick)
- 8 6-inch flour or corn tortillas
- ¼ small head iceberg lettuce, shredded (2 cups)
- 2 medium ripe tomatoes (8 oz. each), cored and chopped (2 cups)
- 1 medium ripe avocado, pitted, peeled, and sliced ¼ inch thick
- ⅓ cup chopped red onion

A chipotle chile is a smoked and dried jalapeño. Ground to a powder, it adds a fiery kick to the creamy sauce for these tacos. Look for ground chipotle in the supermarket spice section. If you don't have a grill, you can cook the steak on a grill pan over medium-high heat.

1. Prepare a medium-hot charcoal or gas grill fire.

2. Combine the sour cream, chipotle, and ¼ tsp. salt in a small bowl. Set aside at room temperature to let the flavors meld.

3. In a small bowl, mix the olive oil, cumin, ½ tsp. salt, and ¼ tsp. pepper. Rub this mixture on all sides of the steak. Grill the steak, covered, flipping once, until medium rare, 3 to 4 minutes per side. Transfer the steak to a large plate to rest for at least 5 minutes.

4. Meanwhile, warm the tortillas on the grill for about 30 seconds per side. Slice the steak across the grain into ¼-inch-thick slices. Fill each tortilla with some of the steak, lettuce, tomato, avocado, and onion. Drizzle with the sauce and serve. —*Adeena Sussman*

PER SERVING: 560 CALORIES | 32G PROTEIN | 42G CARB | 30G TOTAL FAT | 9G SAT FAT | 16G MONO FAT | 3G POLY FAT | 75MG CHOL | 700MG SODIUM | 7G FIBER

Skirt steak has a coarse grained that runs crosswise rather than lengthwise. While it has a texture similar to flank steak, it is more tender and has a beefier flavor. If you can't find skirt steak at the market, substitute hanger or flank steak. Be sure to cook this cut of meat no further than medium rare to keep it from drying out.

new york steaks with martini butter

SERVES 4

- **4** 9- to 10-oz. boneless beef strip steaks, about 1 inch thick, trimmed of excess fat

  Kosher salt and freshly ground black pepper

- **3** Tbs. extra-virgin olive oil

- **¼** cup drained pimiento-stuffed Spanish olives (martini olives), plus 4 olives, sliced, for garnish

- **2** Tbs. gin or vodka

- **1** Tbs. dry vermouth

- **2** tsp. Dijon mustard

- **2** oz. (4 Tbs.) unsalted butter, softened

Top a simple steak, pork chop, or chicken breast with a compound (flavored) butter, and an average dish turns into an exceptional one. Serve these steaks with french fries and steamed broccoli or a Caesar salad.

1. Generously season both sides of the steaks with salt and pepper. Heat the oil in a 14-inch skillet over medium-high heat until shimmering hot (if you don't have a 14-inch skillet, divide the oil between two 10-inch skillets). Add the steaks and cook to your desired doneness, about 4 minutes per side for medium rare (130°F to 135°F).

2. Meanwhile, in a food processor, combine the ¼ cup olives, gin or vodka, vermouth, mustard, ½ tsp. salt, and ¼ tsp. pepper and pulse to coarsely chop. Add the butter and pulse to combine, scraping down the bowl as necessary.

3. Transfer the steaks to a platter or plates and divide the martini butter evenly among the steaks, letting it melt a bit.

4. Garnish with the sliced olives and serve. —*Jill Silverman Hough*

PER SERVING: 550 CALORIES | 50G PROTEIN | 1G CARB | 35G TOTAL FAT | 13G SAT FAT | 16G MONO FAT | 2.5G POLY FAT | 165MG CHOL | 470MG SODIUM | 0G FIBER

Sorting Out Beef Labels

Here are some of the most common terms and what they mean.

• **Grass-fed.** All cattle eat a natural diet of grass at the beginning of their lives. The question is whether the animal was switched to grain to fatten up before slaughter, or whether it continued to eat grass and hay throughout its life. From a health standpoint, exclusively grass-fed beef has more nutrients and less saturated fat, lower rates of the dangerous E. coli O157:H7 bacteria, and no risk of mad cow disease. From a flavor perspective, it's leaner than conventional beef, and it's less forgiving if overcooked; aim for rare or medium rare. Look for terms like "100% grass-fed" or "grass-finished" or for another third-party verifier, such as the American Grassfed Association (whose standards are stricter than those of the USDA).

• **Organic.** Beef that carries the USDA organic logo has met the department's standards, which prohibit the use of growth hormones, antibiotics, genetically modified feed, and animal by-products, among other things. The standards do not require a grass-only diet; the animal may be fed organic grain.

• **Free-range or free-roaming.** These terms have no legal definition when applied to beef (though they do for poultry). While they suggest, at minimum, that the animal had access to the outdoors, there are no standards that producers need to follow.

• **Raised without antibiotics.** This implies just what it says: that antibiotics were not given to the cows. The producer must submit documentation supporting the claim, but unless otherwise noted, it isn't independently verified.

• **No hormones administered.** This suggests that the animal received no growth-stimulating hormones. The producer must submit documentation supporting the claim, but unless otherwise noted, it isn't third-party verified.

• **Natural.** As defined by the USDA, "natural" or "all-natural" beef has been minimally processed and contains no preservatives or artificial ingredients. Since virtually all fresh beef conforms to these standards, the term has no real significance.

• **Naturally raised.** The USDA issued a standard for naturally raised beef that prohibits the use of hormones, antibiotics, and animal by-products but might not address other production concerns, such as animal welfare, diet, or access to pasture. You may see this term accompanied by the USDA "process verified" shield. However, the program is voluntary, so producers may use the term even without verification.

beef tenderloin with mushroom-dill sauce

SERVES 4

- **3** Tbs. unsalted butter
- **12** oz. assorted fresh mushrooms, cleaned, trimmed, and sliced ¼ inch thick
- Kosher salt
- **½** cup minced shallot (about 1 large)
- **2** Tbs. Cognac
- **¾** cup lower-salt beef broth
- **1** Tbs. vegetable oil
- **4** 6-oz. beef tenderloin steaks (about 1 inch thick), preferably at room temperature
- Freshly ground black pepper
- **3** Tbs. sour cream
- **1** tsp. Dijon mustard
- **½** Tbs. minced fresh dill

Topping succulent beef tenderloin steaks with sour-cream-and-Cognac-infused mushrooms turns a weeknight meal into a special occasion. Serve with roasted fingerling potatoes and a light, lemony Boston lettuce salad.

1. Melt the butter in a 12-inch heavy-duty skillet over medium-high heat. Add the mushrooms, season generously with salt, and cook, stirring occasionally, until golden, about 8 minutes. Reduce the heat to medium, add the shallot, and cook until softened, about 3 minutes more. Remove the skillet from the heat and carefully add the Cognac, stirring to deglaze the pan. Add the broth, bring to a boil over medium heat, reduce the heat to low, and simmer for 3 minutes. Cover the skillet, and set aside.

2. Meanwhile, heat the oil in a 12-inch cast-iron skillet over medium-high heat. Pat the steaks dry and season generously on both sides with salt and pepper. When the pan is very hot, add the steaks. Sear until a dark crust forms, 4 to 5 minutes. Turn the steaks, and cook to desired doneness, about 5 minutes more for medium rare. Remove the skillet from the heat, transfer the steaks to a platter, tent with foil, and let rest for 5 minutes.

3. With a rubber spatula, scrape the mushroom mixture into the cast-iron skillet. Add the sour cream and mustard, stirring until heated through and well mixed. If necessary, return the skillet to the stovetop to heat the sauce. Stir in the dill.

4. Transfer the steaks to plates, spoon the sauce over, and serve.
—*Laraine Perri*

PER SERVING: 410 CALORIES | 37G PROTEIN | 7G CARB | 24G TOTAL FAT | 11G SAT FAT | 8G MONO FAT | 2.5G POLY FAT | 120MG CHOL | 410MG SODIUM | 1G FIBER

vietnamese-style beef with garlic, black pepper & lime

SERVES 4

- 2 Tbs. soy sauce
- 2 Tbs. fresh lime juice
- 1½ Tbs. light brown sugar
- 1 Tbs. fish sauce
- 5 cloves garlic, minced
- 3 Tbs. peanut or canola oil
- **Kosher salt and freshly ground black pepper**
- 1½ lb. beef tri-tip steak or tenderloin, cut into ¾-inch pieces
- 1 medium yellow onion, sliced into ¼-inch-thick wedges
- 3 Tbs. chopped salted peanuts, preferably toasted
- 2 scallions, both green and white parts, thinly sliced

Steamed jasmine rice is a good accompaniment to this sweet-savory dish, but you can also serve it with lettuce leaves for wrapping or on a bed of watercress.

1. In a small bowl, combine the soy sauce, lime juice, sugar, and fish sauce; stir until the sugar dissolves. In another small bowl, stir the garlic, 1½ tsp. of the oil, and 1½ tsp. pepper.

2. Season the beef with salt and pepper. In a 12-inch nonstick skillet, heat 1½ tsp. of the oil over medium-high heat until shimmering hot. Swirl to coat the skillet. Add half of the beef in a single layer and cook, without stirring, until well browned, 1 to 2 minutes. Using tongs, turn the pieces over and brown on the other side, 1 to 2 minutes more. Transfer to a medium bowl. Add 1½ tsp. oil to the skillet and repeat with the remaining beef, adding it to the bowl with the first batch when done.

3. Put the remaining 1½ Tbs. oil in the skillet and heat until shimmering hot. Add the onion and cook, stirring frequently, until it begins to soften, 2 to 3 minutes. Add the garlic mixture and cook, stirring constantly, until fragrant, about 30 seconds. Return the beef and any accumulated juices to the pan and stir to combine. Add the soy sauce mixture and cook, stirring constantly, until the beef and onions are coated and the sauce thickens slightly, 2 to 3 minutes. Serve sprinkled with the peanuts and scallions. —*Dawn Yanagihara*

PER SERVING: 460 CALORIES | 40G PROTEIN | 13G CARB | 27G TOTAL FAT | 8G SAT FAT | 13G MONO FAT | 5G POLY FAT | 85MG CHOL | 1,430MG SODIUM | 1G FIBER

braised sausage with balsamic-glazed onions and grapes

SERVES 4

- **3** Tbs. olive oil
- **8** links sweet Italian sausage (about 2 lb.), pricked with a fork
- **1** large yellow onion, thinly sliced (about 2 cups)
- **½** tsp. kosher salt
- **½** cup lower-salt chicken broth
- **2** Tbs. balsamic vinegar
- **20** seedless red grapes, halved
- **2** Tbs. chopped fresh oregano

Sausage and grapes are a classic Italian pairing. The addition of balsamic vinegar and caramelized onions turns this into a quick, warming braise. Piercing the sausages with the tines of a fork will allow them to release some of their juices and infuse the broth. Serve with a crusty baguette and a green salad.

1. Heat 1 Tbs. oil in a large (12-inch) skillet over medium heat until it's shimmering. Add the sausages and cook, turning every couple minutes, until they're browned all over, about 8 minutes. Transfer to a large plate.

2. Add the remaining 2 Tbs. oil and the onion to the pot, sprinkle with the salt, and cook, stirring occasionally, until the onion softens completely and starts to turn light brown, about 7 minutes. Add the chicken broth and balsamic vinegar, and scrape the bottom of the pot with a wooden spoon to incorporate any browned bits. Reduce to a gentle simmer (medium-low or low depending on your stovetop). Add the sausages and grapes, cover the pot with the lid ajar, and cook, stirring occasionally, until the sausages are cooked through (slice into one to check), about 25 minutes. Serve sprinkled with the oregano.

—Tony Rosenfeld

Like bacon, sausage is a great ingredient to have on hand to mix in with vegetables, soups, stews, and pasta. Break up bulk sausage into crumbled pieces and keep in small zip-top bags in the freezer to pull out at a moment's notice.

seared pork medallions in marsala-mushroom sauce

SERVES 4

1½   **lb. pork tenderloin (1 large or 2 small), trimmed of fat and cut on the diagonal into 1½-inch rounds (about 8)**

     Kosher salt and freshly ground black pepper

½   **cup unbleached all-purpose flour**

2   **Tbs. olive oil**

1   **Tbs. unsalted butter**

1   **large shallot, finely diced (about ¼ cup)**

1   **oz. (1½ cups) dried mushrooms, rehydrated and chopped, plus ¾ cup soaking liquid**

⅓   **cup dry Marsala wine**

¼   **cup heavy cream**

2   **Tbs. chopped fresh flat-leaf parsley**

The traditional flavors of chicken Marsala are taken in a completely different direction in this recipe by subbing rounds of pork tenderloin for the chicken cutlets. You can serve the dish over egg noodles or with an herb risotto.

1. Sprinkle the pork with 1 tsp. salt and ½ tsp. black pepper. Put the flour in a small bowl, and then dredge the pork in the flour, shaking off any excess.

2. Heat 1 Tbs. oil and the butter in a large (12-inch) heavy-duty skillet over medium heat until the butter melts. Add the pork and cook, without touching or turning the rounds, until it starts to brown nicely and easily releases from the pan, about 4 minutes. Flip and cook the other sides in the same manner until the pork is cooked through and then transfer to a large serving platter. Cover loosely with foil.

3. To make the sauce, add the remaining 1 Tbs. oil and shallot to the pan, sprinkle with ¼ tsp. salt, and cook, stirring, until the shallot softens and becomes translucent, about 2 minutes. Add the mushrooms and cook, stirring, for 1 minute. Add the Marsala, raise the heat to high, and cook, scraping the bottom of the pan with a wooden spoon to loosen any browned bits, until the liquid has almost completely reduced, about 2 minutes. Stir in the mushroom soaking liquid and cook until it reduces by about half, about 4 minutes. Whisk in the cream and bring to a boil. Take the sauce off the heat and spoon it over the pork. Serve sprinkled with parsley. *—Tony Rosenfeld*

how to rehydrate mushrooms

Bring 2 cups water to a boil in a 2-quart saucepan, add the mushrooms, and boil for 3 minutes; remove the pot from the heat, cover and let sit for 20 minutes, or until the mushrooms become tender. Using a slotted spoon, transfer the mushrooms to a plate. Strain the soaking liquid through a coffee filter or a paper towel and reserve; yields about 1 cup of mushroom liquid.

pork chops with green chiles and onions

SERVES 4

- **1 tsp. ground cumin**
- **1 tsp. pure ancho chile powder or chili powder**
- **Kosher salt and freshly ground black pepper**
- **4 center-cut boneless pork chops, preferably about 1 inch thick (about 1 ½ lb. total)**
- **¾ cup lower-salt chicken broth; more as needed**
- **1 4-oz. can chopped green chiles**
- **3 Tbs. chopped jarred jalapeños (from about 12 slices)**
- **1 Tbs. cider vinegar**
- **¾ cup unbleached all-purpose flour**
- **3 Tbs. olive oil**
- **1 medium yellow onion, thinly sliced**

A double dose of chile—canned and powder—adds pleasant heat to this quick skillet braise. The peppers' light green hue may fade slightly as they simmer, but their spicy essence intensifies into a delicious sauce.

1. In a small bowl, combine the cumin, chile powder, 1¼ tsp. salt, and ¾ tsp. pepper. Sprinkle on both sides of the pork and set aside. In a blender or food processor, purée the chicken broth, green chiles (with their liquid), jalapeños, and vinegar until smooth.

2. Put the flour in a pie plate and dredge the pork chops, shaking to remove any excess. Heat a 12-inch skillet over medium-high heat for 1 minute. Pour in 2 Tbs. of the oil and heat until shimmering hot, about 1 minute. Add the pork chops and cook, without moving, until they're brown around the edges and release easily from the pan, 2 to 3 minutes. Reduce the heat to medium, flip, and cook the other side until browned, about 2 minutes more. Transfer to a large plate.

3. Over medium-high heat, add the remaining 1 Tbs. oil and the onion to the skillet. Sprinkle with ½ tsp. salt and cook, stirring occasionally, until wilted and golden, about 4 minutes. Add the green chile mixture and bring to a boil. Reduce to a simmer and cook, stirring, until the mixture thickens slightly and the onions are completely tender, 2 to 3 minutes more; add a splash of chicken broth if the mixture seems dry. Season to taste with salt and pepper.

4. Return the chops to the pan, nestling them into the onions. Cover and simmer gently until the pork is fairly firm to the touch with just a little give, 3 to 5 minutes. With a paring knife, make a nick in a thicker chop to make sure it's only just a little pink.

5. Serve the pork chops topped with the sauce. *—Tony Rosenfeld*

PER SERVING: 360 CALORIES | 39G PROTEIN | 10G CARB | 18G TOTAL FAT | 4G SAT FAT | 11G MONO FAT | 2G POLY FAT | 115MG CHOL | 810MG SODIUM | 2G FIBER

pork chops stuffed with pine nuts and herbs

SERVES 6

6 **center-cut, bone-in pork loin chops (1¼ to 1½ inches thick)**

½ **cup fresh mint**

½ **cup fresh parsley**

⅓ **cup fresh tarragon**

¼ **oz. (⅓ cup) finely grated pecorino romano**

5 **Tbs. extra-virgin olive oil**

3 **medium cloves garlic, peeled**

1 **tsp. finely grated lemon zest**

½ **tsp. kosher salt**

¼ **tsp. freshly ground black pepper**

¾ **cup pine nuts, toasted**

⅓ **cup golden raisins**

1 **Tbs. unsalted butter, cut into 6 pieces**

A take on traditional pesto, the filling for these pork chops is amped up with sweet raisins and fresh herbs. Roast some potatoes and broccoli to serve with the chops.

1. Position a rack in the center of the oven and heat the oven to 400°F.

2. With a sharp knife, make a horizontal slit in each pork chop to create a 3½-inch-long pocket.

3. In a food processor, combine the mint, parsley, tarragon, pecorino, 3 Tbs. of the oil, the garlic, lemon zest, salt, and pepper. Pulse until finely chopped. Add ½ cup of the pine nuts and pulse until the nuts are roughly chopped. Stir in the remaining ¼ cup pine nuts and the raisins. Season the insides of the pockets with salt and pepper and stuff with the filling. Secure the pockets with toothpicks. Season the outside of the meat generously with salt and pepper.

4. Heat 1 Tbs. of the oil in a 12-inch skillet over medium-high heat until shimmering hot. Sear 3 of the pork chops on both sides until well browned, about 6 minutes total; transfer to a large rimmed baking sheet. Repeat with the remaining 1 Tbs. oil and the remaining pork chops. Top each chop with a piece of butter and roast in the oven until an instant-read thermometer inserted into the thickest part of the pork chops registers 145°F, 10 to 12 minutes. Discard the toothpicks and serve drizzled with the pan juice. —*Samantha Seneviratne*

PER SERVING: 440 CALORIES | 25G PROTEIN | 11G CARB | 33G TOTAL FAT | 7G SAT FAT | 15G MONO FAT | 8G POLY FAT | 65MG CHOL | 230MG SODIUM | 1G FIBER

> **Don't substitute boneless pork chops for this recipe—the bone-in variety is more flavorful and will make the meat less likely to dry out during cooking.**

how to toast pine nuts

There are three ways to toast the nuts, each with its own pros and cons.

OVEN
Spread the nuts on a baking sheet and bake at 375°F, stirring occasionally, until golden brown, 5 to 10 minutes.

PRO: The color of oven-toasted nuts is evenly golden.

CON: You have to heat the oven. Use this method only if you're heating the oven for other reasons, too.

TOASTER OVEN
Spread the nuts on the baking sheet that came with the toaster oven and bake at 325°F, stirring frequently, until golden brown, 3 to 5 minutes.

PRO: Produces results similar to those from a conventional oven, but a toaster oven heats up much faster and is more energy efficient.

CON: Closer proximity to the heating elements in a toaster oven increases the risk of burning the nuts, hence the need for more frequent stirring and a lower baking temperature.

SKILLET
Put the nuts in a dry skillet and cook over medium-low heat, stirring frequently, until golden in spots, about 3 minutes.

PRO: The quickest and most convenient method.

CON: The nuts develop spotty, uneven color and burn more easily than with the two oven methods.

coffee-rubbed pork tenderloin with watermelon rind relish

SERVES 4

FOR THE RELISH

- **4** **lb. watermelon**
- **2** **Valencia oranges**
- **⅔** **cup packed light brown sugar**
- **½** **cup apple cider vinegar**
- **1** **medium shallot, thinly sliced**
- **½** **medium jalapeño, finely chopped (with ribs and seeds)**
- **Kosher salt**

FOR THE PORK

- **1** **Tbs. very finely ground coffee beans (preferably French roast)**
- **2** **tsp. packed light brown sugar**
- **1** **tsp. chili powder**
- **Kosher salt**
- **2** **Tbs. extra-virgin olive oil**
- **2** **1-lb. pork tenderloins, trimmed**

Think twice before you toss out your watermelon rinds; their neutral flavor readily absorbs the sweet-spicy seasonings in this relish. Ground coffee beans infuse the pork with rich, earthy notes.

MAKE THE RELISH

1. Cut the flesh away from the watermelon rind. Cut enough of the flesh into ¼-inch dice to yield ½ cup (reserve the rest for another use). Using a vegetable peeler, remove the dark-green skin from the rind and discard. Cut the rind into ¼-inch dice; you should have about 3 cups.

2. Slice the ends off one of the oranges. Stand the orange on one cut end and cut off the peel and white pith to expose the flesh. Cut the orange segments from the membrane, cut each segment into 3 pieces, and put them in a small bowl. Squeeze the juice from the membrane into the bowl. Repeat with the remaining orange.

3. In a 3-quart saucepan, combine ⅔ cup water with the watermelon flesh and rind, orange segments and juice, brown sugar, vinegar, shallot, jalapeño, and ¼ tsp. salt. Bring to a boil over medium-high heat, stirring occasionally, until the sugar dissolves, about 4 minutes. Reduce the heat to low and simmer, stirring occasionally, until the rind is translucent and the mixture thickens, about 40 minutes. Season to taste with salt, and let cool to room temperature.

MAKE THE PORK

1. In a small bowl, combine the coffee, brown sugar, chili powder, and 2 tsp. salt. Add the olive oil and mix well. Rub the mixture evenly over the pork and set aside.

2. Prepare a medium-high gas or charcoal grill for indirect cooking.

3. Put the tenderloins on the hot side of the grill, cover, and cook, flipping once, until grill marks form on 2 sides, about 4 minutes per side. Move the tenderloins to the cooler side of the grill and continue to cook, covered, until the internal temperature of the pork reaches 140°F to 145°F, 7 to 9 minutes. Transfer to a cutting board, tent with foil, and let rest for about 10 minutes.

4. Slice the pork and serve with the watermelon rind relish.
—*Samantha Seneviratne*

PER SERVING: 540 CALORIES | 44G PROTEIN | 51G CARB | 17G TOTAL FAT | 4.5G SAT FAT | 10G MONO FAT | 1.5G POLY FAT | 110MG CHOL | 790MG SODIUM | 5G FIBER

grilled pork chops with sweet-and-sour onions

SERVES 4

- **4 ¾-inch-thick, bone-in pork loin chops (1¾ to 2 lb.)**
- **¼ cup extra-virgin olive oil**
- **1 Tbs. chopped fresh thyme**
- **Kosher salt and freshly ground black pepper**
- **1½ lb. red onions (about 3 medium), peeled and cut into ¼- to ½-inch-thick disks**
- **½ cup red-wine vinegar**
- **1 Tbs. granulated sugar**

Garlic bread drizzled with a bit of olive oil is the perfect accompaniment.

1. Prepare a medium-high fire on a gas or charcoal grill. In a medium bowl, toss the pork chops with 1 Tbs. of the oil, half of the thyme, 1 tsp. salt, and ½ tsp. pepper. Put the onions on a large plate and sprinkle with 2 Tbs. of the oil and 1½ tsp. salt. In a small bowl, whisk the vinegar, sugar, and the remaining thyme.

2. Grill the onions, covered, flipping once, until crisp-tender, 5 to 6 minutes per side. Return to the plate. Grill the pork, covered, flipping once, until firm to the touch and just cooked through, 3 to 4 minutes per side.

3. Transfer the pork to a large platter, brush with some of the vinegar mixture and tent loosely with foil. Heat the remaining 1 Tbs. oil in a large skillet over medium-high heat until it's shimmering hot. Add the onions and the remaining vinegar mixture and cook, stirring, until they absorb all of the liquid and take on a browned, glazed appearance, 3 to 4 minutes. Serve the pork chops with the onions. *—Tony Rosenfeld*

PER SERVING: 370 CALORIES | 25G PROTEIN | 21G CARB | 21G TOTAL FAT | 4.5G SAT FAT | 13G MONO FAT | 2.5G POLY FAT | 60MG CHOL | 760MG SODIUM | 3G FIBER

how to clean grill grates

To clean grill grates, heat them first to soften the stuck-on gunk and then scrub them with a stiff wire grill brush. Next, fold a paper towel into a little pad, grasp it with long-handled tongs, and dip it in some cooking oil. Quickly swab the grates with the towel, cleaning and oiling them at the same time. Repeat this step until the grates seem clean, and then cover the grill briefly to let it heat up again. If you're grilling something that tends to stick, give the grates another swipe of oil just before the food goes on.

pork chops with cider-dijon pan sauce

SERVES 4

4   **center-cut, bone-in pork chops (2 lb.)**

     Kosher salt and freshly ground black pepper

2   **Tbs. unsalted butter**

1   **medium red apple, such as Pink Lady, Fuji, or Gala, halved, cored, and cut into small dice**

1   **medium shallot, chopped (about ⅓ cup)**

½   **tsp. chopped fresh thyme**

½   **cup apple cider**

½   **cup lower-salt chicken broth**

1   **Tbs. Dijon mustard, preferably country-style (coarse-grained)**

An easy-to-make sauce gives everyday pork chops a flavor boost. Serve with homemade applesauce, rice, or mashed potatoes.

1. Position a rack in the center of the oven and heat the oven to 425°F. Line a large rimmed baking sheet with aluminum foil.

2. Season the chops with 1 tsp. salt and ½ tsp. pepper.

3. Melt the butter in a 12-inch skillet over medium-high heat until the foam subsides. Working in 2 batches, cook the chops until nicely browned, about 2 minutes per side. Transfer to the baking sheet and roast until no longer pink near the bone (use a paring knife to check), about 8 minutes.

4. Meanwhile, lower the heat to medium and add the apple, shallot, and thyme to the skillet and cook, stirring often, until beginning to brown and soften, about 2 minutes. Add the cider, scraping any bits off the bottom of the pan, and cook until reduced by half, about 2 minutes. Add the broth and mustard and continue to cook until slightly reduced, about 2 minutes. Remove from the heat and season to taste with salt and pepper. Serve the sauce over the chops.
—*Melissa Gaman*

PER SERVING: 290 CALORIES | 27G PROTEIN | 12G CARB | 15G TOTAL FAT | 7G SAT FAT | 5G MONO FAT | 1G POLY FAT | 85MG CHOL | 440MG SODIUM | 1G FIBER

pork chops with peach-ginger chutney

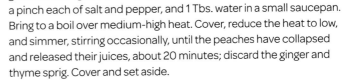

SERVES 4

2 medium peaches (about ¾ lb.), peeled, pitted, and chopped

1 3-inch piece fresh ginger, peeled and cut into 4 thick coins

1 large shallot, chopped

2 tsp. granulated sugar

1 large sprig fresh thyme

Kosher salt and freshly ground black pepper

¾ cup unbleached all-purpose flour

4 ¾-inch-thick boneless pork loin chops

¼ cup extra-virgin olive oil

A serrated peeler makes quick work of peeling peaches. If you don't have one, blanch the peaches in boiling water for about 30 seconds and the skins should come off easily.

1. Combine the peaches, ginger, shallot, sugar, thyme sprig, a pinch each of salt and pepper, and 1 Tbs. water in a small saucepan. Bring to a boil over medium-high heat. Cover, reduce the heat to low, and simmer, stirring occasionally, until the peaches have collapsed and released their juices, about 20 minutes; discard the ginger and thyme sprig. Cover and set aside.

2. Meanwhile, combine the flour, 1 tsp. salt, and ¼ tsp. pepper in a wide, shallow dish and stir to combine. Season the pork chops on both sides with salt and pepper. Dredge the chops in the flour mixture, shake off any excess, and transfer to a clean plate. Discard any remaining flour.

3. Heat the oil in a large (12-inch) skillet over medium heat. Arrange the pork chops in a single layer and cook, turning once, until deep golden brown all over and cooked through, about 12 minutes total.

4. Mash the peach chutney with a potato masher until slightly chunky. Season to taste with salt and pepper.

5. Transfer the pork chops to plates, top with the chutney, and serve.
—*Liz Pearson*

PER SERVING: 450 CALORIES | 20G PROTEIN | 17G CARB | 34G TOTAL FAT | 9G SAT FAT | 18G MONO FAT | 3.5G POLY FAT | 70MG CHOL | 450MG SODIUM | 1G FIBER

More about Ginger

Ginger's aroma, texture, and flavor varies depending upon the timing of its harvest. Early-harvest or young ginger (harvested after 6 months) is tender and sweet, while older, more mature ginger (harvested between 10 and 12 months) is more fibrous and spicy. Mature ginger is usually all that's available in American supermarkets, but young ginger can often be found in Asian markets. It's easily identified by its thin, papery skin, which can be left on, and pink-tinged tips. Look for ginger with skin (the thinner the better) that's smooth, unblemished, and almost translucent. When you break off the piece you want, the interior should be firm, crisp, and not overly fibrous (making it easier to slice). It should have a fresh, spicy fragrance.

stir-fried pork with kimchi and shiitake

SERVES 4

- **1** pork tenderloin (12 to 16 oz.), trimmed of silverskin and cut crosswise ¼ inch thick
- **1** Tbs. soy sauce

  Freshly ground black pepper
- **3** Tbs. peanut or canola oil
- **8** oz. fresh shiitake mushrooms, stems trimmed and caps cut into ¼-inch slices
- **6** scallions, cut into 1½-inch lengths
- **3** large cloves garlic, minced
- **16** oz. napa cabbage kimchi, drained and very coarsely chopped (about 2¾ cups)
- **3** Tbs. mirin (or 2 Tbs. sake or white wine plus 4 tsp. granulated sugar)
- **1** Tbs. Asian sesame oil

  Kosher salt
- **½** Tbs. toasted sesame seeds

There are many types of kimchi (Korean preserved vegetables), but spicy napa cabbage kimchi is the most popular and the best version for this recipe. It can be found at Asian markets and in the produce section of some large supermarkets. Steamed short-grain rice makes a good accompaniment to this dish.

1. In a medium bowl, toss the pork, ½ Tbs. of the soy sauce, and ⅛ tsp. pepper.

2. Heat 1 Tbs. of the oil in a 12-inch nonstick skillet over medium-high heat until you see the first wisp of smoke. Swirl to coat the pan, then add half of the pork and stir-fry until brown in spots and no longer pink, about 2 minutes. Transfer to a bowl. Add another 1 Tbs. of the oil to the skillet and repeat with the remaining pork.

3. Add the remaining 1 Tbs. of the oil to the pan and swirl to coat. Add the mushrooms and scallions and cook, stirring, until the mushrooms are shrunken in size and the scallions are wilted, 2 to 3 minutes. Stir in the garlic and cook until fragrant, about 30 seconds.

4. Add the kimchi, mirin, and the remaining ½ Tbs. soy sauce and cook, stirring frequently, until the liquid released by the kimchi is reduced to about ⅓ cup, about 3 minutes. (The amount of liquid released by the kimchi is somewhat unpredictable—if there is an excessive amount, cook until it reduces or spoon some of it off.) Add the pork and any accumulated juices and cook until heated through, 1 to 2 minutes more. Drizzle with the sesame oil and stir well. Season to taste with salt and pepper, sprinkle with the sesame seeds, and serve.
—*Dawn Yanagihara*

PER SERVING: 340 CALORIES | 23G PROTEIN | 17G CARB | 18G TOTAL FAT | 3.5G SAT FAT | 8G MONO FAT | 3.5G POLY FAT | 55MG CHOL | 1,700MG SODIUM | 3G FIBER

spicy jerk pork chops

SERVES 4

- **2** Tbs. extra-virgin olive oil; more for the pan
- **4** bone-in, center-cut pork chops (¾ inch thick, about 2½ lb. total)
- **2** tsp. kosher salt
- **¾** tsp. freshly ground black pepper
- **4** medium scallions (white and green parts), coarsely chopped
- **2** small Scotch bonnet or habanero chiles, seeded and coarsely chopped (wear gloves)
- **2** small limes, 1 juiced and 1 cut into 8 wedges
- **2** large cloves garlic, coarsely chopped
- **2** Tbs. coarsely chopped fresh ginger
- **1** Tbs. coarsely chopped fresh thyme
- **¾** tsp. ground allspice
- **⅛** tsp. ground cinnamon

This recipe is based on the fiery Jamaican seasoning known as jerk, made of Scotch bonnet chiles, ground spices, garlic, and herbs. Serve with a cabbage slaw and buttered white rice.

1. Position an oven rack about 4 inches from the broiler and heat the broiler to high. Lightly oil a broiler pan or a rack set over a large rimmed baking sheet.

2. Season the pork all over with 1 tsp. salt and the pepper. In a food processor, purée the oil, scallions, chiles, lime juice, garlic, ginger, thyme, allspice, cinnamon, and the remaining 1 tsp. salt. Coat the chops on all sides with the mixture and set on the broiler pan or rack.

3. Broil until the pork begins to brown, about 7 minutes. Flip and cook until browned, the meat is firm to the touch, and an instant-read thermometer inserted close to (but not touching) the bone registers 145°F, about 7 minutes more. Serve with the lime wedges.
—*Tony Rosenfeld*

PER SERVING: 650 CALORIES | 65G PROTEIN | 5G CARB | 41G TOTAL FAT | 14G SAT FAT | 21G MONO FAT | 3.5G POLY FAT | 165MG CHOL | 670MG SODIUM | 1G FIBER

hoisin pork with napa cabbage

SERVES 4

- 1 **lb. pork tenderloin, cut into ¼-inch-thick strips (about 3 inches long)**
- **Kosher salt**
- 3 **Tbs. hoisin sauce (I like Lee Kum Kee brand)**
- 2 **Tbs. soy sauce**
- 1 **Tbs. balsamic vinegar**
- 3 **Tbs. canola or peanut oil**
- 2 **tsp. minced garlic**
- 6 **cups napa cabbage, cut into 1½-inch pieces (about ¾ lb.)**
- 1 **red bell pepper, cored, thinly sliced, and cut into 2- to 3-inch lengths**
- ¼ **cup thinly sliced fresh chives**

Pork tenderloin is the most tender cut of pork and quite lean, too. Long and narrow, whole tenderloin ranges from ¾ lb. to 1½ lb. Because it's relatively inexpensive, widely available, and quick to cook, it's a great choice for weeknight cooking.

1. In a large bowl, season the pork with ½ tsp. salt. In a small bowl, mix the hoisin sauce, soy sauce, and vinegar.

2. Heat 2 Tbs. of the oil in a 12-inch nonstick skillet or large stir-fry pan over medium-high heat until shimmering hot. Add the pork and cook, stirring, until it browns and loses most of its raw appearance, about 2 minutes. Transfer to a plate.

3. Add the remaining 1 Tbs. oil to the skillet. Add the garlic, and once it begins to sizzle, add the cabbage and pepper. Sprinkle with ½ tsp. salt and cook, stirring, until the cabbage starts to wilt, about 2 minutes.

4. Add the hoisin mixture, the pork, and half of the chives and cook, tossing, until heated through, about 1 minute. Let sit for 2 minutes off the heat (the cabbage will exude some liquid and form a rich broth), toss well again, and serve sprinkled with the remaining chives.
—*Tony Rosenfeld*

PER SERVING: 290 CALORIES | 26G PROTEIN | 12G CARB | 15G TOTAL FAT | 2G SAT FAT | 8G MONO FAT | 3.5G POLY FAT | 65MG CHOL | 1,190MG SODIUM | 3G FIBER

More about Napa Cabbage

Napa cabbage has ruffled, thin light green leaves that are as tender as lettuce and crunchy white stems that are similar in texture to green cabbage. Napa cabbage is good when braised, sautéed, or stir-fried or when used raw in salads or slaws. If you can't find napa cabbage, use savoy cabbage, which has a similar crinkly, crunchy texture to its leaves.

Choosing
Look for medium-size cabbages that feel heavy for their size and have plenty of light green leaves.

Prepping
Remove and discard any discolored outer leaves before cutting Napa cabbage as you would green cabbage. Begin by slicing it in half lengthwise and removing its tough core.

Storing
Store whole cabbage in the refrigerator. Shredded cabbage will keep best sealed in a zip-top bag in the crisper drawer.

spicy korean-style pork medallions with asian slaw

SERVES 4 TO 6

1 large or 2 small pork tenderloins (about 1 ¼ lb.)

⅓ cup soy sauce

¼ cup rice vinegar

3 Tbs. light brown sugar

2 medium cloves garlic, minced

1½ Tbs. minced fresh ginger

1 Tbs. Asian sesame oil

1 Tbs. Asian chile sauce (like Sriracha)

1 lb. napa cabbage, thinly sliced (about 6 cups)

1 cup grated carrot (about 2 medium carrots)

4 scallions (both white and green parts), trimmed and thinly sliced

5 Tbs. canola or peanut oil

½ tsp. kosher salt

Medallions (thin rounds) cook quickly, so they're best sautéed on the stovetop, which allows you to control the heat and avoid overcooking the lean, tender meat.

1. Trim the pork of any silverskin and excess fat, and cut on the diagonal into ½-inch-thick medallions.

2. In a small measuring cup, whisk together the soy sauce, 2 Tbs. of the rice vinegar, 2 Tbs. of the brown sugar, the garlic, ginger, ½ Tbs. of the sesame oil, and 2 tsp. of the chile sauce. Toss ½ cup of this mixture with the pork medallions in a large bowl; reserve the remaining mixture to use as a sauce. Let the pork sit at room temperature for 25 minutes or refrigerate for up to 2 hours.

3. Meanwhile, in another large bowl, toss the cabbage and the carrot with half of the scallions, 1 Tbs. of the canola oil, the salt, and the remaining 2 Tbs. rice vinegar, 1 Tbs. brown sugar, ½ Tbs. sesame oil, and 1 tsp. chile sauce. Let sit for 15 minutes, toss again, and transfer to a large serving platter.

4. Heat 2 Tbs. of the canola oil in a 12-inch heavy-based skillet over medium-high heat until shimmering hot. Remove the pork from the marinade, shaking off the excess, and transfer the pork to a clean plate. Discard the marinade. Add half of the pork medallions to the skillet, spacing them evenly. Cook them without touching or turning the medallions until well browned, about 2 minutes. Flip and cook until the pork is just cooked through (slice into a piece to check), about 2 more minutes. Set the pork on top of the slaw. Pour out the oil and wipe the pan with paper towels (if the drippings on the bottom of the pan look like they may burn, wash the pan). Return the pan to medium-high heat. Add the remaining 2 Tbs. canola oil, and cook the remaining medallions in the same manner. Top the slaw with the remaining pork, and pour the reserved soy-ginger sauce over the medallions. Serve immediately, sprinkled with the remaining scallions.
—*Tony Rosenfeld*

PER SERVING: 290 CALORIES | 21G PROTEIN | 12G CARB | 17G TOTAL FAT | 2G SAT FAT, 9G MONO FAT | 4.5G POLY FAT | 55MG CHOL | 1,180MG SODIUM | 2G FIBER

grilled asian pork tenderloin with peanut sauce

SERVES 4 TO 5

- **1** cup light coconut milk
- **½** cup smooth peanut butter, preferably a natural variety
- **¼** cup soy sauce
- **3** Tbs. fresh lime juice
- **3** Tbs. dark brown sugar
- **2** large cloves garlic, minced (2½ tsp.)
- **2** tsp. ground coriander
- **2** small pork tenderloins (about 2 lb. total)

    Vegetable oil for the grill

Serve with steamed jasmine or short-grain rice and stir-fried spinach or snow peas.

1. In a large bowl, whisk the coconut milk, peanut butter, soy sauce, lime juice, brown sugar, garlic, and coriander to make a smooth sauce.

2. Trim the pork of excess fat and silverskin. Butterfly the tenderloins by splitting each one lengthwise almost but not quite all the way through, so the halves remain attached.

3. Open each tenderloin like a book, cover with plastic wrap, and pound to an even ½-inch thickness with a meat mallet or the bottom of a small skillet. Put the pork tenderloins in the bowl with the marinade and turn to coat. Let marinate for 10 to 20 minutes (or up to several hours in the refrigerator).

4. While the pork marinates, heat a gas grill with all burners on high. Clean and oil the grate (see the sidebar on p. 67). Remove the tenderloins from the marinade, letting excess marinade drip back into the bowl (don't discard the marinade). Grill the tenderloins, covered, turning once, until just cooked through, 5 to 7 minutes total (cut into one to check). Transfer to a carving board and let rest for 5 minutes.

5. Meanwhile, pour the marinade into a small saucepan and add 2 Tbs. water; bring to a boil, reduce the heat, and simmer for 3 minutes. Remove from the heat. If the sauce seems too thick, thin it with 1 or 2 tsp. water. Slice the pork and serve with the sauce on the side.
—*Pam Anderson*

PER SERVING: 300 CALORIES | 39G PROTEIN | 7G CARB | 12G TOTAL FAT | 3.5G SAT FAT | 2.5G MONO FAT | 0.5G POLY FAT | 100MG CHOL | 490MG SODIUM | 1G FIBER

lamb chops with lemon, thyme & mustard butter

SERVES 4

4 Tbs. unsalted butter, softened

1 tsp. whole-grain Dijon mustard

1 tsp. fresh thyme leaves, lightly chopped

¾ tsp. finely grated lemon zest

Kosher salt

Freshly ground black pepper

8 lamb loin chops (1½- to 2-inch-thick chops; about 3 lb.), trimmed

Serve the chops with sautéed haricots verts and tiny boiled potatoes.

1. In a small bowl, mash together the butter, mustard, thyme, zest ⅛ salt, and ⅛ pepper until well combined. Refrigerate until ready to use.

2. Position an oven rack 5 to 6 inches from the broiler element and heat the broiler to high. Line the bottom of a broiler pan with foil and replace the perforated top part of the pan. Arrange the chops on the pan. Season both sides of the lamb generously with salt and pepper. Broil until the first side is well browned, about 8 minutes. Turn the chops over with tongs and continue to broil until they're well browned and the center is cooked to your liking, 3 to 5 minutes longer for medium rare (cut into a chop near the bone to check).

3. Transfer the lamb to serving plates and top each chop with a dab of the flavored butter. Serve hot. —*Lori Longbotham*

PER SERVING: 720 CALORIES | 50G PROTEIN | 9G CARB | 57G TOTAL FAT | 27G SAT FAT | 22G MONO FAT | 4G POLY FAT | 225MG CHOL | 500MG SODIUM | 0G FIBER

grilled lamb chops with charred red onion chutney

SERVES 4

- 1 large red onion, cut cross-wise into ½-inch-thick slices
- 3 Tbs. canola oil

  Kosher salt and freshly ground black pepper
- 1 tsp. whole cumin seeds

  Pinch of crushed red pepper flakes
- 1 medium ripe tomato, cored and chopped
- 2 Tbs. apple cider vinegar
- 1 tsp. granulated sugar
- 4 ¾-inch-thick, bone-in lamb shoulder chops (2 to 2½ lb. total)

Grilled onions become a savory chutney after a quick simmer with fresh tomato, a touch of sugar, vinegar, and spices. Serve with grilled or roasted potatoes.

1. Prepare a medium-high gas or charcoal grill fire. Rub the onion slices with 1 Tbs. of the oil, keeping the rings intact, and season with 1 tsp. salt and ¼ tsp. pepper. Arrange them on the grill in a single layer and cook, flipping once, until lightly charred, 8 to 10 minutes. Transfer the onions to a cutting board and chop into small pieces.

2. Heat 1 Tbs. of the oil in a medium saucepan over medium-high heat. Add the cumin and pepper flakes and cook, stirring constantly, until toasted and fragrant, about 1 minute. Add the chopped onions, tomato, vinegar, sugar, ½ tsp. salt, ¼ tsp. pepper, and ⅓ cup water. Bring to a boil, cover, reduce the heat to medium, and boil until the onions are soft, 5 to 7 minutes. Uncover the pot and continue to boil, stirring often, until thickened, about 5 minutes more. Season to taste with salt and pepper.

3. Meanwhile, rub the lamb all over with the remaining 1 Tbs. oil and season with 2 tsp. salt and ½ tsp. pepper. Grill, flipping once, until deep golden brown outside and medium rare inside, about 8 minutes total. Serve topped with the chutney. —*Liz Pearson*

PER SERVING: 330 CALORIES | 29G PROTEIN | 6G CARB | 20G TOTAL FAT | 4G SAT FAT | 11G MONO FAT | 3.5G POLY FAT | 90MG CHOL | 1,070MG SODIUM | 1G FIBER

pistachio-crusted lamb chops

SERVES 4 TO 6

- **1 cup unsalted shelled pistachios**
- **Kosher salt**
- **3 Tbs. honey**
- **1 Tbs. fresh lemon juice**
- **1 tsp. ground cumin**
- **¼ tsp. cayenne**
- **½ tsp. freshly ground black pepper**
- **12 lamb rib chops (about 1½ lb.)**
- **2 Tbs. extra-virgin olive oil**

Serve the lamb chops with lentils and rice and plain Greek yogurt mixed with chopped mint.

1. Position a rack about 4 inches from the broiler and heat the broiler on high.

2. Finely chop the pistachios in a food processor. Combine the pistachios and ½ tsp. salt in a small bowl. In another small bowl, use a fork to mix the honey and lemon juice. In a third small bowl, mix the cumin, cayenne, 1 tsp. salt, and the pepper.

3. Brush the lamb chops with the oil and season on both sides with the spice mixture.

4. Arrange the chops on a foil-lined, rimmed, baking sheet. Broil until lightly browned, 1 to 2 minutes. Flip and broil until the second sides are lightly browned, 1 to 2 minutes. Remove the baking sheet from the oven, and lower the rack to about 6 inches from the broiler. Using a pastry brush, spread about half of the honey mixture on the top sides of the chops. Sprinkle with about half of the nuts, pressing so that they adhere. Broil until the nuts are lightly toasted, about 30 seconds.

5. Flip the chops and repeat the honey-nut coating on the other sides. Broil until the nuts are lightly browned and the lamb is medium rare, about 30 seconds. Let the chops rest for about 2 minutes, and then serve, sprinkling any nuts that may have fallen off the lamb onto each portion. *—Dina Cheney*

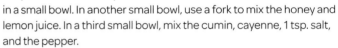
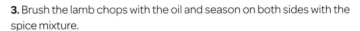

PER SERVING: 300 CALORIES | 19G PROTEIN | 15G CARB | 19G TOTAL FAT | 19G SAT FAT | 10G MONO FAT | 3.5G POLY FAT | 45MG CHOL | 320MG SODIUM | 2G FIBER

broiled lamb skewers with baby arugula and lemon vinaigrette

SERVES 2

2 Tbs. fresh lemon juice

2 tsp. sour cream

1 small clove garlic, minced

Kosher salt

¼ cup plus 1 Tbs. extra-virgin olive oil

¾ lb. boneless lamb shoulder chops or lamb leg steaks, trimmed of extra fat and cut into 1-inch cubes (1½ cups)

Coarsely ground black pepper

4 oz. baby arugula (about 4 cups)

½ cup very thinly sliced red onion (½ small)

1 oz. (¼ cup) crumbled feta or blue cheese

If using bamboo skewers, soak them in water for 30 minutes before threading them.

1. Position an oven rack 4 inches from the broiler element and heat the broiler to high. In a small bowl, combine the lemon juice, sour cream, garlic, and a pinch of salt. Slowly whisk in the ¼ cup olive oil.

2. In a medium bowl, combine the lamb with the 1 Tbs. olive oil, ½ tsp. salt, and ¼ tsp. pepper. Toss to coat evenly. Thread the lamb onto four small (8-inch) bamboo or metal skewers.

3. Put the skewers on a broiler pan and broil the lamb, flipping once, until browned on the outside but still pink inside (medium doneness), 2 to 4 minutes per side. Transfer the skewers to a small, shallow baking dish. Whisk the vinaigrette to recombine and pour 3 Tbs. over the skewers, turning to coat.

4. In a medium bowl, toss the arugula and onion with enough of the remaining vinaigrette to lightly coat (you may not need it all). Season with salt and pepper to taste. Pile the greens on 2 plates, top each salad with 2 lamb skewers, sprinkle with the cheese, and serve immediately. —*Maryellen Driscoll*

PER SERVING: 650 CALORIES | 32G PROTEIN | 8G CARB | 55G TOTAL FAT | 15G SAT FAT | 32G MONO FAT | 4.5G POLY FAT | 115MG CHOL | 760MG SODIUM | 1G FIBER

eggplant, scallop &
broccolini stir-fry
(recipe on p. 85)

fish & seafood

roasted trout with lemon and walnut-browned butter

SERVES 4 TO 6

- **8** rainbow trout fillets (2 to 2½ lb.)
- **2** tsp. kosher salt
- **1** tsp. freshly ground black pepper
- **4** oz. (½ cup) unsalted butter
- **¼** cup finely chopped fresh parsley
- **2** Tbs. finely chopped fresh tarragon
- **24** ⅛-inch-thick lemon slices (2 to 3 lemons)
- **¼** cup chopped walnuts

In the store, rainbow trout are sometimes sold as whole, cleaned fish; if this is how you find them, ask the fish seller to cut them into fillets and remove the fins. This dish is delicious with buttered baby red potatoes tossed with chopped fresh dill.

1. Position a rack in the center of the oven and heat the oven to 450°F.

2. Arrange the trout skin side down on a foil-lined rimmed baking sheet. Sprinkle the salt and pepper evenly over the trout. In a small saucepan, melt the butter and drizzle 4 Tbs. of it evenly over the fillets. Sprinkle the trout evenly with the parsley and the tarragon. Arrange 3 lemon slices over each fillet. Roast until the fillets flake easily when pricked with a fork, 10 to 12 minutes.

3. Meanwhile, set the saucepan with the remaining melted butter over medium heat. Cook until lightly browned and fragrant, 3 to 5 minutes. Immediately remove from the heat and stir in the walnuts; keep warm.

4. When the trout is done, use a large spatula to transfer the fillets to dinner plates—if the skin sticks to the foil, lift up only the flesh. Swirl the walnut butter around and then spoon it over the trout.
—*Julianna Grimes*

BASED ON 6 SERVINGS: 350 CALORIES | 28G PROTEIN | 5G CARB | 25G TOTAL FAT | 12G SAT FAT | 6G MONO FAT, 5G POLY FAT | 120MG CHOL | 440MG SODIUM | 2G FIBER

eggplant, scallop & broccolini stir-fry

SERVES 4

- 1 8-oz. bottle clam juice
- 2 Tbs. lower-sodium soy sauce
- 1 Tbs. Asian sesame oil
- 1 Tbs. red-wine vinegar
- 1 Tbs. cornstarch
- 1 tsp. granulated sugar
- 1 tsp. Asian red chile sauce (such as sambal oelek or Sriracha)
- Freshly ground black pepper
- 3½ Tbs. vegetable oil; more as needed
- 1 lb. long, slender Asian eggplants, trimmed and sliced ¾ inch thick on the diagonal
- 1 to 1¼ lb. all-natural "dry" sea scallops, side muscles removed
- Kosher salt
- 4 scallions, thinly sliced
- 2 Tbs. minced fresh ginger
- 2 tsp. minced garlic
- 1 large bunch (about ½ lb.) broccolini, cut into bite-size pieces

A cross between broccoli and Chinese kale, broccolini has a sweet, slightly peppery flavor. Here, it provides a crisp-tender contrast to the eggplant and scallops. (If you can't find broccolini, substitute small broccoli florets.) A ginger-chile sauce adds spicy heat. Serve over brown jasmine rice.

1. Combine the clam juice, soy sauce, sesame oil, vinegar, cornstarch, sugar, chile sauce, and ½ tsp. pepper in a glass measuring cup or medium bowl.

2. Heat 1½ Tbs. of the vegetable oil in a 12-inch nonstick skillet over medium-high heat. Working in batches, cook the eggplant in a single layer until almost tender and starting to brown, about 3 minutes per side. Transfer each batch to a paper-towel-lined plate when done and add more oil between batches as needed.

3. Heat 1½ Tbs. of the oil in the same skillet over medium-high heat until very hot. Lightly sprinkle the scallops with salt and pepper and cook until brown and almost cooked through, 2 to 3 minutes per side. Transfer to a plate.

4. Add the remaining ½ Tbs. oil and the scallions, ginger, and garlic to the skillet; stir until fragrant, about 30 seconds. Add the broccolini, sprinkle with salt, and stir until heated through, about 1 minute. Cover and cook until crisp-tender, stirring occasionally, 6 to 8 minutes. Stir the broth mixture to combine and add to the skillet. Bring to a simmer, stirring constantly. Add the eggplant and the scallops and simmer just until heated through, 2 to 3 minutes. Serve. —*Kristine Kidd*

PER SERVING: 290 CALORIES | 18G PROTEIN | 21G CARB | 17G TOTAL FAT | 2G SAT FAT | 7G MONO FAT | 7G POLY FAT | 30MG CHOL | 1,180MG SODIUM | 5G FIBER

More about Eggplant

Western, or globe, eggplant is the most common and versatile variety, and you can find it year-round in most parts of the country, though peak season is late summer. Its size varies from ¾ pound to 1¼ pounds, with dark purple skin. A fresh globe eggplant has pale pulp with a few noticeable seeds, which darken and become bitter as the eggplant matures.

Other eggplant varieties are worth seeking out, including Asian eggplant, which is an elongated, slender, quick-cooking type; Italian eggplant, which is smaller than the globe variety and is lobed with dark purple skin; white eggplant, an oval, eggshell-white-hued variety with creamy flesh; and baby, or Indian eggplants, which can be as tiny as a walnut or up to a few inches long. All of these varieties have tender flesh and seeds, and none need peeling.

etta's new crab cakes

**MAKES 8 CRAB CAKES;
SERVES 4**

- **8** slices white sandwich bread
- **3** Tbs. plus 2 tsp. coarsely chopped fresh flat-leaf parsley
- **1** large egg yolk
- **1** Tbs. cider vinegar
- **1** Tbs. Dijon mustard
- **1** Tbs. coarsely chopped red bell pepper
- **1** Tbs. coarsely chopped onion
- **1** tsp. Tabasco® sauce
- **½** tsp. sweet paprika
- **½** tsp. chopped fresh thyme

  Kosher salt and freshly ground black pepper
- **¼** cup extra-virgin olive oil
- **¼** cup sour cream
- **1** lb. fresh or pasteurized blue lump crabmeat, drained and picked clean of shell, or 1 lb. fresh Dungeness crabmeat
- **3** oz. (6 Tbs.) unsalted butter

  Red-Eye Cocktail Sauce (recipe on the facing page)
- **4** lemon wedges

> When making crab cakes, mix the crabmeat gently so you don't break up the lumps. Fold the crabmeat and other ingredients with a rubber spatula as if you're gently folding a cake batter.
>
> If you're using Dungeness, squeeze the crabmeat lightly to remove excess liquid.

You can shape the crab cakes up to 24 hours before you cook them.

1. Tear up the bread and pulse it in a food processor to make fine, soft crumbs (you should have about 3½ cups). Pour the crumbs into a 9x13-inch (or similar size) dish and mix in 3 Tbs. of the parsley.

2. In a food processor, combine the egg yolk, vinegar, mustard, bell pepper, onion, Tabasco, paprika, thyme, ½ tsp. salt, ¼ tsp. pepper, and the remaining 2 tsp. parsley. Pulse to finely mince the vegetables and combine all the ingredients. With the motor running, slowly add the oil through the feed tube until the mixture emulsifies and forms a thin mayonnaise.

3. Transfer the mayonnaise to a large bowl and stir in the sour cream. Use a rubber spatula to gently fold in the crabmeat, taking care not to break up the lumps. Pour the crab mixture onto a large rimmed baking sheet and portion it into eight equal mounds. Gently shape each mound into a patty about 3 inches wide and ½ inch thick. (The mixture will be quite wet.)

4. Using a spatula to move the patties, lightly dredge each patty on both sides in the reserved breadcrumb mixture. Cover the crab cakes with plastic wrap and chill for at least 1 hour. (You can leave the cakes right in the pan of breadcrumbs and chill them as long as overnight.)

5. Heat the oven to 200°F. Heat 3 Tbs. of the butter in a large nonstick skillet over medium heat. When the butter melts, add 4 crab cakes to the pan. Gently fry the crab cakes until they're golden brown on both sides and heated through, turning just once with a spatula, about 4 minutes per side. Transfer the cakes to a plate (don't cover) and keep them warm in the oven. Wipe the skillet clean and cook the remaining crab cakes as above, using the remaining 3 Tbs. butter.

6. Serve hot, accompanied by ramekins of cocktail sauce and lemon wedges. —*Tom Douglas*

PER SERVING WITHOUT SAUCE: 550 CALORIES I 26G PROTEIN I 27G CARB I 37 TOTAL FAT I 15G SAT FAT I 15G MONO FAT I 3.5G POLY FAT I 195MG CHOL I 930MG SODIUM I 2G FIBER

red-eye cocktail sauce

YIELDS ABOUT 1¼ CUPS

1½   tsp. finely ground coffee,
       preferably dark or espresso
       roast

1   cup ketchup

3   Tbs. prepared horseradish

1½   Tbs. fresh lemon juice

2¼   tsp. Worcestershire sauce

This makes enough sauce for a double batch of crab cakes, or you can save the sauce and use it with poached shrimp, pan-fried oysters, or other seafood.

Put the finely ground coffee in a paper coffee filter cone set in a strainer over a Pyrex® measuring cup or small heatproof bowl. Bring a small amount of water to a boil. Pour about 2 Tbs. (the exact amount isn't important) boiling water into the filter cone and allow the liquid coffee to drain off. Discard the liquid and transfer the moistened coffee grounds from the paper cone to a bowl—you may need to scrape the coffee off the paper with a small spoon. Add the ketchup, horseradish, lemon juice, and Worcestershire, and stir. Serve immediately, or cover and refrigerate for up to a week.

Sorting Out Your Crabmeat Choices

You have choices when it comes to crabmeat for crab cakes: You can begin with live crabs and cook and pick the meat yourself. Or you can buy already-picked fresh crabmeat, which comes in cans or plastic tubs. You can find it in the fresh seafood section of many supermarkets and at your local fish market (your best bet).

If you see a package labeled "jumbo lump blue crabmeat," grab it—it makes the best-textured crab cakes because the meat is plump, white, and sweet, with little or no shell. Also very good is "backfin lump crabmeat," lovely big white pieces that come from the crab's backfin and have very little shell. Some cans are labeled simply "lump crabmeat"; that's your next best bet. The word "lump" is your clue that you'll find nice

big, juicy pieces of sweet crabmeat and not shredded stringy bits.

Much of the picked crabmeat on the market comes from blue crabs, the favorite crab variety on the East and Gulf Coasts. But on the West Coast, Dungeness is the crab of choice, and picked is also available.

The saltiness of crabmeat varies. Whichever crabmeat you use for your crab cakes, it's a good idea to taste the meat for salt and adjust the amount of salt in the recipe as needed. Dungeness, in particular, can be quite salty.

braised red snapper puttanesca

SERVES 4

- **4 5-oz. skinless red snapper fillets (about ¾ inch thick)**
- **Kosher salt and freshly ground black pepper**
- **3 Tbs. extra-virgin olive oil**
- **3 medium cloves garlic, minced (about 1 Tbs.)**
- **2 14½-oz. cans petite-diced tomatoes**
- **2 anchovy fillets, minced**
- **3 oz. pitted Kalamata olives, halved lengthwise (about ½ cup)**
- **3 Tbs. coarsely chopped fresh basil leaves**
- **1 Tbs. capers, rinsed**
- **¼ tsp. crushed red pepper flakes**
- **1 Tbs. coarsely chopped fresh mint**
- **2 tsp. red-wine vinegar**

Black sea bass makes a good substitute for snapper in this recipe. Serve with polenta or couscous.

1. Position a rack in the center of the oven and heat the oven to 325°F. Season the snapper all over with salt and pepper. Let sit at room temperature while you prepare the sauce.

2. Heat 2 Tbs. of the olive oil in a 12-inch ovenproof skillet over medium-low heat. Add the garlic and cook, stirring, until softened but not golden, about 1 minute. Add the tomatoes and their juice, anchovies, olives, 2 Tbs. of the basil, capers, and pepper flakes to the pan. Bring the sauce to a brisk simmer and cook, stirring occasionally, until the tomatoes are tender and the juices have reduced to a saucy consistency, about 8 minutes.

3. Nestle the snapper fillets into the sauce, spooning some on top to keep the fish moist. Drizzle with the remaining 1 Tbs. olive oil. Tightly cover the pan with a lid or aluminum foil and braise in the oven until the fish is almost cooked through, 10 to 15 minutes, depending on the thickness.

4. With a slotted spatula, transfer the snapper to 4 shallow serving bowls. If the sauce seems too thin, simmer over medium-high heat until thickened to your liking. Stir the remaining 1 Tbs. basil and the mint and vinegar into the sauce and spoon it over the fish.
—*Allison Ehri Kreitler*

PER SERVING: 320 CALORIES | 31G PROTEIN | 12G CARB | 17G TOTAL FAT | 2.5G SAT FAT | 12G MONO FAT | 2.5G POLY FAT | 50MG CHOL | 1,360MG SODIUM | 0G FIBER

spicy steamed mussels with lemongrass, chile & basil

SERVES 4

- 1 Tbs. vegetable oil
- 2 shallots, thinly sliced into rounds (¼ cup)
- 1 cup lower-salt chicken broth
- 3 stalks lemongrass, trimmed, cut into 2-inch pieces, and lightly smashed (¾ cup)
- 3 ⅛-inch-thick slices fresh ginger

    Zest of ½ lime, peeled off in strips with a vegetable peeler (about 5 strips)

- 2 lb. mussels, scrubbed and debearded
- 1 red serrano (or other small hot red chile), sliced into thin rounds
- ½ cup chopped fresh basil

    Asian chili sauce, such as Sriracha (optional)

Before buying mussels, take a sniff. They should smell like the sea. If they're really fishy smelling, don't buy them.

1. Heat the oil in a large, straight-sided sauté pan or pot over medium heat. Add the shallots and cook, stirring often, until browned, 2 to 3 minutes. Add the broth, lemongrass, ginger, lime zest, and 1 cup water. Bring to a boil over medium-high heat and then reduce to medium low; cover and simmer for 10 minutes.

2. Raise the heat to medium high and add the mussels and chile. Cover and simmer until the mussels open, 2 to 3 minutes. Transfer the mussels to serving bowls, discarding any that haven't opened. Add the basil to the broth and simmer for 1 minute. Add chili sauce to taste, if using. Ladle the broth over the mussels. Don't eat the lemongrass or the ginger. —*Jennifer Armentrout*

PER SERVING: 240 CALORIES | 29G PROTEIN | 11G CARB | 9G TOTAL FAT | 1.5G SAT FAT | 3G MONO FAT | 3G POLY FAT | 65MG CHOL | 670MG SODIUM | 0G FIBER

poached flounder with mint beurre blanc

SERVES 4

- **6 skinless flounder fillets (1½ lb. total)**
- **½ tsp. ground ginger**
- **Kosher salt and freshly ground black pepper**
- **3½ Tbs. coarsely chopped fresh spearmint or ginger mint leaves**
- **¼ cup minced shallots**
- **¼ cup dry white wine**
- **2 Tbs. heavy cream**
- **2 oz. (4 Tbs.) cold unsalted butter, cut into 8 slices**
- **1 Tbs. thinly sliced chives**

This classic shallow-poached fish is served with a minty French butter sauce. It's delicious with a simple rice pilaf and tender green spring vegetables like peas or baby spinach.

1. Lay the fish fillets skinned side up on a cutting board. Slice each fillet in half lengthwise to make 12 strips. In a small bowl mix the ginger, ¼ tsp. salt, and ¼ tsp. pepper. Sprinkle the spice mixture evenly over all the fish and then sprinkle with 2 Tbs. of the chopped mint. Roll each strip into a coil, starting with the fatter end and aligning the roll along the cut edge. Secure with a toothpick, pushing it into the thin end and through the other side.

2. Sprinkle the shallots over the bottom of a 10-inch, straight-sided sauté pan. Arrange the fish coils cut edge down in the pan. Pour in the wine and ⅓ cup water. Turn the heat to medium high and bring the liquid to a simmer. Adjust the heat to maintain a gentle simmer, cover, and poach the fish until cooked through, 4 to 8 minutes. Use a slotted spoon to transfer the fish to a warm plate. Tent with foil while finishing the sauce.

3. Increase the heat to high and boil the liquid until it's reduced to about 3 Tbs. (It should just barely cover the bottom of the pan.) Add the cream and boil for 30 seconds. Reduce the heat to low and whisk in 2 slices of the cold butter, the remaining 1½ Tbs. mint, and the chives. When the butter is almost melted, add another slice and whisk until mostly melted. Repeat with the remaining butter, 1 slice at a time. (Take care not to overheat the sauce or it will separate.) Season to taste with salt and pepper.

4. Remove the toothpicks from each piece of fish. Serve the fish (3 pieces per serving) drizzled with the sauce. *—Jessica Bard*

PER SERVING: 290 CALORIES | 29G PROTEIN | 3G CARB | 16G TOTAL FAT | 9G SAT FAT | 4G MONO FAT | 1.5G POLY FAT | 120MG CHOL | 200MG SODIUM | 0G FIBER

More about Mint

The quintessential herb of spring, mint adds a fresh, crisp flavor to just about anything. There are more than 200 mint varieties, all of which fall into one of two categories: spearmint or peppermint. What you see labeled as simply "mint" in the grocery store is usually spearmint, but shop at a farmers' market and you'll find a mind-boggling variety.

Spearmint is the most versatile of mints, with a natural affinity with fruits and spring vegetables (think peas, asparagus, and artichokes), herbs like basil and cilantro, and spices like ginger, cumin, and cardamom. Its relatively mild flavor makes it ideal for a variety of savory dishes, including grilled and roasted meats. Spearmint varieties include pineapple mint, with a fragrance of fresh pineapple and a slightly sweeter flavor than regular spearmint; apple mint, with a hint of green apple (try it in iced tea); curly mint, with ruffled leaves; and smooth-leaf mint, with soft, velvety leaves.

Peppermint is similar in flavor to spearmint, but it contains menthol, which gives it a stronger flavor and a cooling sensation on the palate. Peppermint is assertive enough to stand up to strong flavors, so it's ideal for chocolate desserts and boldly flavored dishes. Peppermint varieties include orange mint, with overtones of orange and bergamot; chocolate mint, with an unmistakable hint of chocolate; ginger mint; and grapefruit mint.

Prepping
Mint starts to blacken after it's cut, so wait until the last minute before chopping or tearing it and adding it to a dish. When appropriate, tear the leaves gently instead of cutting them, to help prevent blackening.

Storing
Store mint bunches with the cut stems in a glass of water and cover the leaves with a plastic bag. Refrigerate, changing the water every couple of days. It should stay fresh for at least 1 week.

moroccan-spiced seared scallops with green grape and lemon relish

SERVES 4

- **1 medium lemon**
- **Kosher salt**
- **1½ cups seedless green grapes, quartered lengthwise and at room temperature**
- **¼ cup extra-virgin olive oil**
- **2 scallions, thinly sliced**
- **2 Tbs. chopped fresh cilantro**
- **2 Tbs. chopped fresh mint**
- **1 tsp. ground cumin**
- **1 tsp. sweet Hungarian paprika**
- **1 tsp. ground turmeric**
- **¼ tsp. ground cinnamon**
- **¼ tsp. ground ginger**
- **1½ lb. large all-natural "dry" sea scallops, side muscles removed**
- **Freshly ground black pepper**

Lemon zest cooked in salt water brings the flavor of preserved lemons to this succulent relish.

1. Using a vegetable peeler, remove the zest from the lemon in strips (yellow part only). Reserve the lemon. In a small saucepan, combine the lemon zest with ½ cup water and 1 tsp. salt. Bring to a simmer over medium-low heat and cook until the liquid reduces to about 1 Tbs., about 10 minutes. Drain, rinse, drain again, and pat dry. Finely mince the lemon zest and combine it with the grapes, 2 Tbs. of the olive oil, scallions, cilantro, and mint in a medium bowl.

2. In a small bowl, combine the cumin, paprika, turmeric, cinnamon, and ginger.

3. Pat the scallops dry. Season them liberally with salt and pepper and coat them with the spice mixture.

4. Heat 1 Tbs. of the olive oil in a 12-inch nonstick skillet over medium-high heat until shimmering. Add half of the scallops and cook, turning once, until seared on the outside but still translucent in the center, 1 to 2 minutes per side. Transfer to a warm plate. Repeat with the remaining 1 Tbs. oil and scallops.

5. Divide the scallops among 4 plates and serve with the relish. Cut the reserved lemon into quarters and squeeze over the scallops and relish. Serve immediately. —*Jeanne Kelley*

PER SERVING: 320 CALORIES | 29G PROTEIN | 17G CARB | 15G TOTAL FAT | 2G SAT FAT | 10G MONO FAT | 2G POLY FAT | 55MG CHOL | 560MG SODIUM | 2G FIBER

grape varieties

Here's a quick roundup of the most common table grape varieties.

RED FLAME GRAPES are sweet in flavor with a crunchy texture. They're ideal for both eating out of hand and cooking, as they keep their shape well and acquire a deeper flavor when heated.

CONCORD GRAPES have thick skins, juicy flesh, large seeds, and a strong strawberry-like flavor. They come in purple and white varieties and are ideal for juices and jellies.

CHAMPAGNE GRAPES have delicate, sweet, pea-size berries that need gentle handling. These seedless grapes are not used in the homonymous French sparkling wine but are so named because they're thought to resemble tiny bubbles.

GREEN THOMPSON GRAPES are the top seller at the supermarket. Large and seedless, they have firm skins that make them very durable. Their mild flavor pairs well with citrus.

MUSCAT GRAPES usually have seeds and come in black and white varieties. Prized for their honey-floral flavor and perfume, they're used for both eating (they're delicious with cheese) and making wine.

AUTUMN ROYAL GRAPES have large, oval-shaped black berries. Sweet and straightforward, these seedless grapes pair well with salty foods like prosciutto and salted nuts.

smoked salmon hash
with chive sour cream

SERVES 4

- 2 **Tbs. extra-virgin olive oil**
- 3 **large red potatoes (about 1½ lb.), cut into ½-inch dice**
- 1 **small yellow onion, roughly chopped**
- 1 **small green bell pepper, stemmed, cored, seeded, and finely chopped**
- **Kosher salt and freshly ground black pepper**
- ⅔ **cup sour cream**
- 2 **Tbs. thinly sliced fresh chives**
- 1½ **Tbs. fresh lemon juice**
- ½ **tsp. Dijon mustard**
- 14 **oz. hot-smoked salmon fillet, skinned and broken into large flakes (about 1 cup)**

If you're in the mood for "breakfast for dinner," serve this with a fried or poached egg on top. A fresh spinach salad makes a good side.

1. Heat the oil in a 12-inch nonstick skillet over medium-high heat. Add the potatoes, onion, bell pepper, 1 tsp. salt, and ¼ tsp. pepper and cook, stirring often, until golden brown, about 10 minutes. Reduce the heat to medium and continue cooking until the potatoes are tender, about 15 minutes more; season to taste with salt and pepper.

2. Meanwhile, combine the sour cream, 1 Tbs. of the chives, ½ Tbs. of the lemon juice, the mustard, ½ tsp. salt, and ⅛ tsp. pepper in a medium bowl and stir well; set aside.

3. When the potatoes are tender, gently fold in the salmon and the remaining 1 Tbs. lemon juice and continue cooking until heated through, about 2 minutes more. Transfer the hash to plates. Garnish with the remaining 1 Tbs. chives and serve with a dollop of the chive sour cream. *—Liz Pearson*

PER SERVING: 290 CALORIES | 10G PROTEIN | 32G CARB | 15G TOTAL FAT | 5G SAT FAT | 7G MONO FAT | 1.5G POLY FAT | 20MG CHOL | 1,030MG SODIUM | 4G FIBER

pan-seared arctic char with olives and potatoes

SERVES 4

- **4** **small red potatoes (about ¾ lb.), sliced ¼ inch thick**
-    **Kosher salt and freshly ground black pepper**
- **4** **skin-on arctic char fillets (about 5 oz. each), scaled**
- **3** **Tbs. olive oil**
- **2** **sprigs fresh rosemary, each about 3 inches long**
- **½** **cup pitted Kalamata olives**
- **3** **Tbs. roughly chopped fresh flat-leaf parsley**
- **1** **Tbs. balsamic vinegar**
- **4** **lemon wedges**

Looking for a fish you can feel good about eating? Arctic char is a good, sustainable alternative to Atlantic salmon, which it resembles in flavor and texture.

1. In a medium saucepan over high heat, bring the potatoes to a boil in enough salted water to cover them by 1 inch. Reduce the heat to a brisk simmer and cook until tender but not falling apart, about 5 minutes. Drain. Set aside.

2. Pat the fish dry and season with ½ tsp. salt and ¼ tsp. pepper. Heat 1½ Tbs. of the olive oil in a 12-inch nonstick skillet over medium-high heat until shimmering hot. Arrange the fish skin side down in the pan so the fillets fit without touching. Cook undisturbed for 3 minutes. Flip the fillets and cook until the fish is cooked through, an additional 2 to 3 minutes. With a slotted spatula, transfer the fish to a serving platter or plates.

3. Add the remaining 1 ½ Tbs. oil to the pan and heat until shimmering. Add the potatoes and rosemary and cook, flipping occasionally, until the potatoes are tender, 3 to 4 minutes. Add the olives, parsley, balsamic vinegar, and a pinch of salt and pepper and stir gently to heat. Arrange the potato mixture around the fish. Serve garnished with the lemon wedges. *—Jay Weinstein*

PER SERVING: 390 CALORIES | 33G PROTEIN | 17G CARB | 21G TOTAL FAT | 2G SAT FAT | 11G MONO FAT | 1.5G POLY FAT | 0MG CHOL | 540MG SODIUM | 2G FIBER

More about Arctic Char

Caught in Alaska and the Pacific Northwest, char is getting its share of attention because it is a fast-reproducing fish that is available as both wild and farmed (which is a good alternative to wild because it's raised sustainably).

A distant cousin of salmon and trout, char has a mild salmonlike flavor and a beautiful pink color—the result of its natural diet, which includes tiny crustaceans like pink shrimp. Arctic char takes well to virtually any cooking method, and it's hard to overcook thanks to its fatty texture.

tilapia with scallions and black bean sauce

- **3 Tbs. Chinese black bean garlic sauce or black bean chile sauce**
- **1 Tbs. oyster sauce**
- **2 tsp. lower-sodium soy sauce**
- **1 tsp. Asian sesame oil**
- **1 tsp. rice vinegar**
- **1½ lb. tilapia fillets, cut into 2-inch pieces**
- **1 cup long-grain white rice, preferably jasmine**
- **1 Tbs. peanut oil**
- **2 small bunches scallions, trimmed and cut into 1-inch lengths**
- **1 Tbs. Asian chile sauce, such as Sriracha**

You can find Chinese black bean garlic sauce and Asian chile sauce in the Asian section of your supermarket. They're also good additions to marinades and sauces.

1. In a large bowl, stir the black bean sauce, oyster sauce, soy sauce, sesame oil, and rice vinegar. Add the fish and stir gently to coat. Cover and let sit for 20 minutes. Meanwhile, cook the rice according to package directions and keep warm.

2. Heat the oil in a well-seasoned wok or 12-inch nonstick skillet over medium-high heat until the oil shimmers and a piece of scallion dropped in the pan sizzles vigorously. Add the fish all at once, distributing it evenly around the pan. Cook without stirring for 3 minutes. Add the scallions and stir gently. Cook, stirring occasionally and gently, until the thickest part of a piece of fish is opaque throughout (cut to check), 2 to 3 minutes more.

3. Serve with the rice, drizzled with chile sauce. —*Jay Weinstein*

PER SERVING: 410 CALORIES | 39G PROTEIN | 45G CARB | 8G TOTAL FAT | 2G SAT FAT | 3G MONO FAT | 3G POLY FAT | 85MG CHOL | 870MG SODIUM | 1G FIBER

five-spice-glazed salmon with sesame green beans

SERVES 4

¼ cup honey

4 tsp. lower-sodium soy sauce

1½ tsp. five-spice powder

2 large cloves garlic, minced

4 6-oz. skin-on salmon fillets (preferably wild), pin bones and scales removed

Nonstick cooking spray

1 lb. slender green beans, trimmed

2 tsp. canola oil

1 tsp. Asian sesame oil

Kosher salt and freshly ground black pepper

2 Tbs. toasted sesame seeds

1 tsp. lemon juice

Chinese five-spice powder, honey, and soy sauce create a tasty glaze for this simple salmon dish. Broil the green beans and salmon on the same baking sheet, and you have a meal in minutes.

1. In a small bowl, whisk the honey, soy sauce, five-spice powder, and garlic. Put the salmon skin side down on a large plate and pour the honey mixture over it. Flip the fillets so they are skin side up. Let the fish marinate for 15 minutes at room temperature.

2. Position a rack 6 inches from the broiler and heat the broiler on high. Line a large rimmed baking sheet with foil and coat with cooking spray.

3. In a large bowl, toss the green beans with the canola and sesame oils. Arrange the beans on one-half of the prepared baking sheet and season with salt and pepper. Arrange the salmon skin side down on the other half of the baking sheet. Brush the salmon with any remaining marinade from the plate.

4. Broil the salmon and green beans for 3 minutes. Remove the pan from the oven, toss the green beans with tongs, and reposition the salmon pieces as needed so that they cook evenly. Continue to broil until the salmon is just cooked through and the beans are crisp-tender, 2 to 3 minutes. Toss the green beans with the sesame seeds and lemon juice and serve. *—Ivy Manning*

PER SERVING: 400 CALORIES | 41G PROTEIN | 18G CARB | 18G TOTAL FAT | 2.5G SAT FAT | 7G MONO FAT | 7G POLY FAT | 105MG CHOL | 320MG SODIUM | 10G FIBER

seared scallops with cauliflower, brown butter & basil

SERVES 4

- **3** Tbs. extra-virgin olive oil
- **1** small head cauliflower (1 lb.), trimmed and cut into bite-size florets (about 4 cups)
- **1** lb. all-natural "dry" sea scallops
- **1** oz. (2 Tbs.) unsalted butter
- **1** large shallot, minced
- **½** cup dry vermouth
- **¼** tsp. kosher salt
- **¼** tsp. freshly ground black pepper
- **8** large fresh basil leaves, thinly sliced

In this easily assembled meal, vermouth-laced brown butter imbues cauliflower with deep flavor, while a basil garnish adds color and freshness.

1. Heat 1 Tbs. of the oil in a 12-inch nonstick skillet over medium-high heat until shimmering hot. Add the cauliflower and cook, stirring often, until lightly browned, about 4 minutes. Transfer to a bowl.

2. Add the remaining 2 Tbs. oil to the skillet. When shimmering hot, add the scallops in a single layer. Cook until golden brown, about 2 minutes. Flip and cook until the scallops are barely cooked through, about 2 minutes more (if you cut into one, it should still be slightly translucent in the center). Transfer to another bowl.

3. Swirl the butter into the skillet, add the shallot, and cook, stirring often, until the shallot softens and the butter begins to brown, about 1 minute.

4. Add the vermouth and bring it to a boil, scraping up any bits on the bottom of the skillet with a wooden spoon. Return the cauliflower to the skillet and season with the salt and pepper. Cover the skillet and reduce the heat to medium. Cook, stirring once or twice, until the cauliflower florets are tender, about 6 minutes.

5. Return the scallops to the pan and toss to heat through, about 1 minute. Remove from the heat, sprinkle with the basil, and serve.
—*Bruce Weinstein and Mark Scarbrough*

PER SERVING: 300 CALORIES | 21G PROTEIN | 8G CARB | 17G TOTAL FAT | 5G SAT FAT | 9G MONO FAT | 1.5G POLY FAT | 55MG CHOL | 270MG SODIUM | 2G FIBER

More about Scallops

Scallops are bivalves (mollusks with two hinged shells). Although there are hundreds of species of scallops in the world's oceans and bays, only a handful are commonly available. The largest and most popular are sea scallops, harvested primarily in the Atlantic from Eastern Canada to North Carolina, but also from Peru, Japan, and Russia.

Choosing
Ask for "dry" sea scallops, which means that they haven't been soaked in a sodium solution. The solution whitens and plumps the scallops, but when you cook them, all that liquid leaches out, making it impossible to achieve a good sear. Fresh scallops should appear moist but not milky. Refuse any that have a feathery white surface (a sign of freezer burn) or dried and darkened edges (a sign of age). Always ask to smell scallops before buying. They should smell somewhat briny and seaweedy, but not offensive, sharp, or at all like iodine. If the scallops have no smell and a uniform stark white color, chances are they've been soaked in the sodium solution.

Prepping
Remove the tough abductor muscle from the side of each scallop (some scallops are sold with the muscle already removed). If you feel any grit on the scallops, rinse them under cold water (otherwise, avoid rinsing, which can wash away flavor). Pat the scallops dry with paper towels; surface moisture impedes browning.

Storing
Store scallops in the coldest part of your refrigerator. Ideally, nest the bag or container in a larger bowl of ice to ensure that they really stay cold. But avoid direct contact with ice—it will leach flavor and deteriorate the texture of the scallops.

black cod with pine nuts, tomatoes & olives

SERVES 4

- **1** Tbs. extra-virgin olive oil
- **3** medium cloves garlic, chopped
- **½** cup dry white wine
- **3** cups grape tomatoes, halved (quartered if large)
- **1½** cups lower-salt chicken broth
- **½** cup pitted, halved Niçoise olives
- **4** skinless black cod (sablefish) or Pacific cod fillets (about 4 oz. each)

  Kosher salt and freshly ground black pepper
- **1** Tbs. chopped fresh thyme
- **⅔** cup pine nuts, toasted

Toasted pine nuts provide a nice textural contrast to the firm, flaky cod. Serve with a hunk of crusty bread to sop up the tomato sauce.

1. Heat the oil in a 12-inch nonstick skillet over medium-high heat. Add the garlic and cook, stirring, until fragrant, about 1 minute. Add the wine and let simmer until reduced by half, about 2 minutes. Add the tomatoes, broth, and olives. Bring to a simmer and cook, stirring occasionally, until the tomatoes begin to break down, about 8 minutes.

2. Season the fish with salt and pepper. Stir the thyme into the sauce. Nestle the fish into the sauce, return to a simmer, cover, and reduce the heat to low. Cook until the fish is just cooked through, about 4 minutes. Transfer the fish to 4 shallow bowls. Add the pine nuts to the sauce and season to taste with salt and pepper. Spoon the sauce over the fish and serve. —*Samantha Seneviratne*

PER SERVING: 520 CALORIES | 22G PROTEIN | 12G CARB | 42G TOTAL FAT | 6G SAT FAT | 20G MONO FAT | 11G POLY FAT | 55MG CHOL | 700MG SODIUM | 3G FIBER

A dry white wine is any white wine that isn't sweet. But for cooking, choose a white with a high acidity, known in wine parlance as "crisp." Good choices include Sauvignon Blanc, Pinot Grigio, Pinot Gris, and Pinot Blanc. Fuller whites with strong, oaky flavors, like some Chardonnays, don't work as well for cooking: They're lower in acidity and don't lend as much punch as crisper wines. When reduced, the oaky, buttery flavors turn bitter and don't add anything pleasant to a dish.

roasted shrimp with rosemary and thyme

SERVES 4

- 6 Tbs. extra-virgin olive oil
- 6 fresh thyme sprigs
- 3 large fresh rosemary sprigs, halved
- 1 tsp. freshly ground black pepper
- 1½ lb. extra-large shrimp (26 to 30 per lb.), preferably wild, peeled and deveined
- 1½ Tbs. white-wine vinegar
- ½ tsp. kosher salt

If you like, substitute different herb combinations for the rosemary and thyme—try tarragon and chives or lemon verbena and parsley. Serve the shrimp over rice or with some crusty bread to sop up the fragrant olive oil.

1. Position a rack in the center of the oven and heat the oven to 400°F.

2. Pour the oil into a 9x13-inch baking dish. Add the thyme, rosemary, and pepper and bake until the oil mixture is fragrant, about 12 minutes.

3. Add the shrimp to the dish and toss with tongs until coated. Bake the shrimp until pink and firm, 8 to 10 minutes.

4. Add the vinegar and salt, toss well, and let rest at room temperature until the oil cools slightly, about 5 minutes. Discard the herbs (if you choose) and serve. —*Bruce Weinstein and Mark Scarbrough*

PER SERVING: 310 CALORIES | 27G PROTEIN | 1G CARB | 22G TOTAL FAT | 3G SAT FAT | 15G MONO FAT | 2.5G POLY FAT | 250MG CHOL | 430MG SODIUM | 0G FIBER

pan-seared tuna steaks with warm tomato, basil & olive salad

SERVES 4

- **4** 5-oz. boneless, skinless tuna steaks
- Kosher salt and freshly ground black pepper
- **2** Tbs. extra-virgin olive oil
- **1** medium shallot, finely chopped
- **2** cups mixed yellow and red grape or cherry tomatoes, halved
- **⅓** cup sliced pitted green olives, such as picholine or Cerignola
- **2** Tbs. finely chopped fresh basil
- **½** Tbs. fresh lemon juice

Serve this with fluffy couscous for a summery weeknight dinner.

1. Season the tuna with 1 tsp. salt and ¼ tsp. pepper. Heat the oil in a 12-inch skillet over medium-high heat. Arrange the tuna in the skillet in a single layer and cook, turning once, until done to your liking (3 to 4 minutes for medium rare). Transfer the tuna to a large plate.

2. Reduce the heat to medium and add the shallot to the skillet. Cook, stirring, until golden brown, about 1 minute. Add the tomatoes, olives, basil, ½ tsp. salt, and a few grinds of pepper; cook until warmed through and the tomatoes are just softened, about 2 minutes more. Remove the skillet from the heat and gently stir in the lemon juice.

3. Transfer the tuna to plates, top with the tomato salad, and serve.
—*Liz Pearson*

PER SERVING: 300 CALORIES | 34G PROTEIN | 4G CARB | 16G TOTAL FAT | 3G SAT FAT | 8G MONO FAT | 3G POLY FAT, 55MG CHOL | 650MG SODIUM | 1G FIBER

steamed mussels with chorizo, smoked paprika & garlicky croutons

SERVES 4

- **5** Tbs. extra-virgin olive oil
- **6** cloves garlic, 2 minced and 4 thinly sliced
- **1** small yellow onion, thinly sliced

  Kosher salt

- **¾** tsp. smoked sweet paprika
- **1** cup seeded and diced fresh tomato or one 14½-oz. can diced tomatoes, drained
- **1** cup dry white wine
- **6** oz. Spanish-style chorizo, cut into ⅜-inch pieces (1¼ cups)
- **3** sprigs fresh thyme
- **4** lb. mussels, scrubbed and debearded
- **1** baguette, cut on the diagonal into ½-inch slices

  Freshly ground black pepper

The chorizo and mussels cook together, creating a briny, smoky broth that begs to be sopped up with garlic toast. Add a salad and you're done.

1. Combine 3 Tbs. of the olive oil and the minced garlic in a small bowl and set aside.

2. Position an oven rack about 4 inches from the broiler element and heat the broiler on high.

3. In a 6-quart Dutch oven, heat the remaining 2 Tbs. olive oil over medium-high heat until shimmering hot. Add the onion and a pinch of salt and cook, stirring occasionally, until softened but not browned, about 3 minutes. Stir in the sliced garlic and cook until the edges of the onion begin to brown, about 1 minute. Stir in the smoked paprika and cook until fragrant, about 30 seconds. Add the tomatoes, wine, chorizo, and thyme and bring to a simmer, stirring occasionally. Stir in the mussels, coating them with the sauce mixture. Cover and cook, stirring 2 or 3 times, until the mussels have opened, 8 to 10 minutes.

4. Meanwhile, arrange the baguette slices in a single layer on a rimmed baking sheet and brush them with the garlic oil, dividing the bits of garlic evenly among the slices. Sprinkle with salt and pepper and then broil, rotating the baking sheet as needed, until evenly browned and crisp, 1 to 2 minutes.

5. Discard any mussels that have not opened. Serve the mussels with the sauce and the croutons. —*Dawn Yanagihara*

PER SERVING: 820 CALORIES | 44G PROTEIN | 60G CARB | 38G TOTAL FAT | 9G SAT FAT | 21G MONO FAT | 4.5G POLY FAT | 95MG CHOL | 1880MG SODIUM | 3G FIBER

braised cod with fennel, potatoes & littleneck clams

SERVES 4

4   **5-oz. cod fillets (preferably 1 inch thick)**

    Kosher salt and freshly ground black pepper

3   **Tbs. extra-virgin olive oil**

1   **small fennel bulb (about ¾ lb.), trimmed (leave core intact) and cut into ½-inch wedges, plus 1 Tbs. chopped fronds**

2   **large cloves garlic, finely chopped**

1   **medium-large shallot, chopped**

2   **8-oz. bottles clam juice**

8   **oz. small baby red or fingerling potatoes, scrubbed and sliced into ⅛-inch-thick coins, ends discarded (about 6 potatoes)**

1   **large tomato, cut into small dice (12 oz., about 1½ cups)**

2   **Tbs. anisette liqueur, such as Pernod® or Sambuca®**

1   **bay leaf**

1   **large sprig fresh thyme**

¼   **tsp. roughly chopped or coarsely ground fennel seed**

    A generous pinch of saffron, crumbled (about 25 threads)

12   **littleneck clams, scrubbed**

1½   **Tbs. chopped fresh flat-leaf parsley leaves**

You could use halibut in place of the cod. Crusty garlic bread served alongside is perfect for soaking up the flavorful sauce.

1. Position a rack in the center of the oven and heat the oven to 325°F. Season the cod with salt and pepper. Let it sit at room temperature while you prepare the braising mixture.

2. Heat the olive oil in a 12-inch oven-proof skillet over medium-high heat. Add the fennel, sprinkle with a pinch of salt and pepper, and brown on both sides, about 5 minutes total. Remove the pan from the heat and transfer the fennel to a plate. Put the pan over low heat and add the garlic, shallot, ½ tsp. salt, and ¼ tsp. pepper. Cook, stirring, until just softened, 1 to 2 minutes.

3. Add the clam juice, potatoes, tomato, liqueur, bay leaf, thyme, fennel seed, and saffron to the skillet. Raise the heat to medium and bring to a simmer. Simmer for 3 minutes to start the potatoes cooking. Nestle the cod pieces and clams into the sauce, piling the fennel on top of the fish and making sure all of the potatoes are submerged. Tightly cover the pan with a lid or aluminum foil and braise in the oven until the fish is almost cooked through, 10 to 15 minutes, depending on thickness.

4. With a slotted spatula, transfer the cod to 4 shallow bowls. Bring the braising liquid, clams, and vegetables to a brisk simmer on top of the stove, cover the pan, and cook until the clams are opened and the vegetables are tender, 3 to 6 minutes more. Divide the opened clams (discard any unopened ones) and vegetables among the bowls. Add the fennel fronds and parsley to the braising liquid in the pan. Bring to a simmer and pour over the fish and vegetables.

—Allison Ehri Kreitler

PER SERVING: 340 CALORIES | 33G PROTEIN | 21G CARB | 12G TOTAL FAT | 1.5G SAT FAT | 8G MONO FAT | 1.5G POLY FAT | 75MG CHOL | 530MG SODIUM | 4G FIBER

seared scallops with warm radicchio and pancetta

SERVES 2

- 1 **large head radicchio (about 14 oz.)**
- 2 **Tbs. cider vinegar**
- 2 **tsp. granulated sugar**
- 12 **large all-natural "dry" scallops, side muscles removed**

  Kosher salt and freshly ground black pepper
- 6 **oz. pancetta, cut into small dice**

  Olive oil, as needed
- ½ **medium red onion, thinly sliced through the root end**
- 1 **Tbs. minced fresh rosemary**
- 1 **large clove garlic, chopped**

Radicchio's bitterness mellows once it's cooked, making it a sweet, tender bed for the scallops.

1. Remove the outer leaves from the radicchio and cut the head in half through the root end. Cut each half into 4 wedges through the root end and remove the white core.

2. In a small bowl, stir the vinegar and sugar until dissolved.

3. Pat the scallops dry and season with salt and pepper. Heat a 12-inch skillet (preferably cast iron) over medium heat until hot. Add the pancetta and cook, stirring often, until crisp, about 5 minutes. Remove the pancetta from the skillet with a slotted spoon. Pour off all but 3 Tbs. of the fat (if you have less than 3 Tbs., add olive oil to make up the difference).

4. Put the skillet over medium-high heat. Add the scallops and sear until golden brown on one side, 2 to 3 minutes. Flip and continue to cook on the second side until they feel firm when pressed, 2 to 3 minutes more. Transfer to a plate, cover, and keep warm.

5. Add the onion and rosemary to the skillet and cook, stirring often, until the onion is softened, about 3 minutes. Add the garlic and cook, stirring, until fragrant, 15 seconds. Add the radicchio and pancetta, season with salt and pepper, and cook, tossing gently and occasionally, until the radicchio is wilted, 2 to 3 minutes. Remove the skillet from the heat and pour the vinegar mixture over the radicchio. Toss to combine. Serve with the scallops. —*Ivy Manning*

PER SERVING: 220 CALORIES | 13G PROTEIN | 9G CARB | 14G TOTAL FAT | 4.5G SAT FAT | 6G MONO FAT | 1.5G POLY FAT | 40MG CHOL | 1,270MG SODIUM | 1G FIBER

broiled salmon with ginger-shiitake glaze

SERVES 4

- **2 lb. salmon fillet, skin on**
- **3 Tbs. canola oil, more for the baking sheet**
- **¼ tsp. ground coriander**
- **Kosher salt and freshly ground black pepper**
- **½ small red bell pepper, finely diced (about ¼ cup)**
- **3 scallions, trimmed and thinly sliced (white and green parts separated)**
- **2 Tbs. finely chopped ginger**
- **3½ oz. shiitake mushrooms, stemmed and cut into ¼-inch dice (about 1 cup)**
- **¼ cup honey**
- **3 Tbs. rice vinegar**
- **1 Tbs. lower-sodium soy sauce**
- **1 tsp. Asian chili sauce (like Sriracha)**
- **1 tsp. cornstarch**

Though most glazes are applied with a brush, this slightly chunky mixture of sautéed mushrooms and red peppers is spooned over the fish. The honey helps the crust brown, and a splash of vinegar and a spoonful of chili paste perk up the fish, while the vegetables add texture and color.

1. Position an oven rack about 8 inches away from the broiler element and heat the broiler to high.

2. Oil a large, rimmed baking sheet. Set the salmon skin side down on the baking sheet, sprinkle with 1 Tbs oil, the coriander, ½ tsp. salt, and ½ tsp. pepper, and let sit at room temperature while you prepare the sauce.

3. In a large (12-inch) skillet over medium-high heat, cook the red pepper, scallion whites, and ginger in the remaining 2 Tbs. oil, stirring occasionally, until the red pepper and scallions start to soften and brown, about 3 minutes. Add the mushrooms, raise the heat to medium high, sprinkle with ¼ tsp. salt, and cook, stirring, until they soften and start to brown, about 3 minutes. Add the honey, vinegar, soy sauce, chili sauce, and ¼ cup water and bring to a simmer. Whisk the cornstarch with 1 tsp. water and stir into the glaze. Return to a simmer and cook until the glaze thickens, about 1 minute. Remove from the heat.

4. Broil the salmon until it starts to brown and becomes almost firm to the touch, about 8 minutes. Momentarily transfer to the stovetop and spoon the glaze over the salmon. Return to the oven and broil for about 1 minute more so the glaze browns and the salmon almost completely cooks through (check by using a paring knife to flake a thicker part of the fillet). Sprinkle with the scallion greens, transfer to a large platter, and serve. —*Tony Rosenfeld*

fusilli with green beans,
pancetta & parmigiano
(recipe on p. 116)

pasta & noodles

fettuccine with arugula-walnut pesto

SERVES 4 TO 6

- **4 oz. arugula, washed and spun dry (about 3 lightly packed cups)**
- **½ cup freshly grated Parmigiano-Reggiano; more for sprinkling**
- **½ cup walnuts, toasted**
- **2 Tbs. fresh lemon juice**
- **1 clove garlic, smashed and peeled**
- **1 tsp. kosher salt**
- **½ cup extra-virgin olive oil**
- **¼ cup walnut oil**
- **1 lb. dried fettuccine**

Walnut oil smooths out the peppery bite of the arugula, but you can omit it and just use more extra-virgin olive oil instead. A Caesar salad, served either with or after the pasta, is a good complement.

1. Bring a large pot of well-salted water to a boil over high heat.

2. Meanwhile, put the arugula, Parmigiano, walnuts, lemon juice, garlic, and salt into a food processor, and process until the mixture is finely ground, 30 to 60 seconds. In a measuring cup, combine the olive oil and walnut oil. With the food processor running, drizzle the oil through the feed tube, and process the mixture until mostly smooth.

3. Cook the fettuccine in the boiling water until it's al dente, 6 to 8 minutes. Drain. In a medium bowl, toss the fettucine with enough of the pesto to generously coat the pasta. Serve sprinkled with extra Parmigiano, if desired. *—Julianna Grimes*

BASED ON SIX SERVINGS: 600 CALORIES | 13G PROTEIN | 59G CARB | 36G TOTAL FAT | 4.5G SAT FAT | 16G MONO FAT | 13G POLY FAT | 0MG CHOL | 210MG SODIUM | 3G FIBER

pan-fried gnocchi with bacon, onions & peas

SERVES 3

Kosher salt

1 lb. frozen gnocchi

3 oz. thick-cut bacon (about 3 slices), cut into ½-inch-wide pieces

4 Tbs. extra-virgin olive oil

2 medium-small yellow onions, thinly sliced (about 2 cups)

½ cup frozen peas

1 tsp. minced fresh thyme

Freshly ground black pepper

2 Tbs. grated Parmigiano-Reggiano; more for serving

Gnocchi are Italian dumplings made of potatoes or flour (or both) and eggs. Look for them in the frozen foods section of the supermarket.

1. Bring a large saucepan of salted water to a boil. Cook the gnocchi according to package directions. Reserve ½ cup of the cooking water, and drain.

2. Meanwhile, in a large (preferably 12-inch) nonstick skillet, cook the bacon over medium heat until crispy on both sides, about 5 minutes. Transfer to a plate lined with paper towels and set aside. Pour off any fat from the skillet.

3. In the same skillet, heat 2 Tbs. of the oil over medium-high heat. Add the onion and cook until it begins to brown, 3 to 5 minutes. Reduce the heat to medium and continue to cook, stirring occasionally, until the onion is limp and golden brown, 10 minutes more. Stir in the peas and thyme, season with salt and pepper to taste, and transfer to a small bowl.

4. Wipe the skillet clean with a paper towel, and heat the remaining 2 Tbs. oil over medium-high heat. Add the gnocchi and cook, tossing occasionally, until they're lightly brown, about 5 minutes. Gently stir in the onion mixture, bacon, and Parmigiano, along with enough of the reserved cooking water to moisten and coat the gnocchi, about 4 Tbs. Serve immediately, sprinkled with additional Parmigiano.
—Maryellen Driscoll

PER SERVING: 470 CALORIES | 9G PROTEIN | 35G CARB | 33G TOTAL FAT | 10G SAT FAT | 18G MONO FAT | 3G POLY FAT | 40MG CHOL | 880MG SODIUM | 3G FIBER

angel hair pasta with sautéed cherry tomatoes, lemon & tuna

SERVES 4

Kosher salt

2 **Tbs. extra-virgin olive oil**

4 **cups cherry or grape tomatoes (about 1½ lb.; a mix of colors, if possible)**

1 **large clove garlic, minced**

1 **6-oz. can light tuna in oil, drained and separated into chunks**

2 **Tbs. minced jarred peperoncini (about 4 medium peppers), stemmed and seeded**

1 **Tbs. lightly chopped capers**

1 **tsp. fresh lemon juice**

1 **tsp. cold unsalted butter**

½ **tsp. packed, finely grated lemon zest**

8 **oz. dried angel hair pasta**

3 **Tbs. coarsely chopped fresh flat-leaf parsley**

For a real treat, try one of the imported Spanish tunas (Ortiz brand, in particular), which are fairly expensive but very delicious.

1. Bring a large pot of generously salted water to a boil over high heat. Meanwhile, in an 11- to 12-inch skillet, heat the oil over medium-high heat until very hot. Add the tomatoes (be careful because the oil and juice can spatter) and cook until they begin to collapse and their juices run and start to thicken, 6 to 10 minutes. (If you have big, stubborn tomatoes, you may need to crush them a bit with a spatula or pierce them with a knife.) Add the garlic and cook for 30 seconds.

2. Remove the pan from the heat and stir in the tuna, peperoncini, capers, lemon juice, butter, and lemon zest. Season the sauce to taste with salt and keep it warm while you cook the pasta.

3. Cook the pasta in the boiling water according to the package directions. Drain well, arrange in individual pasta bowls, and top with the sauce and the parsley. —*Martha Holmberg*

PER SERVING: 400 CALORIES | 22G PROTEIN | 49G CARB | 13G TOTAL FAT | 2.5G SAT FAT | 7G MONO FAT | 2.5G POLY FAT | 10MG CHOL | 880MG SODIUM | 5G FIBER

linguine with clam sauce

SERVES 2

24	littleneck clams
6	Tbs. extra-virgin olive oil
½	tsp. crushed red pepper flakes
⅓	cup dry white wine
5	Tbs. finely chopped fresh flat-leaf parsley, plus a few whole leaves for garnish
3	large cloves garlic, minced
	Kosher salt
8	oz. linguine or spaghettini
	Freshly ground black pepper

Fresh, in-the-shell clams are the key to getting true clam flavor, and tiny littlenecks are the most tender.

1. Scrub the clams under cold water and set aside. In a heavy 3-quart saucepan, heat 3 Tbs. of the oil over medium heat. Add the pepper flakes and cook briefly to infuse the oil, about 20 seconds. Immediately add the wine, 2 Tbs. of the chopped parsley, and half of the minced garlic. Cook for 20 seconds and add the clams.

2. Cover and cook over medium-high heat, checking every 2 minutes and removing each clam as it opens. It will take 5 to 6 minutes total for all the clams to open. Transfer the clams to a cutting board and reserve the broth. Remove the clams from the shells and cut them in half, or quarters if they're large. Return the clams to the broth. Discard the shells.

3. Bring a large pot of well-salted water to a boil over high heat. Add the pasta and cook until it's almost al dente, 6 to 9 minutes. Don't overcook.

4. While the pasta is cooking, heat the remaining 3 Tbs. olive oil in a 10- or 12-inch skillet over medium heat. Add the remaining 3 Tbs. chopped parsley and the rest of the garlic and cook until the garlic is just soft, about 1 minute. Set the skillet aside.

5. When the pasta is done, reserve about ¼ cup of the pasta cooking water and then drain the pasta. Add the pasta, the clams, and the broth the clams were cooked in to the skillet. Return to low heat, toss the pasta in the sauce, and simmer for another minute to finish cooking it, adding a little of the pasta water if you prefer a wetter dish.

6. Taste for salt and add a large grind of black pepper. Serve immediately, garnished with the parsley leaves. *—Perla Meyers*

PER SERVING: 670 CALORIES | 31G PROTEIN | 63G CARB | 30G TOTAL FAT | 4G SAT FAT | 20G MONO FAT | 4G POLY FAT | 50MG CHOL | 330MG SODIUM | 4G FIBER

cavatappi with artichokes and three cheeses

SERVES 4

Kosher salt

1 lemon

1 Tbs. unsalted butter

1 Tbs. olive oil

½ cup chopped shallot

1 9-oz. package frozen artichoke hearts, cut into ¼-inch slices while frozen

¼ tsp. crushed red pepper flakes

Coarsely ground black pepper

⅓ cup thinly sliced chives

2 Tbs. thinly sliced fresh mint leaves

12 oz. cavatappi

½ cup mascarpone (4 oz.)

½ cup mild goat cheese (3 oz.)

½ cup finely grated pecorino romano; more for serving

Cavatappi resemble elongated elbow macaroni and are the perfect shape for this rich and creamy dish—the herbs, cheeses, and sliced artichoke hearts cling to the spirals. By using a combination of frozen artichoke hearts and fresh chives and mint, you can produce a fast and flavorful vegetarian meal in no time.

1. Bring a large pot of well-salted water to a boil over high heat. From the lemon, grate 1½ tsp. of zest and squeeze 1 Tbs. of juice; set aside. Heat the butter and oil in a 12-inch skillet over medium heat until the butter has melted. Add the shallot and cook until just softened, about 3 minutes. Increase the heat to high and add the frozen artichokes, red pepper flakes, ½ tsp. salt, and ¼ tsp. pepper. Cook until the artichokes are golden brown, 3 to 4 minutes. Remove from the heat and stir in 3 Tbs. of the chives, the mint, and the lemon zest.

2. Meanwhile, cook the cavatappi according to the package directions until al dente. Drain, reserving ½ cup of the water. Return the pasta to the pot and stir in the mascarpone, goat cheese, pecorino, lemon juice, and ¼ cup of the water until smooth. Gently stir in the artichoke mixture and add more water if necessary to moisten the pasta. Season to taste with salt and pepper. Serve sprinkled with the remaining chives and additional cheese. —*Samantha Seneviratne*

PER SERVING: 650 CALORIES | 22G PROTEIN | 74G CARB | 30G TOTAL FAT | 15G SAT FAT | 8G MONO FAT | 1.5G POLY FAT | 65MG CHOL | 730MG SODIUM | 8G FIBER

stir-fried noodles with beef and vegetables

SERVES 4

3 oz. bean threads (cellophane noodles) or thin rice noodles

¼ cup canola or peanut oil

3 Tbs. soy sauce

1½ Tbs. Asian sesame oil

1½ Tbs. rice vinegar

1 Tbs. light brown sugar

½ lb. flank steak

Kosher salt

1 small zucchini (about 6 oz.), halved and thinly sliced crosswise into half circles

1 cup matchstick-cut or grated carrot (1 large carrot)

1 small yellow onion, halved and thinly sliced crosswise into half circles

1 Tbs. toasted sesame seeds

Traditionally, the noodles for this Korean favorite are made of sweet-potato starch, though bean threads or thin rice noodles are also fine.

1. Bring a 3-quart. pot of water to a boil. Add the bean threads or rice noodles, remove from the heat, and let sit until just softened (they should still be plenty toothy), about 3 minutes. Drain in a colander and rinse well under cool, running water. Toss with 1 Tbs. of the canola or peanut oil, and spread out on a tray or large plate lined with paper towels.

2. In a small bowl, mix the soy sauce, sesame oil, rice vinegar, and brown sugar. Trim the beef of excess fat and slice it thinly across the grain. Cut the slices into 2-inch pieces. Season the beef with salt.

3. Heat 1½ Tbs. of the canola or peanut oil in a 12-inch nonstick skillet or large stir-fry pan over medium-high heat until shimmering hot. Add the beef and cook, stirring, until it loses most of its raw appearance, about 1 minute. Transfer to a large plate.

4. Add the remaining 1½ Tbs. oil and the vegetables to the pan. Cook, stirring, until they start to soften, about 2 minutes. Reduce the heat to medium and add the beef and the noodles. Stir the soy mixture and drizzle it over all. Cook, tossing until everything is evenly coated with the sauce and the vegetables are cooked through, about 3 minutes. Serve immediately, sprinkled with the sesame seeds.

—*Tony Rosenfeld*

PER SERVING: 390 CALORIES | 14G PROTEIN | 29G CARB | 24G TOTAL FAT | 3.5G SAT FAT | 12G MONO FAT | 7G POLY FAT | 20MG CHOL | 1,320MG SODIUM | 2G FIBER

fusilli with green beans, pancetta & parmigiano

SERVES 2 TO 3

Kosher salt

½ **lb. fusilli or other twisted pasta**

4 **oz. pancetta, sliced ¼ inch thick and cut into ½-inch squares (¾ cup)**

1 **large clove garlic, smashed and peeled**

½ **lb. green beans, trimmed and cut into 1-inch lengths (2 cups)**

Freshly ground black pepper

1 **oz. (2 Tbs.) unsalted butter, at room temperature**

2 **oz. finely grated Parmigiano-Reggiano (1 cup)**

The pasta's cooking water melts the cheese and turns it into a rich sauce that coats the beans and pulls everything together. If you can't find pancetta, substitute bacon.

1. Bring a medium pot of well-salted water to a boil. Cook the pasta until just barely al dente, about 1 minute less than package timing. Reserve 1 cup of the cooking water, and drain the pasta.

2. While the pasta cooks, put the pancetta in a cold 10-inch skillet and set over medium-high heat. When the pancetta starts sizzling, add the garlic and cook, stirring constantly, until starting to brown, 1 minute. Reduce the heat to medium and continue to cook the pancetta until golden but still chewy at the center (taste a piece if you're not sure), an additional 2 to 3 minutes. If the pancetta has rendered a lot of its fat, spoon off all but 1 Tbs. of the fat from the pan.

3. Add the beans to the pan and cook, stirring constantly, until they're crisp-tender, 3 to 4 minutes. Remove the garlic and season the beans with salt and pepper. With the pan still over medium heat, add the pasta, ½ cup of the pasta water, and the butter. Toss to combine. Add another ¼ cup pasta water and ¾ cup of the Parmigiano. Stir well and season to taste with salt and pepper. If necessary, add a little more pasta water to loosen the sauce.

4. Transfer the pasta to a serving bowl. Grind black pepper over the top and sprinkle with the remaining cheese. —*Maria Helm Sinskey*

PER SERVING: 540 CALORIES | 20G PROTEIN | 62G CARB | 23G TOTAL FAT | 10G SAT FAT | 8G MONO FAT | 2.5G POLY FAT | 50MG CHOL | 1,270MG SODIUM | 6G FIBER

Avoid buying green beans that look withered at either end— it means they've been sitting a while and are losing moisture. Beans relinquish sweetness the longer they're stored, so try to use them right away. If you can't, store them in the refrigerator for up to 4 days in a paper bag or a plastic bag with holes punched in it so the beans can breathe.

fresh pasta with sausage and mushrooms

SERVES 3 TO 4

- ¾ tsp. kosher salt
- 2 Tbs. extra-virgin olive oil
- ¾ lb. sweet Italian chicken sausage, cut into 1-inch pieces
- ½ lb. mixed sliced mushrooms (like oyster, shiitake, and cremini)
- 4 medium scallions (white and green parts), trimmed and thinly sliced
- 2 tsp. chopped fresh rosemary
- ⅛ tsp. crushed red pepper flakes
- Freshly ground black pepper
- 1 cup drained canned diced tomatoes
- 1 cup lower-salt chicken broth
- 1 12-oz. package fresh linguine or fettuccine
- ¾ cup freshly grated Parmigiano-Reggiano

You can find fresh pasta in the refrigerated section of your supermarket. For a spicier dish, use hot Italian chicken sausage.

1. Bring a medium pot of salted water to a boil. Meanwhile, heat the oil in a large, heavy skillet over medium-high heat until shimmering hot. Add the sausage and cook, stirring occasionally, until browned, about 3 minutes. Add the mushrooms, scallions, rosemary, red pepper flakes, salt, and ½ tsp. pepper and cook, stirring often, until the mushrooms soften and start to brown, about 3 minutes. Add the tomatoes and chicken broth, bring to a boil, and then cover and reduce to a gentle simmer. Cook until the sausage is heated through and the flavors are melded, about 5 minutes.

2. Meanwhile, cook the pasta according to the package timing until it's just al dente. Drain well and add to the sauce along with half of the Parmigiano. Cook over medium heat, tossing for 1 minute. Serve sprinkled with the remaining Parmigiano and some black pepper.
—*Tony Rosenfeld*

PER SERVING: 490 CALORIES | 30G PROTEIN | 55G CARB | 17G TOTAL FAT | 4.5G SAT FAT | 5G MONO FAT | 1.5G POLY FAT | 115MG CHOL | 1,280MG SODIUM | 1G FIBER

penne with peas, shrimp & basil

SERVES 4

- **1½ lb. shrimp (21 to 25 per lb.), peeled, deveined, and cut in half lengthwise**
- **½ cup chopped fresh basil**
- **5 Tbs. extra-virgin olive oil**
- **1 Tbs. finely grated lemon zest**

  Kosher salt
- **1½ cups fresh shelled peas (about 1½ lb. unshelled) or frozen peas**
- **¾ lb. dried penne**

  Freshly ground black pepper
- **⅓ cup finely diced shallots**
- **1 tsp. minced garlic**
- **¾ tsp. seeded and minced hot fresh chile, such as Thai bird or serrano**
- **2 oz. arugula, trimmed, washed, and dried (about 2 lightly packed cups)**

Penne is a good pasta for this dish, but you can use other short pastas like rigatoni or ziti.

1. Toss the shrimp with half of the basil, 2 Tbs. of the olive oil, and the lemon zest. Cover and refrigerate for about 30 minutes.

2. Bring a large pot of well-salted water to a boil over high heat. Put the peas in a large metal sieve and dip them into the boiling water. Cook until just tender, 2 to 4 minutes. Lift the sieve from the water, let the peas drain, and then spread them on a baking sheet in a single layer to cool.

3. Add the pasta to the boiling water and cook, following the package directions, until al dente. Reserve ½ cup of the cooking water and drain the pasta.

4. Meanwhile, take the shrimp out of the fridge and season them lightly with salt and pepper. Heat the remaining 3 Tbs. oil in a 12-inch skillet over medium heat. Add the shallot, garlic, chile, and a pinch of salt and cook, stirring occasionally, until the shallot is soft and lightly browned, about 2 minutes. Add the shrimp and continue to cook, stirring, until the shrimp have turned pink and are almost cooked through, 2 to 3 minutes. Stir in the peas and remove from the heat.

5. Return the drained pasta to its pot and add the shrimp mixture and 2 Tbs. of the pasta water. Cook over medium heat until the shrimp are completely cooked through, about 1 minute more. Toss the arugula and the remaining basil into the pasta. Add more pasta water as necessary to keep the pasta moist, and continue tossing until the arugula is wilted, about 1 minute. Season to taste with salt and pepper and serve immediately. *—Annie Wayte*

PER SERVING: 680 CALORIES | 43G PROTEIN | 74G CARB | 20G TOTAL FAT | 3G SAT FAT | 13G MONO FAT | 3G POLY FAT | 250MG CHOL | 880MG SODIUM | 7G FIBER

quick skillet mac and cheese

SERVES 4

Kosher salt

12 oz. dried spiral pasta, such as cavatappi, rotini, or double elbows

1.5 oz. (3 Tbs.) unsalted butter

3 Tbs. unbleached all-purpose flour

2 cups low-fat (2%) milk

4 oz. grated Emmentaler (1¼ cups)

4 oz. grated Gruyère (1¼ cups)

1 Tbs. Dijon mustard

1 Tbs. Worcestershire sauce

½ tsp. dried thyme

Freshly ground black pepper

3 oz. finely grated Parmigiano-Reggiano (3 cups)

Who says you can't have indulgent comfort food on a weeknight? Be sure to use a broiler-safe skillet, such as a cast-iron one.

1. Bring a large pot of well-salted water to a boil over high heat. Add the pasta and cook according to the package directions until just tender. Drain well and set aside.

2. Meanwhile, melt the butter in a 12-inch ovenproof skillet (preferably cast iron) over medium heat. Whisk in the flour and continue whisking until well combined, about 15 seconds. Whisk in the milk and continue to cook, whisking constantly, until the mixture thickens, 1 to 2 minutes.

3. Add the Emmentaler, Gruyère, mustard, Worcestershire sauce, and thyme and whisk until the cheese is melted and the mixture is smooth, 2 minutes. Stir in the pasta to coat with the sauce. Off the heat, season to taste with salt and pepper. Sprinkle the Parmigiano-Reggiano evenly over the pasta.

4. Position a rack about 4 inches from the broiler and heat the broiler on high. Broil the pasta until the top is browned, 3 to 4 minutes, and serve. —*Bruce Weinstein and Mark Scarbrough*

PER SERVING: 750 CALORIES | 36G PROTEIN | 77G CARB | 32G TOTAL FAT | 19G SAT FAT | 8G MONO FAT | 2G POLY FAT | 95MG CHOL, | 930MG SODIUM | 4G FIBER

More about Emmentaler

Named for Switzerland's Emmental Valley, Emmentaler, a cow's-milk cheese, has a nutty-sweet, mellow flavor, making it perfect for snacking and cooking. It is light gold in color, has marble-size holes, and has a natural light brown rind.

orecchiette with brussels sprouts, gorgonzola & brown-butter pecans

SERVES 4 TO 6

Kosher salt

20 oz. Brussels sprouts, trimmed (4 cups)

3½ Tbs. extra-virgin olive oil

½ tsp. freshly ground black pepper

1 lb. dried orecchiette

1½ Tbs. unsalted butter

½ cup coarsely chopped pecans

2 large shallots, minced (¾ cup)

¾ cup heavy cream

4 oz. Gorgonzola, crumbled (1 cup)

1 Tbs. fresh lemon juice

For a sweet, nutty flavor, roast the Brussels sprouts until they're just this side of charred.

1. Position a rack in the lower third of the oven, set a heavy, rimmed baking sheet on the rack, and heat the oven to 500°F. Bring a large pot of well-salted water to a boil over high heat.

2. In a food processor fitted with the medium (4 mm) slicing disk, slice the Brussels sprouts. Transfer them to a large bowl, drizzle with the oil, sprinkle with 1¼ tsp. salt and the pepper, and toss until well coated. Remove the hot baking sheet from the oven and spread the Brussels sprouts on it in a single layer. Roast, stirring once about halfway through the cooking time, until the Brussels sprouts are tender and flecked with charred bits, 15 to 20 minutes.

3. Meanwhile, cook the orecchiette according to the package directions until just al dente.

4. In a medium heavy-duty skillet, melt ½ Tbs. of the butter over medium heat. Add the pecans and cook, stirring frequently, until the butter is deeply browned and the pecans are toasted, about 3 minutes. Transfer to a plate and set aside.

5. Melt the remaining 1 Tbs. butter in the skillet over medium heat. Add the shallot and cook, stirring occasionally, until softened, 2 to 3 minutes. Add the cream and bring to a simmer. Off the heat, add 3 oz. (¾ cup) of the Gorgonzola and stir until melted.

6. Drain the orecchiette and return it to the pot. Add the Brussels sprouts, Gorgonzola sauce, and lemon juice and toss well. Serve, sprinkled with the pecans and the remaining Gorgonzola.
—Dawn Yanagihara

PER SERVING: 670 CALORIES | 19G PROTEIN | 67G CARB | 36G TOTAL FAT | 14G SAT FAT | 15G MONO FAT | 4.5G POLY FAT | 70MG CHOL | 700MG SODIUM | 8G FIBER

More about Brussels Sprouts

Brussels sprouts—they get their name because it's believed they were first cultivated in Belgium—look like tiny cabbages (and are a member of the cabbage family) and have a flavor that's both assertive and somewhat sweet. They take well to a variety of cooking methods, including roasting, steaming, braising, and sautéing. It's key not to overcook them or, like cabbage, they will become unpleasantly pungent.

Choosing
Look for sprouts from early fall through spring, and choose tight heads with little decay or yellowing. Sprouts that are loose and ruffly have most likely been grown in too much heat and won't be as intensely sweet and nutty. You'll sometimes find the whole stalk, which is gorgeous in a sculptural way but a pain to store once you get it home.

Prepping
Use a small paring knife to trim off the lower part of the stem and any tatty outer leaves. Brussels sprouts can be cooked whole, halved, quartered, or sliced. You can also separate the individual leaves, which is a little tedious but a lovely presentation.

Storing
Store sprouts in the coldest part of the refrigerator, where they should last at least a week or more. The longer they're stored, the more the outer leaves will yellow, so just peel them off before cooking.

udon with tofu and stir-fried vegetables

SERVES 4

Kosher salt

¾ **lb. dried udon noodles**

3 **cups lower-salt chicken broth**

1 **Tbs. plus 2 tsp. oyster sauce**

1 **Tbs. plus 2 tsp. rice vinegar**

4 **tsp. Asian sesame oil**

¼ **cup minced fresh ginger**

2 **Tbs. canola oil**

¾ **lb. bok choy, cut crosswise into ¾-inch pieces (4 cups)**

3½ **oz. shiitake mushrooms, stemmed and thinly sliced (1½ cups)**

½ **lb. extra-firm tofu, cut into ½-inch cubes**

2 **medium carrots, cut into matchsticks**

3 **medium scallions, trimmed and thinly sliced, for garnish**

Udon, wheat-based Japanese noodles, are available both dried (used in this recipe) and fresh. Dried udon are flatter than their fresh counterparts and closer in texture to linguine.

1. Bring a medium pot of well-salted water to a boil. Add the noodles and cook, stirring, until tender, about 8 minutes. Transfer to a colander and run under cold water to cool slightly. Drain well.

2. In a medium bowl, mix the chicken broth, oyster sauce, vinegar, and 2 tsp. of the sesame oil.

3. Heat the ginger and canola oil in a large skillet over medium-high heat until the ginger sizzles steadily for about 30 seconds. Add the bok choy and mushrooms, sprinkle with the remaining 2 tsp. sesame oil and ¾ tsp. salt and cook, tossing after 1 minute, until the bok choy turns dark green and begins to soften, 3 to 5 minutes. Add the chicken broth mixture, tofu, and carrots and bring to a boil. Reduce to a simmer, cover, and cook until the carrots are soft and the tofu is heated through, 5 to 7 minutes.

4. Distribute the noodles among 4 bowls. Spoon the vegetables, tofu, and broth over the noodles. Sprinkle with the scallions and serve.
—*Tony Rosenfeld*

PER SERVING: 540 CALORIES | 24G PROTEIN | 71G CARB | 19G TOTAL FAT | 2G SAT FAT | 9G MONO FAT | 4.5G POLY FAT | 0MG CHOL | 820MG SODIUM | 8G FIBER

More about Udon

These thick Japanese noodles are made from white wheat flour, salt, and water, and are usually served in a soup or with a dipping sauce.

Prepping
Cook both fresh and dried udon in well-salted boiling water until just tender (about 3 minutes for fresh, 8 minutes for dried). Drain the noodles and rinse them briefly under cold water before using in soup or another dish; this stops the cooking and also removes some of the surface starch, preventing them from sticking together.

Storing
Keep fresh udon refrigerated and use by their expiration date. Dried udon will keep nearly indefinitely on the pantry shelf.

spaghetti with creamy braised garlic and leeks

SERVES 4

- 1 oz. (2 Tbs.) unsalted butter
- 1 Tbs. extra-virgin olive oil
- 6 medium leeks (light green and white parts only), halved and sliced crosswise into ½-inch pieces (10 cups)
- 10 medium cloves garlic, halved
- Kosher salt
- ¼ tsp. freshly ground black pepper
- ½ cup dry white wine
- 1 cup lower-salt chicken broth
- 12 oz. dried spaghetti
- ½ cup heavy cream
- ½ oz. (⅓ cup) grated pecorino romano
- ¼ cup chopped fresh flat-leaf parsley

Whole heads of garlic stay fresh longer than peeled garlic cloves found in jars. Keep garlic in its mesh bag in a cool, dark, dry place for up to 2 weeks.

Braising the garlic in this recipe takes away some of its punch, rendering it sweet and ultra tender.

1. Heat the butter and oil in a 12-inch skillet over medium-high heat until the butter has melted. Add the leeks, garlic, ½ tsp. salt, and the pepper and cook, stirring often, until the leeks begin to brown, 3 to 5 minutes. Add the wine and simmer until reduced by half, about 1 minute. Add the chicken broth and bring to a simmer. Reduce the heat to low and press a 12-inch round piece of parchment over the leek mixture to cover completely (see the sidebar below). Cover the skillet and cook, stirring occasionally (you will have to lift the parchment), until the leeks are very soft but not falling apart and the garlic is very soft, about 40 minutes.

2. Meanwhile, bring a large pot of well-salted water to a boil and cook the spaghetti according to the package directions until al dente. Drain, reserving ½ cup of the pasta cooking water.

3. Uncover the skillet and remove the parchment. Stir in the cream and cook, stirring occasionally, until the sauce thickens slightly, about 3 minutes. Add the cooked pasta and toss. If necessary, add the reserved pasta water 1 Tbs. at a time to make a silky sauce that clings to the pasta.

4. Off the heat, stir in the cheese and parsley. Season to taste with salt and pepper, and serve. —*Samantha Seneviratne*

PER SERVING: 540 CALORIES | 17G PROTEIN | 87G CARB | 24G TOTAL FAT | 12G SAT FAT | 8G MONO FAT | 2G POLY FAT | 60MG CHOL | 540MG SODIUM | 6G FIBER

use parchment for a richer braise

Place a piece of parchment between the braising vegetables and the lid. The parchment reduces the head-room in the pan, so the vapors travel less and become more concentrated as they drip back down, giving you a richer sauce.

linguine with lemon-garlic shrimp

SERVES 3

Kosher salt

½ lb. dried thin linguine

1 lemon

1 lb. extra-large (26 to 30 per lb.) shrimp, peeled and deveined

Freshly ground black pepper

1 oz. (2 Tbs.) unsalted butter

3 medium cloves garlic, thinly sliced (1 Tbs.)

⅛ to ¼ tsp. crushed red pepper flakes

¼ cup dry white wine, such as Pinot Grigio

½ cup mascarpone

2 Tbs. thinly sliced chives

This easy pasta gets its luxurious creaminess from mascarpone, an Italian cream cheese (see the sidebar on p. 126).

1. Bring a large pot of well-salted water to a boil over high heat. Cook the linguine in the boiling water according to the package directions until al dente. Reserve about ¾ cup of the cooking water and then drain the pasta.

2. Meanwhile, finely grate 1¼ tsp. of zest from the lemon and squeeze 2 Tbs. of juice. Toss the shrimp with ½ tsp. of the zest and ¼ tsp. each salt and pepper.

3. In a 12-inch skillet, melt the butter over medium-high heat until the foam subsides. Add the garlic and red pepper flakes and cook until the garlic just begins to brown, about 1 minute. Add the shrimp and cook until just opaque, about 3 minutes. Add the wine and lemon juice, bring to a boil, and cook until slightly reduced, 1 minute.

4. Add the drained pasta, mascarpone, and ½ cup of the cooking water. Toss well, adding more cooking water as needed, until the pasta and shrimp are coated and the sauce looks creamy. Remove from the heat. Toss in the remaining ¾ tsp. lemon zest and the chives. Season to taste with salt and pepper and serve. *—Melissa Gaman*

PER SERVING: 830 CALORIES | 40G PROTEIN | 62G CARB | 45G TOTAL FAT | 24G SAT FAT | 12G MONO FAT | 2.5G POLY FAT | 340MG CHOL | 640MG SODIUM | 4G FIBER

For best results when zesting, choose thick-skinned lemons, which tend to have pebbly-textured skin. Before zesting, scrub the lemon's skin well to remove any residue (a soak in warm water can help remove any wax coating). Remove just the thin yellow layer of rind, not the white pith below. Use a vegetable peeler to get wide strips of zest and a rasp-style grater for finely grated zest.

pasta puttanesca

SERVES 4

Kosher salt

3 Tbs. extra-virgin olive oil

4 large cloves garlic, minced

3 oil-packed anchovy fillets, finely chopped (scant 1 Tbs.)

¼ tsp. crushed red pepper flakes

1 28-oz. can crushed tomatoes

1 lb. dried spaghetti

½ cup pitted brine-cured black olives, such as Kalamata, coarsely chopped

2 Tbs. nonpareil capers, rinsed and drained

1 Tbs. chopped fresh oregano or marjoram

Freshly ground black pepper

Many of the ingredients for this classic flavor-packed pasta may already be in your pantry, making this a perfect weeknight meal.

1. Bring a large pot of well-salted water to a boil over high heat.

2. Meanwhile, heat 1 Tbs. of the olive oil with the garlic in a 3-quart saucepan over medium heat. Cook, stirring frequently, until the garlic is sizzling, about 2 minutes. Add the anchovies and red pepper flakes and cook, stirring frequently, until the garlic is very pale golden, 1 to 2 minutes more. Stir in the tomatoes. Increase the heat to medium high, bring to a boil, and then reduce the heat to medium low and simmer, stirring occasionally, until the sauce is slightly thickened, 8 to 10 minutes.

3. After adding the tomatoes to the pan, add the pasta to the boiling water and cook according to the package directions until al dente.

4. When the tomato sauce is ready, add the olives, capers, and oregano and stir. Simmer until just heated through, about 2 minutes. Stir in the remaining 2 Tbs. olive oil and season the sauce to taste with salt and pepper.

5. When the pasta is ready, reserve ½ cup of the cooking water and drain well. Return the pasta to the pot, set it over medium-low heat, pour in the sauce, and toss, adding cooking water as needed for the sauce to coat the pasta. Serve immediately. —*Dawn Yanagihara*

PER SERVING: 720 CALORIES | 30G PROTEIN | 103G CARB | 22G TOTAL FAT | 3.5G SAT FAT | 13G MONO FAT | 3.5G POLY FAT | 30MG CHOL | 2,590MG SODIUM | 10G FIBER

asparagus ravioli with brown butter sauce

Sea salt

1 **lb. thick asparagus, trimmed, spears cut into 1-inch pieces, and tips reserved**

6 **Tbs. mascarpone**

⅓ **cup whole milk ricotta**

¼ **cup freshly grated Parmigiano-Reggiano; more for serving**

1 **tsp. anchovy paste**

½ **tsp. minced garlic**

Pinch of cayenne

Kosher salt and freshly ground black pepper

36 **wonton wrappers**

4 **oz. (½ cup) unsalted butter**

½ **cup blanched almonds, chopped**

Finely grated lemon zest to taste

Wonton wrappers are a quick alternative to homemade pasta for ravioli. The rich brown butter, bright lemon zest, and crunchy almond garnish perfectly complement the creamy asparagus filling.

1. Bring a medium pot of well-salted water to a boil over high heat. Have ready a medium bowl of ice water. Boil the asparagus tips until tender but still bright green, about 2 minutes. With a slotted spoon, transfer to the ice water. When cool, transfer with the slotted spoon to a small bowl and set aside. Cook and cool the asparagus spears in the same manner; dry them on paper towels. In a food processor (or by hand), chop 1½ cups of the spears very finely and transfer to a medium bowl. Add the remaining spears to the tips.

2. Add the mascarpone, ricotta, Parmigiano, anchovy paste, garlic, and cayenne to the chopped asparagus; mix well. Season to taste with salt and pepper.

3. Arrange 18 wonton wrappers on a work surface. Put 1 level Tbs. of the asparagus filling in the center of each wrapper. Using a pastry brush, moisten the edges of each with water. Top each with another wrapper and press the edges firmly to seal, expelling any air bubbles as you seal. If you don't plan to cook the ravioli immediately, cover them with a damp cloth.

4. Bring a large pot of well-salted water to a rolling boil over high heat. Meanwhile, melt the butter in a 10-inch skillet over medium heat and add the almonds, shaking the pan. Cook until the butter turns light brown, about 6 minutes, and then immediately transfer to a small bowl.

5. Add the ravioli to the boiling water. When they rise to the surface, after about 1 minute, use a slotted spoon to transfer them to warm plates or pasta bowls. Spoon the brown butter mixture over the ravioli. Top with the reserved asparagus pieces, a grinding of pepper, a sprinkle of Parmigiano, and a little lemon zest and serve. —*John Ash*

PER SERVING: 510 CALORIES | 13G PROTEIN | 33G CARB | 38G TOTAL FAT | 19G SAT FAT | 12G MONO FAT | 3G POLY FAT | 90MG CHOL | 620MG SODIUM | 3G FIBER

More about Mascarpone

Mascarpone is a thick and buttery double- to triple-cream cow's milk cheese (containing over 60% and often over 75% milk fat). It's slightly sweet with a faint yellow hue and spans dishes from starters to sweets.

Try mixing mascarpone into pasta or fold it into polenta. For simple desserts, serve mascarpone with fresh figs, pears, or berries, or dollop a spoonful alongside fruit pies or tarts.

spicy peanut noodles with ground pork and shredded vegetables

SERVES 4

Kosher salt

½ **lb. dried ¼-inch-wide rice noodles (pad thai noodles)**

1 **Tbs. Asian sesame oil**

¾ **lb. lean ground pork**

½ **cup crunchy peanut butter, preferably natural**

¼ **cup seasoned rice vinegar**

1½ **Tbs. fish sauce**

1 **or 2 jalapeños, stemmed and finely chopped (seeded, if desired)**

2 **medium carrots (about 6 oz.), grated**

2 **large yellow squash or zucchini (about 1 lb.), grated**

⅔ **cup coarsely chopped fresh mint**

Lime wedges, for serving

Grated carrots, squash, and chopped mint balance the spicy heat of the jalapeños. For a milder dish, use only 1 chile and remove its seeds and ribs—they're hotter than the flesh itself.

1. Bring a large pot of salted water to a boil. Add the rice noodles and cook, stirring often, until just tender, about 5 minutes. Drain and rinse under cold running water; leave to drain in a colander.

2. Meanwhile, heat 2 tsp. of the oil in a large skillet over medium-high heat. Add the pork and ½ tsp. salt and cook, stirring to break up the meat, until just cooked through, 4 to 8 minutes; set aside.

3. In a large bowl, whisk the peanut butter, vinegar, fish sauce, the remaining 1 tsp. oil, and 3 Tbs. warm water until smooth. Add the drained noodles, pork, jalapeños, carrots, squash, and all but 2 Tbs. of the mint and toss gently. Garnish with the remaining mint, and serve at room temperature with the lime wedges on the side. —*Liz Pearson*

PER SERVING: 620 CALORIES | 26G PROTEIN | 655G CARB | 29G TOTAL FAT | 6G SAT FAT | 6G MONO FAT | 3G POLY FAT | 500MG CHOL | 1,000MG SODIUM | 5G FIBER

orecchiette with ham and peas in cheese sauce

SERVES 8

Kosher salt

1 lb. orecchiette or other small shell pasta

4 oz. (½ cup) unsalted butter, more for the dish

1 large shallot, finely diced (about ¼ cup)

¼ cup unbleached all-purpose flour

3 cups whole milk, warmed

2 cups freshly grated Grana Padano

2 tsp. chopped fresh thyme

1¾ tsp. freshly ground black pepper

¼ tsp. Tabasco

¾ lb. ham steak, cut into ½-inch dice

2 cups frozen peas, thawed

½ cup coarse fresh breadcrumbs

1 Tbs. olive oil

In this dressed-up macaroni and cheese, orecchiette takes the place of tiny elbows, peas and ham add flavor and texture, and Grana Padano stands in for the usual Cheddar.

1. Position a rack in the center of the oven and heat the oven to 375°F. Butter a 9x13-inch baking dish. Bring a large pot of well-salted water to a boil and add the pasta; cook according to the package directions until al dente. Reserve ½ cup of the pasta water, drain the pasta well, and return the pasta to the pot.

2. Meanwhile, for the cheese sauce, melt the butter in a medium (3-quart) saucepan over medium heat. Add the shallot, sprinkle with ¼ tsp. salt, and cook, stirring occasionally, until it softens and becomes translucent, about 3 minutes. Add the flour and cook, stirring, until it turns golden and smells nutty, about 1 minute. Whisk in the milk in a slow, steady stream, and cook, whisking occasionally to avoid sticking on the bottom of the pan, until the mixture thickens, about 10 minutes. Remove from the heat and stir in all but ½ cup of Grana Padano, the thyme, 1½ tsp. pepper, ½ tsp. salt, and the Tabasco. Stir the ham and peas into the béchamel; taste and add more salt and pepper if needed.

3. Stir ¼ cup of the pasta water into the béchamel so it loosens a bit and then toss with the pasta in the pasta pot. Add more pasta water as needed. Transfer to the prepared baking dish. In a small bowl, mix the breadcrumbs, olive oil, ¼ tsp. salt, and the remaining ¼ tsp. pepper with the remaining ½ cup cheese, and sprinkle over the pasta. Bake the pasta until it bubbles and browns around the edges, about 20 minutes (cover with foil if the top browns too quickly). Let cool for a couple of minutes and then serve. *—Tony Rosenfeld*

rigatoni with sun-dried tomato and fennel sauce

SERVES 4

Kosher salt

2 Tbs. extra-virgin olive oil

1 cup chopped fennel (about ½ medium bulb)

2 medium cloves garlic, very coarsely chopped

1 cup heavy cream

1 cup lower-salt chicken broth

⅓ cup drained oil-packed sun-dried tomatoes, very coarsely chopped

¼ tsp. crushed red pepper flakes

1 Tbs. Pernod (optional)

1 lb. rigatoni

The sauce in this pasta dish is enhanced by the subtle licorice flavor of Pernod, but any pastis or anise-flavored liqueur could work. Add sliced, cooked sweet Italian sausage for a more substantial meal (its flavors work well with the sauce).

1. Bring a large pot of well-salted water to a boil. Meanwhile, heat the olive oil in a 10- to 11-inch, straight-sided sauté pan over medium heat. Add the fennel and garlic and cook, stirring occasionally, until the fennel starts to soften and brown, about 5 minutes. Stir in 1 cup water, the cream, chicken broth, sun-dried tomatoes, red pepper flakes, and 1 tsp. salt. Bring to a boil, reduce the heat, and simmer briskly, uncovered, until the tomatoes are plump and soft, about 15 minutes.

2. Remove from the heat and stir in the Pernod, if using. Let cool slightly and then purée in a blender until smooth. Wipe out the skillet, return the sauce to the skillet, season to taste with salt, and keep hot.

3. Cook the rigatoni until just barely al dente, 1 to 2 minutes less than the package instructions. Drain well and return to the pot. Add the sauce and toss over medium-low heat for a minute or two so the pasta finishes cooking and absorbs some of the sauce. —*Tony Rosenfeld*

More about Fennel

The general name "fennel" applies to two varieties: Florence fennel, or finocchio, and common fennel. Florence fennel has a bulbous base, long celerylike stalks, and delicate bright green fronds. The bulb is crunchy with a pleasantly sweet aniseed, or licoricelike flavor, and can be eaten raw or cooked. The stalks and fronds can also be used in cooking. Common fennel is the variety of the plant from which fennel seeds are harvested. Though common fennel doesn't have a bulb, its stalks and fronds can be used like those of Florence fennel.

Choosing
Choose clean, firm bulbs with no sign of browning. Any attached greenery should look fresh and bright green in color.

Prepping
If you buy Florence fennel with the stalks intact, cut them off close to the bulb, so you'll have a more manageable vegetable. Next, peel the stringy fibers off the outer layer of the bulb with a peeler or sharp paring knife. Then cut the bulb as called for in your recipe.

Storing
Refrigerate fennel tightly wrapped in a plastic bag for up to 5 days.

penne with spinach, gorgonzola & walnuts

SERVES 4

Kosher salt

8 oz. fresh baby spinach leaves (10 lightly packed cups)

¼ cup coarsely chopped walnuts

12 oz. dried penne (3 ½ cups)

¾ cup heavy cream

2½ oz. crumbled Gorgonzola (½ cup)

Freshly ground black pepper

3 Tbs. thinly sliced fresh chives

Chopped nuts are unusual in pasta, but they pair brilliantly with the earthy Gorgonzola in this creamy fall dish. Toasting the nuts deepens their flavor, so don't skip this step.

1. Position a rack in the center of the oven and heat the oven to 350°F. Meanwhile, bring a large pot of generously salted water to a boil. Put the spinach in a colander in the sink.

2. Toast the walnuts on a rimmed baking sheet in the oven until dark golden brown, 6 to 8 minutes. Set aside.

3. Cook the penne according to package directions. Reserve about ½ cup of the cooking water and drain the pasta in the colander over the spinach.

4. Put the cream, Gorgonzola, ¼ tsp. pepper, and a pinch of salt in a 12-inch nonstick skillet and bring to a boil over medium-high heat. Cook, stirring frequently, until slightly thickened, 2 to 3 minutes. Reduce the heat to medium, add the pasta, spinach, and 2 Tbs. each of the walnuts and chives. Cook, stirring constantly, until some of the sauce is absorbed by the pasta, about 2 minutes. If necessary, add some of the cooking water to moisten the pasta. Season to taste with salt and pepper. Transfer to serving bowls, sprinkle with the remaining 2 Tbs. walnuts and 1 Tbs. chives, and serve. *—Lori Longbotham*

PER SERVING: 620 CALORIES | 19G PROTEIN | 72G CARB | 28G TOTAL FAT | 14G SAT FAT | 7G MONO FAT | 5G POLY FAT | 80MG CHOL | 560MG SODIUM | 7G FIBER

grilled shrimp salad with
feta, tomato & watermelon
(recipe on p. 153)

main dish salads

roasted butternut squash and pear salad with spiced-pecan vinaigrette

SERVES 6

- ½ **cup pecans, very coarsely chopped**
- 1 **oz. (2 Tbs.) unsalted butter, melted**
- ½ **tsp. ancho chile powder**
- 3 **cups ¾-inch-diced, peeled butternut squash (from about a 2-lb. squash)**
- ⅓ **cup plus 2 Tbs. extra-virgin olive oil**
- 1½ **tsp. kosher salt**
- ¼ **cup very thinly sliced shallots**
- 3 **Tbs. balsamic vinegar**
- 1 **Tbs. Dijon mustard**
- 2 **tsp. light brown sugar**
- 6 **cups loosely packed mixed salad greens**
- 1 **small ripe pear, halved, cored, and thinly sliced**

This salad combines fall's sweetest flavors: mellow butternut squash, crisp buttery pears, and crunchy pecans, with a slightly spicy kick from the vinaigrette.

1. Position a rack in the center of the oven and heat the oven to 450°F.

2. Put the pecans and butter in an 8-inch-square Pyrex dish and toss to coat. Sprinkle with the chile powder and toss. Bake the nuts until toasted, about 5 minutes. Set aside to cool.

3. Put the squash on a heavy-duty, rimmed baking sheet. Drizzle 2 Tbs. of the oil over the squash and sprinkle with ¾ tsp. salt. Toss to coat. Roast the squash until browned on the bottom, about 20 minutes. Flip with a metal spatula and continue to roast until the squash is tender and nicely browned on a second side, 5 to 10 minutes more. Set aside to cool.

4. Put the shallot in a small bowl, cover with hot water, and let soak for 15 minutes; drain in a colander.

5. Combine the vinegar, mustard, brown sugar, and ¼ tsp. salt in a small bowl. While whisking vigorously, slowly pour in the remaining ⅓ cup oil.

6. Combine the salad greens and shallot in a large bowl; sprinkle with ½ tsp. salt. Drizzle just enough of the dressing over the salad to coat lightly, and toss gently. Divide the greens among 6 plates and scatter the pecans, squash, and pears over the greens. Drizzle with a little more dressing if desired and serve. —*Julianna Grimes*

PER SERVING: 310 CALORIES I 3G PROTEIN I 17G CARB I 28G TOTAL FAT I 5G SAT FAT I 17G MONO FAT I 4G POLY FAT I 10MG CHOL I 370MG SODIUM I 5G FIBER

steak, egg & blue cheese salad

SERVES 4

- **1** small clove garlic

    Kosher salt

- **3** Tbs. red-wine vinegar

- **1½** tsp. Dijon mustard

- **½** cup plus 1 Tbs. extra-virgin olive oil

    Freshly ground black pepper

- **1** lb. beef sirloin steak tips

- **2** heads Boston lettuce, washed, spun dry, and torn into bite-size pieces (about 6 cups loosely packed)

- **4** medium- or hard-cooked eggs, peeled and quartered lengthwise

- **¾** cup crumbled blue cheese (about 4 oz.)

- **1** medium carrot, peeled and very thinly sliced crosswise

- **6** medium red radishes, thinly sliced

- **¼** cup 1-inch-long-sliced fresh chives

This steak is also delicious cooked on the grill. If you have a mandoline, use it to cut the carrots and radishes into very thin slices.

1. Roughly chop the garlic, sprinkle it with a generous pinch of salt, and mash it into a paste with the side of a chef's knife. Transfer the garlic to a small bowl and whisk in the vinegar and mustard. Whisk in the ½ cup oil in a thin, steady stream. Season the vinaigrette to taste with salt and pepper. Drizzle the sirloin tips with 2 Tbs. of the vinaigrette and let sit while preparing the other salad ingredients. Reserve the remaining vinaigrette for dressing the salad.

2. Season the meat all over with 1 tsp. salt and ½ tsp. pepper. Heat the remaining 1 Tbs. oil in a 10-inch skillet (preferably cast iron), over high heat. When the oil is shimmering hot, add the meat and sear on both sides until cooked to your liking, about 3 minutes per side for medium rare. Let the meat rest briefly on a cutting board while assembling the salad.

3. Put the lettuce in a large serving bowl. Whisk the vinaigrette and toss the lettuce with just enough of the vinaigrette to coat. Slice the sirloin tips on the diagonal into ½-inch-thick medallions. Scatter the meat (and any accumulated juices), eggs, cheese, carrot, radishes, and chives on top of the lettuce. Drizzle the toppings with some of the remaining vinaigrette to taste (you may not need it all) and toss gently at the table. Serve any remaining vinaigrette on the side.
—Allison Ehri Kreitler

PER SERVING: 600 CALORIES | 37G PROTEIN | 7G CARB | 48G TOTAL FAT | 12G SAT FAT | 28G MONO FAT | 4.5G POLY FAT | 285MG CHOL | 1,130MG SODIUM | 2G FIBER

grilled corn, shrimp & chorizo salad

SERVES 8

FOR THE VINAIGRETTE

- ⅔ cup extra-virgin olive oil; more for drizzling
- 4 to 5 large cloves garlic, peeled and grated on the small holes of a box grater to yield about 2 Tbs.
- Kosher salt
- 1 tsp. sweet smoked paprika (Spanish pimentón)
- ⅓ cup sherry vinegar
- Freshly ground black pepper

FOR THE SALAD

- 8 large ears fresh corn, husked
- Extra-virgin olive oil
- Kosher salt
- 1 cup thinly sliced scallions, both white and green parts (about 1 large bunch)
- 24 easy-peel shrimp in the shell (16 to 20 per lb.)
- 4 Spanish chorizo sausages (about 14 oz. total), split lengthwise
- 1 pint cherry or grape tomatoes, cut in half
- Freshly ground black pepper
- 1 recipe Grilled Garlic Bread (recipe on the facing page)

This one-dish meal marries the best flavors from summer shore dinners—seafood and corn—with the smokiness of Spanish paprika and chorizo.

MAKE THE VINAIGRETTE

1. Combine the olive oil and the grated garlic in a small saucepan. Cook over low heat until the garlic begins to brown slightly, about 10 minutes. Add a pinch of salt and stir to dissolve. Remove from the heat and let sit until the oil cools a bit, about 3 minutes. Add the paprika and let it infuse the oil for about 12 minutes more. Strain the oil through a fine-mesh sieve and discard the garlic. (If making in advance, store in the refrigerator for up to 2 days.)

2. Put the vinegar in a small bowl. Add a pinch of salt and a couple of grinds of black pepper and whisk to combine. Slowly drizzle in the garlic-paprika oil, whisking constantly until well incorporated. Taste and adjust the seasonings if necessary.

MAKE THE SALAD

1. Prepare a medium-high charcoal or gas grill fire. Brush the corn all over with olive oil and season with salt. Grill, covered, turning occasionally until all sides are charred and deeply blistered in places, 6 to 10 minutes. Remove from the grill, cut the kernels off the cobs while still warm, and put the kernels in a large bowl. Add half the vinaigrette and toss to coat the kernels. Stir in the scallions and set aside.

2. Reduce the grill temperature to medium, or if using charcoal, let the coals die down a bit. Grill the shrimp and the sausage, turning once halfway through the cooking time, until the shrimp are pink, curled, and cooked through, 4 to 6 minutes, and the sausages are plump and well browned, 5 to 8 minutes. Transfer the shrimp and sausages to separate platters and cover with foil to keep warm.

3. While still warm, peel the shrimp and gently fold into the salad, along with the rest of the vinaigrette. Slice the sausages into ⅓-inch-thick half-moon-shaped pieces and mix into the salad. Add the tomatoes and mix gently. Taste and season with pepper and more salt if necessary. Serve the salad warm or at room temperature spooned over slices of grilled garlic bread. —*Elizabeth Karmel*

PER SERVING: 700 CALORIES | 21G PROTEIN | 57G CARB | 45G TOTAL FAT | 9G SAT FAT | 29G MONO FAT | 5G POLY FAT | 60MG CHOL | 1,010MG SODIUM | 6G FIBER

grilled garlic bread

SERVES 8

8 **¾- to 1-inch-thick slices crusty, artisan-style bread, like ciabatta**

¼ **cup extra-virgin olive oil for brushing**

1 **to 2 large cloves garlic, peeled and halved**

Sea salt or kosher salt

Prepare a medium-low charcoal or gas grill fire. Brush both sides of the bread with the oil and grill, covered, turning once, until golden and marked on both sides, 1 to 3 minutes per side. Off the heat but while the bread is still hot, lightly rub one side of each bread slice with the cut sides of the garlic—heat and friction from the bread will cause the garlic to "melt" into the bread. Sprinkle with salt and serve.

PER SERVING: 190 CALORIES | 5G PROTEIN | 26G CARB | 7G TOTAL FAT | 1G SAT FAT | 5G MONO FAT | 0.5G POLY FAT | 0MG CHOL | 440MG SODIUM | 1G FIBER

village-style greek salad with chicken and lemon-mint vinaigrette

SERVES 4

½ **medium red onion, thinly sliced (about 1 cup)**

1½ **lb. chicken tenders**

1 **tsp. kosher salt**

¾ **tsp. freshly ground black pepper**

⅓ **cup plus 2 tsp. extra-virgin olive oil**

⅓ **cup chopped fresh mint**

2 **Tbs. fresh lemon juice**

1 **medium clove garlic, minced**

½ **tsp. finely grated lemon zest**

12 **oz. feta, cut into ½-inch cubes (2 ¾ cups)**

2 **cups cherry tomatoes, washed and halved**

1 **large cucumber, peeled, seeded, and cut into ½-inch chunks**

⅔ **cup pitted Kalamata olives, halved**

Village-style salads, called horiatiki *in Greece, usually omit the lettuce and leave the other ingredients in rough chunks. Serve this salad with warmed pita.*

1. Put the sliced onion in a small bowl and add enough cold water to cover.

2. Trim off any exposed tendon ends from the wide tips of the tenders, if necessary. Season the tenders with ¾ tsp. salt and ½ tsp. pepper. Heat 2 tsp. of the oil in a 12-inch nonstick skillet over medium-high heat until hot. Cook the tenders until well browned on both sides and just cooked through, about 3 minutes per side. Transfer the chicken to a cutting board and let rest while you make the dressing.

3. In a large bowl, combine the mint, lemon juice, garlic, lemon zest, and ¼ tsp. each salt and pepper. Slowly whisk in the remaining ⅓ cup oil. Set aside 2 Tbs. of the vinaigrette in a small bowl.

4. Drain the onion and press gently to remove any excess water. Add the onion to the large bowl of vinaigrette, along with the feta, tomatoes, cucumber, and olives. Slice the chicken crosswise into ½-inch pieces and add it to the salad. Toss everything to coat. Divide the salad among 4 serving plates, drizzle with the reserved vinaigrette, and serve immediately. —*Adam Reid*

PER SERVING: 690 CALORIES | 48G PROTEIN | 13G CARB | 49G TOTAL FAT | 17G SAT FAT | 25G MONO FAT | 4.5G POLY FAT | 170MG CHOL | 1,740MG SODIUM | 2G FIBER

five easy ways to build a better salad

1. Discard damaged or coarse outer lettuce leaves or save them for something else.
2. Wash greens well (use a big bowl and do two or three soaks, lifting the leaves up each time so that grit settles to the bottom) and spin-dry them. Store the leaves delicately packed into large zip-top bags lined with paper towels. Most greens will keep for several days like this.
3. Don't overdress your salad or it'll be soggy. You can always add more dressing, but you can't take it away.
4. Toss with a light hand so that you don't damage delicate greens.
5. Season your greens with a little salt and pepper as you toss them with dressing. Even though the dressing is already seasoned, a little more salt and pepper at this point makes a huge flavor difference.

cobb salad with fresh herbs

SERVES 6

- **2** Tbs. mayonnaise
- **1** tsp. Dijon mustard

  Kosher salt and freshly ground black pepper

- **3** large boneless, skinless chicken breast halves (7 to 8 oz. each), tenderloins separated if still attached
- **2** heads Boston lettuce (about 12 oz. total), trimmed, torn into bite-size pieces, washed, and dried
- **1½** cups lightly packed fresh parsley leaves, torn if large
- **¾** cup lightly packed mint leaves, torn if large
- **1** recipe Lemon-Sherry Vinaigrette (recipe on the facing page)
- **3** large avocados
- **2½** cups (about 1 lb.) halved grape tomatoes
- **1** heaping cup (6 oz.) crumbled Roquefort
- **⅔** cup toasted pine nuts
- **12** slices bacon, cooked, cooled, and crumbled
- **½** cup sliced chives (¾ inch long)

This salad comes together quickly, but toast the pine nuts ahead and you'll have dinner on the table in a snap.

GRILL THE CHICKEN

Heat a gas grill to medium high. In a mixing bowl, combine the mayonnaise, mustard, ½ tsp. salt, and ¼ tsp. pepper. Add the chicken and toss to coat. Grill until well marked and cooked through, 4 to 6 minutes per side for the breasts, and 2 to 3 minutes per side for the tenderloins. Let cool and cut into small dice.

ASSEMBLE THE SALADS

1. Set 6 large dinner plates on your counter. Combine the lettuce, parsley, and mint in a large mixing bowl. Toss with just enough of the vinaigrette to coat lightly, 4 to 5 Tbs. Season with a little salt and pepper and toss again. Divide among the plates, arranging the lettuce in a circle with a small hole in the center.

2. Peel, pit, and cut the avocados into medium dice and toss them in a medium bowl with 2 Tbs. of the vinaigrette. Combine about a sixth each of the avocados, tomatoes, Roquefort, pine nuts, and chicken in the mixing bowl. Season with a little salt and pepper and toss with about 1 Tbs. of the vinaigrette. (You won't use all the dressing.) Mound the mixture in the center of a salad. Repeat for the rest of the salads. Sprinkle on the bacon and chives and serve. —*Susie Middleton*

PER SERVING: 800 CALORIES | 37G PROTEIN | 8G CARB | 67G TOTAL FAT | 14G SAT FAT | 34G MONO FAT | 11G POLY FAT | 95MG CHOL | 1,280MG SODIUM | 10G FIBER

lemon-sherry vinaigrette

YIELDS 1¼ CUPS

- ¾ **cup plus 2 Tbs. extra-virgin olive oil**
- ¼ **cup sherry vinegar**
- 2 **tsp. finely grated lemon zest (from about 1 large lemon)**
- 1 **tsp. granulated sugar**
- 1 **tsp. minced fresh garlic**
- ½ **tsp. Dijon mustard**
- ½ **tsp. kosher salt**
- ¼ **tsp. Worcestershire sauce**
- ¼ **tsp. freshly ground black pepper**

Put all the ingredients in a glass measuring cup or a jar with a tight-fitting lid and whisk or vigorously shake to combine. You can store the vinaigrette in the refrigerator for up to 5 days; let come to room temperature and shake or whisk before using.

grilled shrimp and calamari salad with arugula and orange vinaigrette

SERVES 4

- **1** medium orange
- **¼** cup plus 2 Tbs. extra-virgin olive oil
- **2** tsp. chopped fresh thyme
- **2** tsp. white-wine vinegar

  Kosher salt and freshly ground black pepper
- **¼** lb. (4 to 6) cleaned calamari bodies (no tentacles), rinsed and patted dry
- **16** jumbo shrimp (21 to 25 per lb.), peeled, deveined, rinsed, and patted dry
- **1** red bell pepper, quartered lengthwise and cored
- **1** medium fennel bulb (about 1 lb.), trimmed, quartered, cored, and thinly sliced crosswise
- **5** oz. baby arugula (about 5 cups)

If you don't like calamari, you can substitute extra shrimp.

1. Prepare a medium-high gas or charcoal grill fire.

2. Finely grate 1 tsp. of zest from the orange and then squeeze ⅓ cup juice. In a small bowl, whisk the juice and zest with ¼ cup of the oil, 1 tsp. of the thyme, the vinegar, ½ tsp. salt, and ¼ tsp. pepper.

3. Using a sharp pairing knife, cut open the calamari bodies lengthwise and lightly score both sides in a cross-hatch pattern. Put them in a medium bowl with the shrimp and red pepper and toss with the remaining 2 Tbs. oil, 1 tsp. thyme, ½ tsp. salt, and ¼ tsp. pepper. Thread the shrimp on 3 or 4 metal skewers.

4. Grill the shrimp and peppers (skin side up), covered, until they have good grill marks, 2 to 3 minutes. Flip both and continue to grill until the shrimp are just firm and opaque, about 2 minutes more. Move the shrimp to a clean plate and let the peppers continue to cook until they're soft and the skin is charred, about 5 minutes more. Meanwhile, grill the calamari until barely cooked through, about 1 minute per side. When the calamari and peppers are done, move them to the plate with the shrimp.

5. Cut the calamari into quarters lengthwise and remove the shrimp from the skewers. Peel and thinly slice the red peppers. In a large bowl, toss the fennel and arugula with half of the vinaigrette. Season to taste with salt and pepper. Distribute the greens on 4 plates and top with the shrimp, calamari, and red peppers. Drizzle with some of the remaining vinaigrette and serve. —*Tony Rosenfeld*

PER SERVING: 320 CALORIES | 20G PROTEIN | 11G CARB | 22G TOTAL FAT | 3G SAT FAT | 15G MONO FAT | 2.5G POLY FAT | 190MG CHOL | 480MG SODIUM | 3G FIBER

grilled steak salad with pineapple-ginger dressing

SERVES 4

FOR THE DRESSING

- 5 Tbs. pineapple juice
- 1 Tbs. soy sauce
- 1 Tbs. peanut oil
- 1 Tbs. Asian sesame oil
- 2 tsp. fresh lime juice
- ½ tsp. honey
- ½ tsp. finely grated fresh ginger
- 1 small clove garlic, minced
- 1 large pinch crushed red pepper flakes
- ¼ cup small-diced fresh pineapple
- 1 Tbs. finely chopped fresh cilantro

FOR THE STEAK

- 1 lb. flank steak
- 1½ Tbs. vegetable oil; more for the grill
- Kosher salt and freshly ground black pepper

FOR THE SALAD

- 6 oz. torn butter lettuce leaves (about 6 lightly packed cups)
- 1 medium cucumber, seeded and thinly sliced
- 3 radishes, thinly sliced
- Kosher salt and freshly ground black pepper
- ¼ cup thinly sliced scallions (both white and light green parts)

Look for peeled and cut fresh pineapple in the produce section of your supermarket; it's a great time-saver.

Heat a gas grill to medium high.

MAKE THE DRESSING

In a small bowl, whisk the pineapple juice, soy sauce, peanut oil, sesame oil, lime juice, honey, ginger, garlic, and pepper flakes to blend. Stir in the pineapple and cilantro.

COOK THE STEAK

Rub the steak with the oil and season with 1 tsp. each salt and pepper. Clean and oil the grill grates. Grill the steak, covered, until it has nice grill marks on one side, 5 to 6 minutes. Flip and reduce the heat to medium. Cook, covered, until done to your liking, an additional 4 to 5 minutes for medium rare. Transfer to a cutting board and let rest for 5 to 10 minutes.

ASSEMBLE THE SALAD

1. In a large bowl, toss the lettuce, cucumber, and radishes with about half of the dressing. Season to taste with salt and pepper. Divide among 4 large plates.

2. Thinly slice the steak across the grain and drape it over the greens. Drizzle some of the remaining dressing over the beef, sprinkle with the scallions, and serve. —*Maryellen Driscoll*

PER SERVING: 360 CALORIES | 33G PROTEIN | 8G CARB | 22G TOTAL FAT | 6G SAT FAT | 9G MONO FAT | 5G POLY FAT | 60MG CHOL | 760MG SODIUM | 1G FIBER

grilled-chicken caesar salad
with garlic croutons

SERVES 6

Vegetable oil for the grill

6 **boneless, skinless chicken thighs, trimmed of any excess fat (1 lb.)**

1 **recipe Creamy Caesar Dressing (recipe on the facing page)**

Kosher salt and freshly ground black pepper

8 **½- to ¾-inch-thick slices dense peasant bread**

¼ **cup extra-virgin olive oil**

1 **large clove garlic, cut in half and peeled**

3 **hearts of romaine, trimmed, cut into 1½-inch pieces, washed, and dried (about 13½ cups)**

¾ **cup coarsely grated Parmigiano-Reggiano (use the larger holes on a box grater)**

2 **large endives, trimmed, halved lengthwise, cored, and thinly sliced crosswise (3 cups)**

1 **half medium head frisée, trimmed, torn into bite-size pieces, washed, and dried (2 lightly packed cups)**

⅓ **cup fresh parsley leaves, washed, dried, and torn into smaller pieces if large**

This classic salad gets a fresh update thanks to the variety of greens on the plate.

GRILL THE CHICKEN

Prepare a medium-high gas or charcoal grill fire. When hot, clean the grate with a stiff wire brush and then wipe it down with a folded paper towel dipped in oil. In a medium bowl, toss the chicken with 1 Tbs. of the dressing, ½ tsp. salt, and ¼ tsp. pepper. Grill, covered, turning once, until nicely browned and cooked through, 3 to 5 minutes per side. Let cool and slice thinly just before serving.

MAKE THE CROUTONS

Reduce the grill to medium-low heat (or let the fire die down). Generously brush the bread slices on both sides with the oil and sprinkle with a little salt. Grill the bread, covered, until golden brown on both sides, 1 to 3 minutes per side. Rub the bread on both sides with the cut sides of the garlic. Let the bread cool for a few minutes and then cut into ½-inch cubes.

ASSEMBLE THE SALAD

1. Set 6 large dinner plates on the counter. Arrange a sliced chicken thigh in the center of each plate and position some of the slices near the edge of the plate so they'll be visible after the salad is mounded on top. Spoon about a teaspoon of the Caesar dressing over each of the sliced thighs. Put the romaine in a large mixing bowl and toss with about 6 Tbs. of the dressing. Add 6 Tbs. Parmigiano and a big pinch each of salt and pepper to the bowl and toss again. Arrange the romaine over the chicken on each plate. Sprinkle about half of the croutons over the plates. Toss the endive in the mixing bowl with 2 to 3 Tbs. dressing. Add 2 Tbs. Parmigiano and a pinch each of salt and pepper and toss again. Arrange the endive in the center of the romaine on each plate.

2. Toss the frisée in the mixing bowl with about 2 Tbs. of the dressing. Add 2 Tbs. Parmigiano and a pinch each of salt and pepper and toss again. Pile the frisée in the center of the salads. Sprinkle the remaining cheese, croutons, and the parsley over the salads. Serve.
—*Susie Middleton*

PER SERVING: 590 CALORIES | 29G PROTEIN | 37G CARB | 38G TOTAL FAT | 7G SAT FAT | 24G MONO FAT | 6G POLY FAT | 105MG CHOL | 1,400MG SODIUM | 10G FIBER

creamy caesar dressing

Substitute a pasteurized yolk for the raw egg if desired.

YIELDS A SCANT 1 CUP

3	oil-packed anchovies, rinsed and patted dry
2	large cloves garlic, smashed and peeled
1	large egg yolk
2½	Tbs. fresh lemon juice
1	Tbs. Dijon mustard
1½	tsp. finely grated lemon zest
¼	tsp. kosher salt
¼	tsp. freshly ground pepper
½	cup extra-virgin olive oil

Put all the dressing ingredients except the oil in a blender. Blend until thoroughly combined. With the motor running, carefully pour in the oil in a slow, steady stream. You can store the dressing, tightly covered, in the refrigerator for up to 3 days.

spinach and artichoke salad with couscous cakes and feta

SERVES 3

FOR THE DRESSING

- 2   **Tbs. fresh lemon juice**
- 1   **Tbs. sour cream**
- 1   **tsp. finely chopped fresh mint**
- 5   **Tbs. extra-virgin olive oil**
-   **Kosher salt and freshly ground black pepper**

FOR THE COUSCOUS CAKES

- ¾   **cup couscous**
- 2   **tsp. kosher salt**
- 1   **large clove garlic, peeled**
- ¼   **cup packed fresh flat-leaf parsley leaves**
- ½   **cup canned chickpeas, rinsed and drained**
- 2   **large eggs, lightly beaten**
-   **Finely grated zest of 1 medium lemon (about 1½ tsp.)**
- 3   **Tbs. vegetable or canola oil**

FOR THE SALAD

- 8   **oz. baby spinach, washed and dried (about 6 lightly packed cups)**
- 1   **14-oz. can artichoke bottoms, drained, rinsed, and sliced**
- 15   **cherry tomatoes, halved**
-   **Kosher salt and freshly ground black pepper**
- 1   **oz. crumbled feta**

(about ¼ cup)

Quick-to-cook couscous cakes make this meatless main-course salad satisfying.

MAKE THE DRESSING

In a small bowl, combine the lemon juice, sour cream, and mint. Slowly whisk in the olive oil. Season to taste with salt and pepper.

MAKE THE COUSCOUS CAKES

1. Put the couscous and 1 tsp. salt in a medium bowl. Add 1 cup boiling water to the couscous, cover the bowl with a pan lid or plate, and let sit for 4 to 5 minutes.

2. Coarsely chop the garlic in a food processor. Add the parsley and pulse until finely chopped. Add the chickpeas and 1 tsp. salt and pulse until coarsely chopped.

3. Uncover the couscous and fluff with a fork. Stir in the chickpea mixture, eggs, and lemon zest until well combined. Press the couscous mixture into a ¼-cup measure, smooth the top, and invert the measuring cup to release the cake onto a plate. Repeat with the remaining couscous mixture to make 9 cakes.

4. Heat 1½ Tbs. of the vegetable oil in a large skillet over medium heat until shimmering hot. Add 5 of the couscous cakes to the skillet and use a spatula to lightly flatten the cakes so they're about ¾ inch thick. Cook, flipping once, until crisp and golden brown on both sides, 2 to 3 minutes per side. Transfer to a paper-towel-lined plate. Add the remaining 1½ Tbs. vegetable oil to the skillet and cook the remaining cakes the same way.

ASSEMBLE THE SALAD

In a large bowl, toss the spinach, artichokes, and tomatoes with about three-quarters of the dressing. Season to taste with salt and pepper and divide among 3 large plates. Top each salad with 3 couscous cakes, sprinkle each salad with feta, and drizzle with the remaining dressing. —*Maryellen Driscoll*

PER SERVING: 710 CALORIES | 20G PROTEIN | 63G CARB | 44G TOTAL FAT | 8G SAT FAT | 24G MONO FAT | 9G POLY FAT | 155MG CHOL | 1,580MG SODIUM | 9G FIBER

sweet potato, ham & goat cheese salad

SERVES 4

- **1 medium yellow onion,** halved lengthwise and cut into ½-inch wedges
- **1 medium sweet potato,** peeled and cut into ¼-inch rounds
- **½ cup extra-virgin olive oil**
- **1¼ tsp. chopped fresh rosemary**
- **Kosher salt and freshly ground black pepper**
- **¾ lb. ham steak (preferably "ham with natural juices"),** cut into ¾-inch cubes (2 cups)
- **2 Tbs. pure maple syrup**
- **2 Tbs. balsamic vinegar**
- **5 oz. mesclun salad mix**
- **4 oz. fresh goat cheese,** crumbled

Look for high-quality, all-natural ham steak for the best flavor and texture.

1. Position a rack in the center of the oven and heat the oven to 450°F. Line a rimmed baking sheet with foil. On the baking sheet, toss the onion, sweet potato, 2 Tbs. of the oil, 1 tsp. of the rosemary, ½ tsp. salt, and ¼ tsp. pepper and spread in a single layer. Roast until the vegetables start to become tender, about 15 minutes.

2. In a small bowl, toss the ham with the maple syrup. Push the vegetables on the baking sheet aside to make room for the ham and bake until the ham and onion are browned in places, about 10 minutes.

3. Meanwhile, in a small bowl, whisk the remaining 6 Tbs. oil with the vinegar, the remaining ¼ tsp. rosemary, and ¼ tsp. each salt and pepper. In a large bowl, toss the mesclun with ¼ cup of the vinaigrette. Season to taste with salt and pepper.

4. Divide the mesclun among 4 plates. Top with the roasted vegetables and ham. Sprinkle each salad with some of the goat cheese. Drizzle with the remaining vinaigrette and serve. *—Tony Rosenfeld*

PER SERVING: 520 CALORIES | 24G PROTEIN | 19G CARB | 39G TOTAL FAT | 11G SAT FAT | 23G MONO FAT | 3.5G POLY FAT | 60MG CHOL | 1,460MG SODIUM | 2G FIBER

niçoise salad with grilled tuna and potatoes

SERVES 6

- **18** small (baby) red potatoes (about 1 ¼ lb.)
- **3½** tsp. kosher salt
- **12** oz. haricots verts (thin green beans), trimmed
- **3** Tbs. mayonnaise
- **2** tsp. honey
- **1½** lb. 1-inch-thick fresh tuna steaks
- **¼** tsp. freshly ground black pepper
- **2** tsp. Dijon mustard
- **4** oz. small inner leaves of red leaf lettuce, washed, dried, and torn into bite-size pieces (4½ lightly packed cups)
- **3** oz. baby arugula, washed and spun dry (3¾ lightly packed cups)
- **16** large basil leaves, torn into small pieces
- **1** recipe Basil Vinaigrette (recipe on the facing page)
- **1¼** lb. small ripe red, yellow, and orange tomatoes, cut into wedges
- **1** cup Niçoise olives (or other black olives)
- **3** hard-cooked eggs, peeled and quartered

Artfully arrange the ingredients on individual plates for an impressive presentation.

BOIL THE POTATOES AND HARICOTS VERTS

1. Put the potatoes and 2 tsp. salt in a large saucepan, add enough water to cover by 1 inch, and bring to a boil. Reduce to a simmer and cook until easily pierced with a wooden skewer, 15 to 20 minutes. Drain and let cool.

2. Fill the saucepan three-quarters full of fresh water and bring to a boil. Add the haricots verts and ½ tsp. salt to the water and cook until you can just bite through a bean with little resistance, 3 to 4 minutes. Drain, rinse with cool water to stop the cooking, and set aside.

GRILL THE POTATOES AND TUNA

1. Heat a gas grill to high or prepare a hot charcoal fire.

2. Combine 1 Tbs. of the mayonnaise and the honey in a small bowl. Season the tuna steaks with ½ tsp. salt and the pepper and coat both sides with the mayonnaise mixture. When the grates are very hot, grill the tuna until dark marks form on both sides, 1 to 2 minutes per side for medium rare. (If you prefer medium tuna, grill over medium-high heat for about 3 minutes per side.) Transfer to a cutting board and let rest for 5 minutes. Slice into ¼-inch-thick strips.

3. Cut the potatoes in half and toss them in a mixing bowl with the remaining 2 Tbs. mayonnaise, the mustard, and ½ tsp. salt. Turn the grill to medium high or let the fire die down some. Grill the potatoes without disturbing except to flip, until brown grill marks form on both sides, 1 to 2 minutes per side.

ASSEMBLE THE SALAD

1. Set 6 large dinner plates on your counter. Put the red leaf lettuce, the arugula, and half of the basil in a large mixing bowl and toss with 2 to 3 Tbs. of the vinaigrette.

2. Divide the lettuce among the plates, piling it in neat, tall mounds at twelve o'clock. Combine the tomatoes and the remaining basil in the mixing bowl and toss with 2 to 3 Tbs. of the vinaigrette. Tuck the tomatoes in to the left of the lettuce and arrange the tuna to the right of the lettuce. Put the olives in the middle of each plate. Toss the green beans in the bowl with about 2 Tbs. of the vinaigrette. Arrange the grilled potatoes and the green beans at the bottom of each plate and tuck in the hard-cooked egg quarters wherever they look best. Drizzle a few teaspoons of the vinaigrette over the tuna and the potatoes on every plate. Serve right away. —*Susie Middleton*

PER SERVING: 690 CALORIES | 34G PROTEIN | 31G CARB | 48G TOTAL FAT | 8G SAT FAT | 28G MONO FAT | 6G POLY FAT | 150MG CHOL | 1,330MG SODIUM | 5G FIBER

basil vinaigrette

YIELDS ABOUT 1 CUP

- ¾ **cup extra-virgin olive oil**
- ¼ **cup red-wine vinegar**
- 3 **Tbs. finely chopped fresh basil**
- 1 **large clove garlic, minced**
- 1 **Tbs. Dijon mustard**
- 1 **tsp. fresh lemon juice**
- ½ **tsp. honey**
- ¼ **tsp. kosher salt**
- ⅛ **tsp. freshly ground pepper**

Put all the ingredients in a glass measuring cup or a jar with a tight-fitting lid and whisk or vigorously shake to combine. Whisk again just before using. You can store the vinaigrette in the refrigerator for up to 5 days, but don't add the basil until 15 to 30 minutes before using.

vietnamese-style chicken salad

SERVES 4

- **3** small shallots, coarsely chopped (½ cup)
- **1** jalapeño, chopped (seed first if you want less heat)
- **1** Tbs. granulated sugar
- **¼** tsp. freshly ground black pepper
- **¼** cup rice vinegar
- **3** Tbs. fish sauce
- **1** lb. boneless, skinless, thin-sliced (¼ to ½ inch thick) chicken breast cutlets
- **¼** tsp. kosher salt
- **6** oz. package coleslaw mix
- **1** cup fresh mint leaves, torn if large
- **¼** cup fresh cilantro leaves
- **¼** cup salted peanuts, coarsely chopped

If you don't have a grill, you can cook the chicken indoors on a ridged grill pan over medium-high heat for the same amount of time.

1. Prepare a medium grill fire.

2. With a mortar and pestle, pound the shallots, jalapeño, sugar, and ⅛ tsp. pepper until the shallot is very soft (but not puréed) and liquid is released. Transfer to a large serving bowl and stir in the vinegar and fish sauce.

3. Season the chicken with the salt and ⅛ tsp. pepper and grill, turning once, until just cooked through, about 2 minutes per side. Let cool and then shred the chicken with your fingers into long thin strips, pulling the meat along its natural grain.

4. Toss the coleslaw mix into the vinegar mixture. Add the chicken, mint, and cilantro and combine well. Top with the peanuts and serve at room temperature. *—Lori Longbotham*

PER SERVING: 220 CALORIES | 27G PROTEIN | 11G CARB | 7G TOTAL FAT | 1.5G SAT FAT | 3G MONO FAT | 2G POLY FAT | 65MG CHOL | 1,260MG SODIUM | 2G FIBER

lentil salad with fennel and smoked salmon

YIELDS ABOUT 4 CUPS; SERVES 4

- 1 cup French green lentils du Puy, rinsed and picked over for stones
- 1 medium clove garlic

  Kosher salt
- ½ medium shallot, finely chopped (about 1½ Tbs.)
- 3 Tbs. Champagne vinegar
- 2 tsp. finely grated fresh ginger (use the small holes on a box grater)
- 1 tsp. Dijon mustard
- ½ tsp. fennel seed, coarsely ground

  Freshly ground black pepper
- ⅓ cup canola oil
- 9 small radishes, halved and thinly sliced (about 1 cup)
- ½ small bulb fennel, quartered lengthwise and thinly sliced crosswise (about 1 cup), plus 1 Tbs. chopped fennel fronds
- 2 Tbs. sliced fresh chives; more for garnish
- 4 oz. cold-smoked salmon, cut into ½-inch squares (about ½ cup)

If you can't find French green lentils du Puy, substitute brown lentils. Cook them until just tender so they don't fall apart when you toss the salad.

1. In a medium saucepan, combine the lentils with 4 cups water. Simmer over medium heat until just tender, 20 to 30 minutes. Drain in a colander and let cool to room temperature.

2. Roughly chop the garlic, sprinkle it with a pinch of salt, and mash to a paste with the flat side of a chef's knife. In a medium bowl, whisk the garlic paste, shallot, vinegar, ginger, mustard, fennel seed, 1½ tsp. salt, and ¼ tsp. pepper. Whisk in the oil.

3. In a large bowl, toss the lentils, radishes, fennel, fennel fronds, and chives with just enough of the vinaigrette to coat everything lightly (you may not need it all). Season to taste with salt and pepper. (You can prepare the salad to this point up to 4 hours ahead.) Just before serving, gently stir in the salmon and a few grinds of pepper. Garnish with chives and serve. —*Allison Ehri Kreitler*

PER SERVING: 250 CALORIES | 12G PROTEIN | 21G CARB | 14G TOTAL FAT | 1G SAT FAT | 8G MONO FAT | 4G POLY FAT | 5MG CHOL | 690G SODIUM | 8G FIBER

More about Cold-Smoked Salmon

Often mislabeled as lox, cold-smoked salmon is fresh salmon that's cured with salt, sugar, and seasonings and then smoked at temperatures below 80°F. It's best not to cook cold-smoked salmon because heat alters its smooth, delicate texture. (And don't confuse cold-smoked salmon with hot-smoked salmon, which is smoked over higher heat to an internal temperature of 145°F for a drier, flakier result.)

When opening, cut the plastic wrapping away from the salmon, but keep its cardboard backing intact. This way, you can store any uneaten salmon on the cardboard, wrapping the entire package in clean plastic. Cold-smoked salmon will keep in the refrigerator, tightly wrapped, for up to a week.

southwestern grilled chicken salad with tomato and black bean salsa

SERVES 4

- 1 boneless skinless chicken breast half (6 to 7 oz.), trimmed
- ½ Tbs. chili powder
- 1 tsp. light or dark brown sugar
- ½ tsp. ground coriander
- ½ tsp. ground cumin
- Kosher salt
- 6 Tbs. extra-virgin olive oil; more for the grill
- 2 Tbs. plus 2 tsp. fresh lime juice
- 1 Tbs. plus 2 tsp. chopped fresh cilantro, plus leaves for garnish
- 2 tsp. honey
- Freshly ground black pepper
- Green Tabasco (optional)
- 1 cup canned black beans, rinsed and drained
- 4 oz. small cherry or grape tomatoes, quartered or halved (about ¾ cup)
- 1 large scallion, thinly sliced
- 2 small heads Bibb lettuce, torn into bite-size pieces (about 9 cups)
- 1 medium firm-ripe avocado
- ¼ cup toasted pine nuts or pepitas

This quick dinner is heavy on the veggies and light on the meat. The spicy salsa amps up the flavor.

1. Prepare a medium-high gas or charcoal grill fire.

2. Trim and then butterfly the chicken breast by slicing it horizontally almost but not entirely in half so you can open it like a book.

3. Combine the chili powder, brown sugar, coriander, cumin, and ¾ tsp. salt in a small bowl. Rub some of the spice mix over both sides of the butterflied chicken breast (you won't need it all) and let sit while the grill heats.

4. Clean and oil the grill grate. Grill the breast until the edges of the top side are white, about 3 minutes. Flip and cook until just done, 1 to 2 minutes more. Let the chicken rest for 5 to 10 minutes.

5. In a small bowl or a glass jar with a tight lid, combine the olive oil, lime juice, 1 Tbs. of the cilantro, the honey, ½ tsp. salt, a few grinds of pepper, and a few shakes of green Tabasco (if using). Whisk or shake well to combine.

6. Combine the black beans, tomatoes, scallion, the remaining 2 tsp. cilantro, and a pinch of salt in a small bowl. Add 2 Tbs. of the dressing and toss gently.

7. Put the lettuce in a bowl, season with a little salt, and toss with just enough of the dressing to lightly coat. (Reserve a little to drizzle on the chicken.) Arrange the lettuce on a platter or 4 dinner plates. Slice the chicken breast very thinly. Pit and slice the avocado. Arrange the chicken, avocado, and salsa on the lettuce. Drizzle a little of the remaining dressing over the chicken and avocado. Garnish with the pine nuts or pepitas and the cilantro leaves. —*Susie Middleton*

PER SERVING: 470 CALORIES | 18G PROTEIN | 28G CARB | 33G TOTAL FAT | 5G SAT FAT | 21G MONO FAT | 5G POLY FAT | 25MG CHOL | 510MG SODIUM | 9G FIBER

grilled shrimp salad with feta, tomato & watermelon

SERVES 4

1½   lb. raw extra-jumbo shrimp (16 to 20 per lb.), peeled (leave tail segment intact) and deveined

¼   cup plus 2 Tbs. fresh lemon juice

1   tsp. smoked sweet paprika

Kosher salt and freshly ground black pepper

¼   cup extra-virgin olive oil

1½   tsp. honey

Vegetable oil, for the grill

½   medium head frisée, torn into bite-size pieces (4 cups)

3   cups small-diced seedless watermelon (about 1 lb.)

3   medium ripe red or yellow tomatoes, cored and cut into wedges

2   cups yellow cherry or pear tomatoes, halved

6   oz. feta, cut into small dice (1¼ cups)

30   fresh basil leaves, thinly sliced (½ cup)

Ripe, in-season ingredients are the key to this summery main-course salad, so use the best tomatoes and watermelon you can find.

1. Prepare a hot gas or charcoal grill fire.

2. In a medium bowl, toss the shrimp with 2 Tbs. of the lemon juice and the paprika; marinate at room temperature for 5 minutes. Thread the shrimp onto metal skewers or wooden skewers that have been soaked in water for at least 30 minutes. Season the shrimp on both sides with ½ tsp. salt and ¼ tsp. pepper.

3. In a small bowl, combine the remaining ¼ cup lemon juice with the olive oil, honey, and a pinch each of salt and pepper. Whisk well.

4. Clean and oil the grill grates. Grill the shrimp, flipping once, until firm and opaque throughout, 4 to 6 minutes total.

5. In a large bowl, gently toss the frisée with 3 Tbs. of the dressing. In a medium bowl, gently toss the watermelon, tomatoes, feta, basil, 2 Tbs. dressing, ¼ tsp. salt, and ⅛ tsp. pepper. Divide the frisée among 4 plates and spoon one-quarter of the watermelon mixture over each. Top with the shrimp skewers, drizzle with the remaining dressing, and serve.   —*Dina Cheney*

PER SERVING: 430 CALORIES | 36G PROTEIN | 20G CARB | 24G TOTAL FAT | 9G SAT FAT | 12G MONO FAT | 2.5G POLY FAT | 290MG CHOL | 990MG SODIUM | 3G FIBER

quinoa salad with apples, walnuts, dried cranberries & gouda

SERVES 6

1½ cups quinoa, preferably red

Sea salt

5 Tbs. extra-virgin olive oil; more as needed

1 large red onion, quartered lengthwise and thinly sliced crosswise

2 Tbs. balsamic vinegar

4 oz. arugula, trimmed and thinly sliced (about 3 cups)

4 oz. aged Gouda, finely diced (about 1 cup)

3 medium celery stalks, thinly sliced

1 large, crisp apple, such as Fuji or Pink Lady, cut into ½-inch dice

1 cup walnuts, coarsely chopped

1 cup finely diced fennel

¾ cup dried cranberries

3 Tbs. sherry vinegar

Freshly ground black pepper

With its dried fruit, walnuts, and apples, this sweet-and-savory dish is reminiscent of a Waldorf salad. It's a great meat-free lunch or dinner.

1. In a bowl, rinse the quinoa with water, rubbing it between your fingers for about 10 seconds. Drain and transfer it to a 3-quart pot. Add 2½ cups water and ½ tsp. sea salt and bring to a boil over medium-high heat. Reduce the heat to medium low and simmer, covered, until the quinoa is tender but still delicately crunchy, about 15 minutes.

2. Drain the quinoa and return it to the pot. Cover and let the quinoa rest for 5 minutes; then fluff it with a fork. Let cool to room temperature.

3. While the quinoa cooks, heat 2 Tbs. of the olive oil in a 12-inch non-stick skillet over medium-high heat. Add the onion and a pinch of salt; cook, stirring frequently, until tender and brown around the edges, 6 to 8 minutes. Add the balsamic vinegar and toss with the onion until the vinegar cooks away, about 1 minute. Remove from the heat and let cool to room temperature.

4. In a large bowl, mix the quinoa, onions, arugula, cheese, celery, apple, walnuts, fennel, and cranberries.

5. In a small bowl, whisk the remaining 3 Tbs. olive oil with the sherry vinegar, ½ tsp. sea salt, and a few grinds of pepper. Add the dressing to the salad and gently mix it in. Let rest a moment; then season to taste with salt and pepper. Add more olive oil if the salad seems dry.
—*Anna Thomas*

PER SERVING: 330 CALORIES | 9G PROTEIN | 34G CARB | 19G TOTAL FAT | 4G SAT FAT | 7G MONO FAT | 7G POLY FAT | 15MG CHOL | 350MG SODIUM | 4G FIBER

More about Quinoa

Known as the "mother grain" of the Incan empire, quinoa (pronounced keen-wah) is a small, flat seed. It's a staple for millions in South America and is available in a gorgeous array of colors, from golden tan to brick red. It's an excellent source of protein and fiber, as well as iron, zinc, potassium, calcium, and vitamin E.

Quinoa is mild, sweet, and slightly astringent, with an intriguing texture that's both soft and crunchy. The seeds are coated in a bitter natural substance called saponin, which is usually washed off before the grain is sold; still, it's best to give quinoa a rinse before cooking. It cooks like rice (but more quickly) and makes an excellent addition to pilafs, soups, and salads.

Store quinoa in an airtight container in a cool, dry place for up to a year.

grilled asparagus and steak salad with hoisin vinaigrette

SERVES 4

FOR THE STEAK AND ASPARAGUS

- ½ Tbs. black peppercorns
- 1 tsp. coriander seeds
- 1 tsp. fennel seed
- Kosher salt
- 1 lb. thick-cut New York strip steak
- 1½ Tbs. olive oil
- 1 lb. thick asparagus, trimmed
- Freshly ground black pepper

FOR THE VINAIGRETTE

- 3 Tbs. lower-salt chicken broth; more as needed
- 2½ Tbs. hoisin sauce
- 2 Tbs. olive oil
- 2 Tbs. white-wine vinegar
- 1½ tsp. lower-sodium soy sauce
- 2 tsp. minced fresh ginger
- 1 tsp. Dijon or Chinese mustard
- 1 tsp. minced garlic
- Kosher salt and freshly ground black pepper to taste

FOR THE SALAD

- 4 cups upland cress or watercress
- 1 large mango, peeled and slivered into thin wedges, or 2 large navel oranges, peeled and sliced into thick rounds
- ½ small red onion, thinly sliced and soaked briefly in ice water
- Daikon or radish sprouts for garnish (optional)

This salad packs bright flavor with minimal fuss. If you don't want to grill outside, cook the steak and asparagus on a stovetop grill pan instead.

PREPARE THE STEAK AND ASPARAGUS

1. Put the peppercorns, coriander, fennel, and ½ tsp. salt in a spice grinder and grind to a fine powder. Coat the steak with ½ Tbs. of the olive oil and then the peppercorn mixture. Set aside for at least 30 minutes and up to 1½ hours.

2. Toss the asparagus with the remaining 1 Tbs. of olive oil and season with salt and pepper; set aside.

MAKE THE VINAIGRETTE

In a blender, combine all of the ingredients and pulse 2 or 3 times to mix, adding more broth if necessary to achieve a silky consistency.

GRILL THE STEAK AND ASPARAGUS

1. Prepare a high gas or charcoal grill fire. Grill the steak until nice grill marks form, about 5 minutes. Flip and cook the steak on the second side until an instant-read thermometer inserted in the steak reads 125°F for rare, about 4 minutes. Remove the steak from the grill and put on a cutting board. Tent with foil to keep warm. Let the meat rest while you grill the asparagus.

2. Spread out the asparagus on the grill and cook, turning a couple of times, until crisp-tender, about 5 minutes.

ASSEMBLE THE SALAD

Arrange the asparagus, cress, and mango on 4 plates or a platter. Thinly slice the steak across the grain and arrange over the salad. Drizzle with the vinaigrette and garnish with the red onion and daikon sprouts (if using). —*John Ash*

PER SERVING: 350 CALORIES | 29G PROTEIN | 19G CARB | 19G TOTAL FAT | 4.5G SAT FAT | 12G MONO FAT | 2G POLY FAT | 55MG CHOL | 610MG SODIUM | 3G FIBER

buying & storing asparagus

- Choose spears that are firm, straight, and smooth, with tightly closed tips. Stalks should not be dry at the cut ends or limp. Open tips or ridges along the stem indicate old age; these stalks will be less flavorful and have a tough, woody texture. Thicker spears are usually more tender than skinny ones.

- To prep, trim away the tough, white woody base from the end of the asparagus spears. To ensure you've trimmed enough, cut off a sliver of the end and eat it: It should be tender. You can also snap off the bottom of the spear with your hands (it should break naturally where the stem starts to toughen), though you'll probably waste more tender asparagus than necessary.

- To store, stand trimmed spears upright in a jar with an inch or so of water. Cover with a plastic bag and store in the refrigerator for up to 3 days.

The Color of Asparagus

There are about 300 species of asparagus plants within the Asparagus genus, but we eat just one: *Asparagus officinalis*. While the green variety is most common, purple and white asparagus can also be found in some farmers' markets and specialty stores.

Green

Its sweet, grassy notes become more vegetal with age. Although it's available in supermarkets much of the year, it's best consumed from early to late spring, when it's more likely to be harvested from a local source.

Purple

It's sweeter, more tender, and produces fewer stalks per plant than its green cousin. Also known as Violetto d'Albenga, this variety originated in northwestern Italy (these days, it's also grown in California). To preserve its color, use it raw or cook it briefly; the longer it cooks, the more likely it'll turn from purple to green.

White

Milder than other varieties, it has just a touch of pleasant bitterness. White asparagus is buried in the soil and kept out of the sun to prevent it from developing chlorophyll, which would turn it green.

southeast asian grilled eggplant salad

SERVES 4

¼ cup peanut oil

¼ cup fresh lime juice

3 Tbs. minced shallot

1 Tbs. fish sauce

1¾ tsp. granulated sugar

1 to 2 Thai bird chiles, minced, or 1½ to 2 serrano chiles, seeded and minced

Kosher salt and freshly ground black pepper

2 Tbs. minced fresh ginger

1½ Tbs. soy sauce

1¼ lb. long, slender Asian eggplants, trimmed and halved lengthwise

4 oz. baby lettuces (about 5½ cups)

10 to 12 oz. cherry or grape tomatoes, halved (about 2 cups)

1 cup packed fresh basil leaves (preferably Thai basil)

⅓ cup packed fresh mint leaves

This salad is a delicious way to show off the lovely slender shape of Asian eggplants, which readily absorb the ginger-soy dressing that's spooned over the top.

1. Prepare a medium-high gas or charcoal grill fire.

2. In a small bowl, whisk 3 Tbs. of the peanut oil with the lime juice, 2 Tbs. of the shallot, the fish sauce, ¾ tsp. of the sugar, and the chiles. Season to taste with salt and pepper.

3. In another small bowl, combine 2 tsp. water with the ginger, soy sauce, the remaining 1 Tbs. shallot, and 1 tsp. sugar.

4. Arrange the eggplant halves on a rimmed baking sheet, brush both sides with the remaining 1 Tbs. peanut oil, and sprinkle with salt and pepper. Grill the eggplant, covered, until tender, 3 to 5 minutes per side.

5. Combine the lettuces, tomatoes, basil, and mint in a large bowl. Rewhisk the lime dressing and toss just enough into the salad to lightly coat the greens. Season the salad to taste with salt and pepper. Transfer the salad to a platter and arrange the eggplant over the salad. Spoon the ginger mixture over the eggplant, and serve immediately. —*Kristine Kidd*

PER SERVING: 120 CALORIES | 3G PROTEIN | 12G CARB | 8G TOTAL FAT | 1.5G SAT FAT | 3.5G MONO FAT | 2.5G POLY FAT | 0MG CHOL | 650MG SODIUM | 5G FIBER

sourdough panzanella with grilled chicken

SERVES 4

- ½ **cup olive oil; more for the grill**
- 4 **¾-inch-thick slices sourdough bread**
- 1 **tsp. finely chopped fresh oregano**
- ½ **tsp. smoked sweet paprika**
- **Kosher salt and freshly ground black pepper**
- 1 **lb. boneless, skinless chicken breast halves, trimmed**
- 3 **Tbs. red-wine vinegar**
- 1 **anchovy fillet, rinsed**
- 1 **small clove garlic**
- 4 **medium tomatoes, cut into ¾-inch pieces (3 cups)**
- 1 **medium cucumber, peeled, halved lengthwise, seeded, and cut into ¾-inch pieces (1½ cups)**
- ½ **small red onion, chopped (½ cup)**
- ¼ **cup chopped fresh mixed herbs, such as basil, parsley, cilantro, or mint**

> For balanced texture, be sure to slice the tomatoes, cucumbers, chicken, and bread about the same size.

In this classic Italian salad, sourdough bread soaks up the flavors of fresh herbs, late-summer tomatoes, and a savory vinaigrette. Adding grilled chicken turns it into a full meal.

1. Prepare a medium-high charcoal or gas grill fire. Clean and oil the grill grate.

2. Brush the bread on both sides with 2 Tbs. of the olive oil. Grill the bread until well marked, about 1 minute per side. Transfer to a cutting board, cut into ¾-inch cubes, and set aside.

3. In a small bowl, mix the oregano, smoked paprika, ½ tsp. salt, and ½ tsp. pepper. Sprinkle evenly over the chicken breasts. Grill, turning once, until an instant-read thermometer inserted into the thickest part of each breast registers 165°F, 10 to 12 minutes total. Transfer to a cutting board, let rest for 5 minutes, and then cut into ¾-inch cubes.

4. In a large bowl, whisk the remaining 6 Tbs. olive oil and the vinegar. Press the anchovy fillet and garlic clove through a garlic press into the bowl (or mince by hand). Add the bread, chicken, tomatoes, cucumber, red onion, and herbs and toss well. Season to taste with salt and pepper and serve. —*Bruce Weinstein and Mark Scarbrough*

PER SERVING: 700 CALORIES | 39G PROTEIN | 62G CARB | 33G TOTAL FAT | 5G SAT FAT | 21G MONO FAT | 4.5G POLY FAT | 70MG CHOL | 1,110MG SODIUM | 5G FIBER

curried turkey and israeli couscous salad with dried cranberries

SERVES 4

- ¼ cup freshly squeezed orange juice
- ½ cup dried cranberries
- Kosher salt
- 1 cup Israeli couscous
- 6 oz. skinless roast turkey meat, cut into medium dice (1½ cups)
- ½ cup toasted almonds, chopped
- 2 medium celery stalks, finely chopped
- 2 scallions, thinly sliced
- 3 Tbs. extra-virgin olive oil
- 4 tsp. white-wine vinegar
- 1½ tsp. curry powder
- Freshly ground black pepper

You can use light or dark turkey meat in this citrusy, sweet, subtly spiced salad. No turkey on hand? Use rotisserie chicken instead.

1. In a 1-quart saucepan, bring the orange juice to a boil over medium-high heat. Add the dried cranberries, stir, and set aside.

2. In a 3-quart saucepan, bring 2 quarts of well-salted water to a boil over high heat. Add the couscous and simmer until al dente, about 8 minutes. Drain and rinse with cold water until the couscous is cool. Drain again thoroughly and transfer to a large serving bowl. Add the cranberries and orange juice, turkey, almonds, celery, and scallions.

3. In a small bowl, whisk the olive oil, vinegar, and curry powder. Add to the couscous mixture and toss to combine. Season to taste with salt and pepper and serve. —*Ivy Manning*

PER SERVING: 470 CALORIES | 22G PROTEIN | 53G CARB | 20G TOTAL FAT | 2.5G SAT FAT | 13G MONO FAT | 3G POLY FAT | 35MG CHOL | 610MG SODIUM | 4G FIBER

Israeli couscous is similar to regular couscous but is larger and pearl-shaped. If you don't have any, use orzo or another tiny pasta shape instead.

endive and apple salad with warm goat cheese

SERVES 4

- 1 **cup pomegranate juice**
- 6 **oz. goat cheese**
- ½ **cup finely chopped hazelnuts**
- 1.5 **oz. (3 Tbs.) unsalted butter**
- 2 **large Belgian endives, halved lengthwise with core left intact, each half cut lengthwise into 4 pieces**
  Kosher salt and freshly ground black pepper
- 2 **firm, medium-sweet apples (like Fuji or Honeycrisp), peeled, cored, and cut into ½-inch dice (about 3 cups)**
- 1 **medium shallot, finely diced (about 3 Tbs.)**
- 1 **Tbs. cider vinegar**
- 1 **tsp. Dijon mustard**
- 6 **Tbs. extra-virgin olive oil**
- 4 **oz. (4 lightly packed cups) baby spinach**
- ⅓ **cup fresh pomegranate seeds (optional)**
- 2 **Tbs. thinly sliced fresh chives**

Crisp and somewhat bitter when raw, Belgian endives develop a mellow, slightly nutty flavor when cooked. Pair them with sautéed apples, rounds of hazelnut-coated goat cheese, and a sweet-tart dressing for a salad that's sure to become a weeknight favorite.

1. Position a rack in the center of the oven and heat the oven to 425°F.

2. In a small saucepan over high heat, reduce the pomegranate juice to about ¼ cup (it should be syrupy), about 15 minutes.

3. Meanwhile, mash the goat cheese in a small bowl with a fork until smooth. Form the cheese into four 2-inch-diameter rounds. Put the hazelnuts on a small plate and press the goat cheese rounds into the nuts on all sides to coat. Transfer the cheese to a small baking sheet and bake until the nuts brown and the cheese softens, 8 to 10 minutes.

4. While the goat cheese bakes, melt 2 Tbs. of the butter in a 12-inch heavy-duty skillet over medium-high heat. Arrange the endives flat in the pan (they'll fit snugly), sprinkle with ½ tsp. each salt and pepper, and cook, undisturbed, until browned, 2 to 3 minutes. Flip and cook until the other side starts to soften, 1 to 2 minutes. Transfer to a large plate.

5. Melt the remaining 1 Tbs. butter in the skillet, add the apples and shallot, sprinkle with ¼ tsp. salt and cook, shaking the pan often, until the apples start to soften, 2 to 3 minutes.

6. Transfer the pomegranate juice to a medium bowl. Add the vinegar, mustard, and ½ tsp. each salt and pepper; whisk until combined. Gradually whisk in the oil and season with more salt and pepper to taste.

7. In a large bowl, toss the spinach and apples with half of the vinaigrette and season to taste with salt and pepper. Arrange the endives on 4 large serving plates, top with a mound of the spinach mixture, and then the goat cheese. Sprinkle with the pomegranate seeds (if using) and the chives and drizzle with the remaining vinaigrette.
—*Tony Rosenfeld*

PER SERVING: 570 CALORIES | 12G PROTEIN | 31G CARB | 47G TOTAL FAT | 15G SAT FAT | 26G MONO FAT | 4G POLY FAT | 40MG CHOL | 590MG SODIUM | 6G FIBER

> Pomegranate juice gives the dressing its sweet-tart flavor. You can also reduce the juice to make a glaze for chicken or a syrup for cocktails, or use it in a sorbet. Look for it in your grocery store's produce section.

watermelon and cress salad with grilled shrimp and hearts of palm

SERVES 2

- 5   Tbs. extra-virgin olive oil
- 1   Tbs. Dijon mustard
- 2   tsp. finely grated lemon zest

     Kosher salt and freshly ground black pepper

- 8   oz. jumbo shrimp (21 to 25 per lb.), peeled and deveined, tails left intact
- 3   canned hearts of palm, drained and patted dry (about half a 14-oz. can)
- 1   Tbs. Champagne vinegar
- 1   tsp. minced shallot
- 6   oz. watercress or upland cress, separated into small sprigs, thicker stems trimmed
- ½   cup packed fresh basil, thinly sliced
- 12   oz. watermelon, thinly sliced into narrow wedges, rind removed, seeded if necessary
- 3   oz. ricotta salata, crumbled (about ¾ cup)

Watermelon's crunch and subtle sweetness provide a nice contrast to the savory, tender shrimp and hearts of palm. Ricotta salata (salted, pressed fresh ricotta) is similar to feta in texture but not as salty.

1. Prepare a medium-high gas or charcoal grill fire.

2. Meanwhile, in a medium bowl, whisk 1½ Tbs. of the olive oil, 2 tsp. of the mustard, the lemon zest, ¼ tsp. salt, and ¼ tsp. pepper. Toss the shrimp in the marinade and let sit for about 10 minutes.

3. Thread the shrimp onto metal skewers. Toss the hearts of palm with ½ Tbs. of the olive oil and ¼ tsp. each salt and pepper. Grill the shrimp and hearts of palm, flipping once, until they have nice grill marks and the shrimp are just cooked through, about 4 minutes total. When cool enough to handle, halve the hearts of palm lengthwise, and then cut crosswise into thirds. Remove the shrimp from the skewers.

4. In a small bowl, whisk the remaining 1 tsp. mustard with the vinegar, shallot, and ¼ tsp. each salt and pepper. Whisk in the remaining 3 Tbs. olive oil in a thin stream. Add more salt and pepper to taste.

5. In a large bowl, toss the cress and basil with just enough of the dressing to lightly coat. Season to taste with salt. Divide the greens between 2 plates. Top with the watermelon wedges and drizzle lightly with the remaining dressing. Top with the hearts of palm, shrimp, and crumbled ricotta salata. *—Samantha Seneviratne*

PER SERVING: 550 CALORIES | 28G PROTEIN | 14G CARB | 44G TOTAL FAT | 10G SAT FAT | 27G MONO FAT | 4G POLY FAT | 160MG CHOL | 1,780MG SODIUM | 3G FIBER

pan-seared salmon with baby greens and fennel

SERVES 4

FOR THE DRESSING

2½ **Tbs. Champagne or white-wine vinegar**

2 **Tbs. fresh orange juice**

1 **tsp. finely grated orange zest**

  Kosher salt and freshly ground black pepper

¼ **cup dried cherries**

½ **cup extra-virgin olive oil**

FOR THE SALMON

4 **6-oz. skinless salmon fillets, preferably center cut**

1 **tsp. kosher salt**

¼ **tsp. freshly ground black pepper**

1½ **Tbs. extra-virgin olive oil**

FOR THE SALAD

8 **oz. mixed baby salad greens (about 8 lightly packed cups)**

1 **small fennel bulb, trimmed, halved lengthwise, cored, and very thinly sliced crosswise**

  Kosher salt and freshly ground black pepper

If you have fleur de sel, use it to season the finished salad. The salt flakes are an appealing contrast to the sweet and citrusy dressing.

START THE DRESSING

In a small bowl, combine the vinegar with the orange juice and zest, ¼ tsp. salt, and a few grinds of pepper. Stir in the dried cherries and set aside.

COOK THE SALMON

Season the salmon fillets on both sides with 1 tsp. salt and ¼ tsp. pepper. Heat the oil in a 12-inch skillet over medium-high heat. Cook the salmon, flipping once, until barely cooked through and a rich golden brown crust develops on both sides, 4 to 5 minutes per side. Set aside on a plate.

FINISH THE DRESSING

Using a fork or slotted spoon, remove the cherries from the orange juice mixture and set aside. Slowly whisk the ½ cup olive oil into the orange juice mixture until blended. Season to taste with salt and pepper.

ASSEMBLE THE SALAD

Combine the greens and fennel in a large bowl. Add about half of the vinaigrette to the salad, toss, and season to taste with salt and pepper. Divide the salad among 4 large plates or shallow bowls. Set a piece of salmon on each salad and sprinkle the cherries around the fish. Drizzle some of the remaining vinaigrette over each fillet and serve.

—*Maryellen Driscoll*

PER SERVING: 620 CALORIES | 41G PROTEIN | 14G CARB | 38G TOTAL FAT | 8G SAT FAT | 24G MONO FAT | 9G POLY FAT | 155MG CHOL | 1,580MG SODIUM | 9G FIBER

almond-crusted chicken and nectarine salad with buttermilk-chive dressing

FOR THE DRESSING

- ¼ cup buttermilk
- 1 Tbs. sour cream
- 1 Tbs. white balsamic vinegar
- ½ tsp. honey
- 2 Tbs. extra-virgin olive oil
- 1 Tbs. thinly sliced fresh chives
- 1 tsp. kosher salt
- ¾ tsp. freshly ground black pepper

FOR THE CHICKEN

- 2 large eggs
- 1¾ cups sliced almonds
- ½ cup unbleached all-purpose flour
- 1½ lb. chicken tenderloins, pounded ¼ inch thick
- 1 tsp. kosher salt
- ¾ tsp. freshly ground black pepper
- 2 to 3 Tbs. vegetable oil

FOR THE SALAD

- 6 cups torn tender lettuce (such as butter lettuce, oakleaf, Red Sails) or arugula or both
- 2 small to medium ripe nectarines (or peaches), halved, pitted, and sliced ¼ inch thick

  Kosher salt and freshly ground black pepper

If you can't find chicken tenderloins, look for thin cutlets, which work just as well.

MAKE THE DRESSING

In a medium bowl or liquid measuring cup, combine the buttermilk, sour cream, vinegar, and honey. Slowly whisk in the oil to blend. Stir in the chives and season to taste with salt and pepper.

COOK THE CHICKEN

1. Lightly beat the eggs in a wide, shallow dish. Pulse the almonds and flour together in a food processor until the almonds are chopped; transfer the almond mixture to another wide, shallow dish. Season the chicken on all sides with the salt and pepper. Dip one piece of chicken at a time in the eggs. Shake off the excess and dredge in the almond mixture, pressing lightly to help it adhere. Set aside on a wire rack.

2. Heat 2 Tbs. of the oil in a large skillet over medium heat until shimmering hot. Working in batches, cook the chicken until light golden brown on both sides and just cooked through, 3 to 4 minutes per side. Transfer the chicken to a paper-towel-lined plate when done. Between batches, remove any stray almonds from the pan and add more oil if necessary.

ASSEMBLE THE SALAD

In a large bowl, toss the lettuce, arugula, or both and the nectarines with about half of the dressing. Season to taste with salt and pepper. Divide among 4 dinner plates. Divide the chicken among the plates, overlapping the pieces on top of the salad. Drizzle additional dressing over the chicken and serve. —*Maryellen Driscoll*

PER SERVING: 680 CALORIES | 50G PROTEIN | 31G CARB | 41G TOTAL FAT | 6G SAT FAT | 23G MONO FAT | 10G POLY FAT | 200MG CHOL | 700MG SODIUM | 7G FIBER

farmers' market quesadillas
(recipe on p. 178)

meatless mains

seared baby bok choy with tofu and shiitakes

SERVES 2

- ½ lb. extra-firm tofu
- ⅓ cup lower-salt chicken broth
- 1½ Tbs. minced jarred jalapeño slices
- 2 tsp. Asian sesame oil
- 1 tsp. granulated sugar
- 3 Tbs. canola oil
- ½ lb. baby bok choy (about 2), split in half lengthwise
- 1 tsp. kosher salt
- 1½ inch piece fresh ginger, peeled and thinly sliced (about 2 Tbs.)
- 2 cloves garlic, thinly sliced (about 1 Tbs.)
- 3½ oz. fresh shiitakes, stemmed

If you're trying to eat less meat but aren't crazy about giving up its texture and flavor, this stir-fry will please you. The combination of extra-firm tofu and earthy shiitakes is an apt stand-in for chicken or beef, and the slight bitterness of the bok choy holds its own alongside the assertive flavors of jalapeños and sesame oil.

1. Drain and cut the tofu into ¾-inch-thick slices. Cut each slice crosswise into ½-inch-wide sticks (you should have fat, rectangular sticks). Put the tofu on paper towels and set aside. In a small bowl, mix the broth, jalapeño, sesame oil, and sugar.

2. Set a 12-inch skillet over medium-high heat until hot, about 1 minute. Add 1½ Tbs. of the canola oil and once it's shimmering hot, add the bok choy, cut side down. Sprinkle with ½ tsp. salt and cook, without touching, until browned, about 2 minutes. Continue to cook, tossing, until the bok choy stems start to soften and wilt, about 2 minutes more. Transfer to a plate.

3. Add the remaining 1½ Tbs. canola oil and the ginger to the skillet and cook, stirring, until golden, about 1 minute. Add the garlic and let it sizzle for 10 seconds. Add the tofu and shiitakes, sprinkle with the remaining ½ tsp. salt, and cook, stirring occasionally, until the mushrooms brown and soften, about 3 minutes.

4. Return the bok choy to the pan, add the broth mixture, and cook, tossing, until the sauce evenly coats the vegetables and the bok choy is tender, about 2 minutes. Serve immediately. —*Tony Rosenfeld*

PER SERVING: 400 CALORIES | 15G PROTEIN | 16G CARB | 33G TOTAL FAT | 3G SAT FAT | 19G MONO FAT | 9G POLY FAT | 0MG CHOL | 700MG SODIUM | 3G FIBER

More about Tofu

Tofu is made from soybeans, water, and a coagulant, such as calcium sulfate, magnesium chloride (an extract of sea salt), calcium chloride (derived from a mineral ore), vinegar, or lemon or lime juice. It has a soft texture that's vaguely similar to cheese, but its mild, slightly vegetal flavor is not at all cheesy. It's a staple of Japanese cuisine and is also popular as a meat substitute.

Tofu comes in a variety of textures that are used for different purposes. Silken tofu is smooth and custardy. It blends into a lush, creamy texture that's good for dressings, dips, creamy desserts like cheesecake and puddings, and smoothies. Soft tofu isn't as smooth as silken, but it also blends well into dips, sauces, and soups. Both firm and extra-firm tofu are dense and hold their shape better. Their porous texture allows them to absorb marinades really well. Try cutting firm tofu into cubes or slices for grilling, broiling, sautéing, or stir-frying.

Most grocery stores carry the fresh-water-packed tofu in a refrigerator case in the produce section. Be sure to check the expiration date before buying.

Prepping

Before using, all water-packed tofu needs draining. Cut a slit in the packaging, turn upside down over the sink, and drain as much as possible before fully opening. That's all you need to do with silken tofu, since it'll fall apart with any more handling. Rinse and pat dry soft, firm, and extra-firm tofu. For a stir-fry, you may want to firm up your tofu a bit more by pressing it: Sandwich the tofu between paper or cloth towels and put it on a plate or something else to contain the water. Set a heavy skillet or pot on top and refrigerate for as little as 10 minutes or up to an hour, depending on how much drier and firmer you want the tofu to be.

Storing

Store unopened fresh tofu in the fridge. After opening, keep leftover tofu covered and submerged in fresh water. Change the water daily, keep it cold, and the tofu should last for about a week. Throw it out when it begins to smell sour. If you have leftover firm or extra-firm tofu, you can drain and freeze it, which actually gives it a meatier texture. Frozen, well-wrapped tofu stays good for 3 to 5 months.

portobello mushrooms with creamy spinach-artichoke filling

SERVES 4

- 3 Tbs. olive oil
- 3 medium cloves garlic, minced (1 Tbs.)
- 4 medium portobello mushrooms, stemmed, and gills removed

  Kosher salt and freshly ground black pepper
- 4 oz. cream cheese, softened
- 3 Tbs. mayonnaise
- 1½ tsp. fresh thyme
- 9 to 10 oz. frozen chopped spinach, thawed and squeezed dry
- 9 oz. frozen artichokes, thawed, lightly squeezed dry, and chopped
- ½ cup fresh breadcrumbs or panko
- ⅓ cup finely grated Parmigiano-Reggiano

This vegetarian main course brings together the addictive flavors of stuffed mushrooms and spinach and artichoke dip. If you can't find frozen artichoke hearts, substitute a 14-oz. can of artichoke hearts, drained and patted dry.

1. Position a rack in the center of the oven and heat the oven to 450°F.

2. In a small bowl, combine 2 Tbs. of the oil and about two-thirds of the minced garlic. Brush the insides of the mushroom caps with the garlic oil and sprinkle generously with salt and pepper. Arrange the mushrooms oiled side up on a rimmed baking sheet and roast until just tender, about 10 minutes.

3. Meanwhile, in a medium bowl, mix the cream cheese, mayonnaise, and ½ tsp. of the thyme with the back of a wooden spoon. Stir in the spinach and artichokes and season to taste with salt and pepper. In another medium bowl, combine the remaining garlic, 1 Tbs. oil, and 1 tsp. thyme with the breadcrumbs and cheese.

4. Spoon the artichoke mixture evenly into the mushroom caps and sprinkle with the breadcrumb mixture. Bake until the crumbs are golden brown and the filling is hot, about 10 minutes. Serve immediately. —*Pam Anderson*

PER SERVING: 370 CALORIES | 11G PROTEIN | 17G CARB | 31G TOTAL FAT | 9G SAT FAT | 12G MONO FAT | 6G POLY FAT | 40MG CHOL | 650MG SODIUM | 6G FIBER

grilled vegetable tacos with cilantro pesto

SERVES 8

FOR THE GRILLED VEGETABLES

- 2 small zucchini, cut length-wise into ¼-inch-thick slices
- 2 small yellow squash, cut lengthwise into ¼-inch-thick slices
- 2 medium chayote, peeled, seeded, and sliced into ¼-inch-thick slices
- 3 Tbs. sunflower or vegetable oil
- 1 tsp. minced garlic
- 1 serrano chile, minced
- Kosher salt and freshly ground black pepper

FOR ASSEMBLING THE TACOS

- 8 6-inch corn tortillas, warmed
- 1 recipe Cilantro Pesto (recipe below)
- ¾ cup crumbled queso fresco or feta (optional)
- Coarsely chopped fresh cilantro (optional)

If you can't find the squashlike Mexican chayote, substitute an additional zucchini and yellow squash.

GRILL THE VEGETABLES

1. Prepare a medium-high gas or charcoal grill fire.

2. In a large bowl, combine the zucchini, yellow squash, and chayote. Add the oil, garlic, serrano, 1 tsp. salt, and 1 tsp. pepper and toss gently to coat. Grill, covered, until the vegetables become tender and have grill marks on both sides, 2 to 3 minutes per side. The chayote will soften but won't become limp like the zucchini and squash.

3. Let the vegetables cool slightly and then slice crosswise into thin strips. Season to taste with more salt and pepper.

ASSEMBLE THE TACOS

Spoon some of the vegetable mixture on top of each tortilla and top with a drizzle of the pesto and some crumbled cheese and chopped cilantro (if using). The filling can be warm or at room temperature.
—*Sue Torres*

PER SERVING: 290 CALORIES | 6G PROTEIN | 18G CARB | 23G TOTAL FAT | 3.5G SAT FAT | 5G MONO FAT | 14G POLY FAT | 5MG CHOL | 260MG SODIUM | 3G FIBER

cilantro pesto

YIELDS ABOUT ⅔ CUP

- 1 cup packed coarsely chopped fresh cilantro
- ½ cup sunflower or vegetable oil
- 2 Tbs. toasted pine nuts
- 1 medium clove garlic
- ½ tsp. kosher salt

Combine all the ingredients in a blender and purée until smooth. Set aside, or refrigerate in an airtight container for up to 3 days.

asparagus and fried eggs on garlic toast

SERVES 4

4 ½-inch-thick slices sourdough bread (from a
round loaf)

1 large clove garlic, halved

1 Tbs. extra-virgin olive oil,
more for brushing the toast

1 lb. asparagus, trimmed of
tough, woody stems

Kosher salt

4 large eggs

Freshly ground black pepper

1 oz. pecorino romano, shaved
into large shards with a
vegetable peeler

*The softly cooked egg yolks in
this dish, which works well for
a light dinner, become a delicious sauce for the toast and
asparagus.*

1. Lightly toast the bread. Rub
one side of each slice with the
garlic and brush lightly with olive oil. Put 1 slice on each of 4 plates.

2. Put the asparagus in a 12-inch nonstick skillet with ½ cup water, the
olive oil, and ½ tsp. salt. Cover, bring to a boil over medium-high heat,
and cook until tender, about 5 minutes.

3. Meanwhile, crack the eggs into a shallow bowl. When the asparagus
is ready, pat dry and divide it among the pieces of toast. Wipe out the
skillet with paper towels if wet; then slide the eggs into the hot skillet,
sprinkle each with a pinch of salt and pepper, cover, and cook over
low heat until the whites are firm but the yolks are still runny, about
2 minutes.

4. Top each toast with an egg. Garnish with the shaved pecorino
and serve. —*Allison Ehri Kreitler*

PER SERVING: 420 CALORIES | 22G PROTEIN | 59G CARB | 11G TOTAL FAT | 4G SAT FAT |
4G MONO FAT | 2G POLY FAT | 195MG CHOL | 780MG SODIUM | 4G FIBER

red-cooked tofu

SERVES 4

- 4 medium scallions, thinly sliced (white and green parts separated)
- 2 medium carrots, cut into small dice
- 1 cup lower-salt chicken broth or (preferably home-made) vegetable broth
- 6 Tbs. lower-sodium soy sauce; more as needed
- ¼ cup Shaoxing (Chinese cooking wine) or dry sherry
- 1½ Tbs. minced fresh ginger
- 2 tsp. granulated sugar
- ¼ tsp. freshly ground black pepper
- 2 14-oz. packages firm tofu, cut into 1-inch pieces
- 2 Tbs. seasoned rice vinegar
- 2 tsp. arrowroot or cornstarch

Red-cooking is a traditional Chinese braising technique that uses soy sauce, sugar, and rice wine to flavor the food and give it a dark red color. This easy, aromatic stew is delicious served over cooked rice or mustard greens.

1. In a large saucepan, combine the scallion whites, carrots, broth, soy sauce, Shaoxing, ginger, sugar, and pepper. Bring to a simmer over medium-high heat, stirring once or twice. Cover, reduce the heat to low, and simmer gently for 5 minutes. Add the tofu, cover, and continue to simmer gently until the tofu is heated through and has absorbed some of the other flavors, 10 minutes.

2. In a small bowl, whisk the vinegar and arrowroot until smooth and then stir the mixture into the stew, taking care not to break up the tofu. Stir gently until thickened, about 1 minute. Add more soy sauce to taste, sprinkle with the scallion greens, and serve.
—*Bruce Weinstein and Mark Scarbrough*

PER SERVING: 350 CALORIES | 34G PROTEIN | 20G CARB | 18G TOTAL FAT | 2.5G SAT FAT | 4G MONO FAT | 10G POLY FAT | 0MG CHOL | 960MG SODIUM | 6G FIBER

vegetables and tofu with spicy peanut sauce

SERVES 2 TO 3

- **4** medium red potatoes (12 oz.), cut into ⅓-inch-thick slices
- **2** medium carrots (4 oz.), peeled and cut on the diagonal into ⅓-inch-thick slices
- **7** oz. package pressed, baked tofu (regular or Thai flavor), sliced into 1-inch-square pieces, ½ inch thick
- **1** small crown broccoli (7 oz.), cut into 1-inch florets
- **3** oz. green beans, trimmed and halved crosswise on the diagonal
- **½** cup natural unsalted peanut butter (smooth or chunky)
- **1** Tbs. soy sauce
- **1½** tsp. Asian chile paste, such as sambal oelek; more to taste
- Kosher salt

On the Indonesian island of Java, this hearty, main course—known as gado-gado—is sold by street vendors, who carry the ingredients on yokelike poles, assembling each serving to order. It's surprisingly easy to make.

1. Put a steamer basket in a large pot and fill the pot with water to just reach the bottom of the basket.

2. Put the potatoes in a single layer in the steamer basket, set the pot over medium-high heat, and bring the water to a boil. Cover the pot and cook for 4 minutes, then carefully remove the lid, move the potatoes to one side of the pot, and add the carrots in a snug, slightly overlapping layer. Cover the pot and steam until the carrots and potatoes are just tender, another 6 to 7 minutes. Transfer the potatoes and carrots to a platter. Put the tofu, broccoli, and beans in the steamer; cover and cook until the tofu is hot and the broccoli and beans are just tender, about 4 minutes. Transfer to the platter with the other vegetables.

3. In a medium bowl, combine the peanut butter, soy sauce, chile paste, and ½ cup hot water from the pot. Whisk to combine, adding more water as needed to create a thick but fluid sauce. Add more chile paste and salt to taste. Serve with the sauce on the side.
—*Dabney Gough*

PER SERVING: 530 CALORIES | 30G PROTEIN | 41G CARB | 29G TOTAL FAT | 4G SAT FAT | 0G MONO FAT | 0G POLY FAT | 0MG CHOL | 1,070MG SODIUM | 10G FIBER

sesame-ginger tofu and shiitake kebabs

MAKES 8 KEBABS; SERVES 4

- 1 **14-oz. package water-packed extra-firm tofu, well drained**
- ¼ **cup reduced-sodium soy sauce**
- 3 **Tbs. rice wine (sake or Shaoxing)**
- 3 **Tbs. hoisin sauce**
- 2 **Tbs. peanut oil**
- 2 **Tbs. Asian sesame oil**
- 2 **Tbs. chopped fresh ginger**
- 1 **Tbs. honey**
- 40 **medium shiitake mushrooms (about 1 lb.), stems trimmed**
- 2 **bunches scallions (white and light green parts only), cut into 1-inch lengths to yield 40 pieces**
- 1 **orange**
- **Nonstick cooking spray**

Serve these kebabs with brown rice or somen noodles.

1. In a shallow pan, soak eight 12-inch bamboo skewers in water while you work. Sandwich the tofu between paper towels and put on a plate. Set a small heavy pot or cutting board on the tofu to press out excess moisture. Let sit for 20 to 30 minutes.

2. Cut the tofu into 40 cubes by first slicing the tofu block in half horizontally and then cutting each half into 20 cubes.

3. In a large bowl, whisk the soy sauce, rice wine, hoisin sauce, peanut oil, sesame oil, ginger, and honey. Add the tofu, mushrooms, and scallions. Marinate at room temperature for 30 to 45 minutes, stirring frequently but gently.

4. Trim the ends of the orange, cut it lengthwise into quarters, and then slice each quarter crosswise into 6 slices, to yield 24 slices total.

5. Line a large heavy-duty, rimmed baking sheet with foil and coat the foil with cooking spray. Position a rack 8 inches from the broiler element and heat the broiler on high.

6. Thread 5 scallion pieces, 5 shiitakes, 5 pieces of tofu, and 3 orange slices onto each skewer in an alternating pattern. Arrange the skewers on the baking sheet. Broil until nicely browned on one side, 5 to 6 minutes. Gently turn the kebabs over and cook until golden brown on the other side, 5 to 6 minutes more.

7. Meanwhile, pour the remaining marinade into a small (1-quart) saucepan. Bring to a boil over medium-high heat. Reduce the heat to maintain a gentle simmer and cook until slightly reduced and the flavors meld, about 2 minutes.

8. Arrange the kebabs on a serving platter or on individual plates. Drizzle with the sauce and serve. —*Susie Middleton*

PER SERVING: 230 CALORIES | 13G PROTEIN | 29G CARB | 10G TOTAL FAT | 1G SAT FAT | 6G MONO FAT | 2G POLY FAT | 0MG CHOL | 200MG SODIUM | 5G FIBER

artichoke, leek, & taleggio frittata

SERVES 4

5   baby artichokes, trimmed

5   Tbs. extra-virgin olive oil

Kosher salt and freshly ground black pepper

2   medium leeks (white and light green parts only), trimmed, washed, and thinly sliced (1½ cups)

6   large eggs

3   oz. Taleggio, cut into ¼-inch cubes (about ½ cup)

¼   cup chopped fresh flat-leaf parsley

½   tsp. chopped fresh thyme

Taleggio is a semisoft Italian cheese. Look for it in well-stocked supermarkets and specialty stores.

1. Dry the artichokes, cut in half lengthwise, and slice lengthwise about ½ inch thick.

2. Heat 2 Tbs. of the olive oil in a 10-inch nonstick skillet over medium heat. Add the artichokes, a pinch of salt, and a couple of grinds of pepper. Cook the artichokes until lightly browned on one side, about 4 minutes. With a wide spatula, turn them over and cook until lightly browned on the other side, about 1 minute. Add ¼ cup water and bring to a boil. Reduce the heat to low, cover, and simmer until tender, about 4 minutes. Remove the cover and cook until any remaining liquid is evaporated. Transfer to a small bowl.

3. Add 2 Tbs. of the oil and the leeks to the pan with a pinch of salt. Increase the heat to medium low and cook, stirring occasionally, until soft and tender, 10 to 12 minutes. Transfer to the bowl with the artichokes.

4. Whisk the eggs in a medium bowl. Add the artichokes, leeks, Taleggio, parsley, thyme, and ½ tsp. salt.

5. Position an oven rack 6 inches from the broiler and heat the broiler on high. Wipe out the skillet and heat the remaining 1 Tbs. oil over medium-low heat. Pour in the egg mixture and cook until the bottom is light golden (use a spatula to peek), about 4 minutes. Slide the spatula under the bottom to keep it from sticking. Put the pan under the broiler and cook until the eggs are set and the top is golden brown, about 3 minutes more. Slide onto a serving platter and serve warm or at room temperature. —*Sara Jenkins*

PER SERVING: 190 CALORIES | 8G PROTEIN | 6G CARB | 15G TOTAL FAT | 4G SAT FAT | 8G MONO FAT | 1.5G POLY FAT | 165MG CHOL | 280MG SODIUM | 2G FIBER

how to clean and trim artichokes

BABY ARTICHOKES

Snap off the dark green outer leaves of the artichoke until only the pale, tender inner leaves remain.

Cut off the top ¼ inch of the artichoke.

Trim the stem end and any dark parts around the bottom.

Rub a lemon half over all the cut ends.

WHOLE ARTICHOKES

Cut off the bottom of the stem, leaving about ½ inch.

Pull off any small, fibrous dark leaves around the base.

Cut off the top ½ inch of the artichoke.

Using scissors, trim off the sharp, pointed tips of the remaining leaves.

ARTICHOKE HEARTS

Snap off the dark green outer leaves of the artichoke until only the pale, tender inner leaves remain.

Cut off the top third of the artichoke and all but 1 inch of the stem.

Using a paring knife, peel away the tough outer layer of the stem and remove the base of the leaves all around.

Cut the artichoke in half lengthwise. With a spoon or melon baller, scoop out and discard the hairy choke and thorny inner leaves.

ARTICHOKE BOTTOMS

Snap off the dark green outer leaves of the artichoke until only the pale, tender inner leaves remain.

Cut off the leaves at the base.

Using a paring knife, cut off the stem and remove the base of the leaves all around.

With a spoon or melon baller, scoop out and discard the hairy choke and thorny inner leaves.

farmers' market quesadillas

MAKES 4 QUESADILLAS

- **5** Tbs. vegetable oil
- **1** cup small-diced fresh, mild chiles, such as Anaheim or poblano (from about 2 large chiles)
- **1½** cups small-diced summer squash (from about 2 small zucchini, yellow squash, or yellow crookneck)

  Kosher salt and freshly ground black pepper
- **1** cup fresh corn kernels (from 2 medium ears)
- **⅛** tsp. chipotle chile powder
- **1** cup diced tomato (from 2 small tomatoes)
- **¼** cup chopped fresh cilantro
- **1** Tbs. fresh lime juice
- **4** 9-inch flour tortillas
- **2** cups grated sharp Cheddar (8 oz.)

  Sour cream, for serving (optional)

These quick quesadillas are loaded with the best of the season: summer squash, fresh corn, and diced tomatoes. Fresh chiles and chipotle powder give the dish some smoky heat.

1. Heat the oven to 200°F. Fit a cooling rack over a baking sheet and put in the oven.

2. Heat 1 Tbs. of the oil in a 12-inch skillet over medium-high heat until hot. Add the chiles and cook, stirring, until soft, 3 to 4 minutes. Add the squash, season with salt and pepper, and cook, stirring, until the squash softens and starts to brown, 3 to 4 minutes. Stir in the corn and chipotle powder and cook for 2 minutes more. Spoon into a bowl, let cool for a few minutes, and then fold in the tomato, cilantro, and lime juice. Season to taste with salt and pepper. Set aside ¾ cup of the mixture.

3. Lay several layers of paper towel on a work surface. Wipe out the skillet, put it over medium-high heat, and add 1 Tbs. of the oil. When it's hot, put 1 tortilla in the pan. Quickly distribute ½ cup of the cheese evenly over the tortilla and about a quarter of the remaining vegetable mixture over half the tortilla. When the underside of the tortilla is browned, use tongs to fold the cheese-only side over the vegetable side. Lay the quesadilla on the paper towels, blot for a few seconds, and then move it to the rack in the oven to keep warm while you repeat with the remaining oil and tortillas. Cut the quesadillas into wedges and serve immediately with the reserved vegetable mixture and sour cream. —*Martha Holmberg*

PER SERVING: 660 CALORIES | 22G PROTEIN | 51G CARB | 42G TOTAL FAT | 15G SAT FAT | 16G MONO FAT | 9G POLY FAT | 60MG CHOL | 1,090MG SODIUM | 5G FIBER

> Chipotles are dried smoked jalapeños, and in any form they add an intriguing depth to dishes. McCormick® makes ground chipotle, and The Spice Hunter® sells a crushed chipotle, which would be a fine substitute in this recipe; just add a bit more than you would of the ground.

matzo brei with fresh chives

SERVES 4 TO 6

- 4 pieces unsalted matzo (about 4 oz.)
- 5 large eggs, beaten
- ¼ cup thinly sliced fresh chives
- 1 tsp. kosher salt
- ¼ tsp. freshly ground black pepper
- 5 Tbs. unsalted butter

Matzo brei is a simple dish of eggs, butter, and matzo (an unleavened crackerlike bread). Although typically served during Passover, it makes a delicious meal anytime. If using salted matzo, halve the amount of salt in the recipe.

1. In a small saucepan, bring 1¼ cups of water to a boil. In a large bowl, crumble the matzo into 1-inch (or smaller) pieces and pour the boiling water over them. Let sit until the matzo softens but doesn't turn to mush, about 20 seconds. Using a large slotted spoon, press the matzo against the bowl and pour off any excess liquid (there may not be any). Stir in the eggs, chives, salt, and pepper.

2. Melt the butter in a 10- to 12-inch nonstick skillet over medium-high heat. When the foam starts to subside, add the matzo mixture. Use a heatproof spatula to gently scramble and break up the eggs, cooking until they are softly set, 3 to 4 minutes. Season with more salt and pepper and serve immediately. —*Tony Rosenfeld*

PER SERVING: 220 CALORIES | 7G PROTEIN | 16G CARB | 14G TOTAL FAT | 7G SAT FAT | 4G MONO FAT | 1G POLY FAT | 200MG CHOL | 250MG SODIUM | 1G FIBER

rice and beans with fried eggs

SERVES 4

- ¾ cup long-grain white rice
- Kosher salt
- 2 Tbs. canola oil
- 1 small yellow onion, cut into small dice
- ½ medium red bell pepper, seeded and cut into small dice
- 2 large cloves garlic, minced
- ½ tsp. ground cumin
- ¼ cup canned tomato sauce
- 1 15½-oz. can black beans, drained and rinsed
- 3 Tbs. Salsa Lizano®; more to taste
- Freshly ground black pepper
- 8 large eggs
- 2 Tbs. chopped fresh cilantro

Served with soft corn tortillas, this traditional Costa Rican dish is perfect for breakfast, lunch, or dinner. If you can't find Salsa Lizano, substitute Worcestershire.

1. Put the rice, a big pinch of salt, and 1½ cups of water in a 3-quart saucepan. Bring to a boil over medium-high heat, reduce the heat to low, cover, and cook until the rice has absorbed the water and is tender, about 15 minutes. Remove from the heat and set aside with the lid on.

2. Meanwhile, heat 1 Tbs. of the oil in a 4-quart saucepan over medium heat. Add the onion, bell pepper, garlic, and a pinch of salt; cook, stirring occasionally, until softened, about 3 minutes. Add the cumin and cook until fragrant, about 30 seconds. Add the tomato sauce and stir for 1 minute. Add the beans and 1 cup of water and simmer until the liquid reduces to the level of the beans, about 4 minutes.

3. Add the rice to the beans and mix well. Stir in the Salsa Lizano and season to taste with salt and pepper. Keep warm.

4. Heat the remaining 1 Tbs. of oil in a 12-inch nonstick skillet over medium heat, swirling the pan to coat evenly. Gently crack the eggs into the pan. Season with salt and pepper, cover, and cook until the yolks' edges have just begun to set, 2 to 3 minutes. (The eggs should cook gently, so lower the heat if needed.) Separate the eggs with the edge of a spatula.

5. To serve, put a heaping spoonful of the rice and beans on a plate and slide 2 eggs on top. Sprinkle with the cilantro. —*Julissa Roberts*

PER SERVING: 460 CALORIES | 21G PROTEIN | 54G CARB | 17G TOTAL FAT | 3.5G SAT FAT | 8G MONO FAT | 3.5G POLY FAT | 425MG CHOL | 710MG SODIUM | 6G FIBER

What Is Salsa Lizano?

Found in nearly every Costa Rican home, restaurant, and roadside food stand, Salsa Lizano is a smooth, light brown, vegetable-based sauce with a touch of sweetness and a hearty punch of spice, including cumin, mustard, and turmeric. It's most commonly served as a condiment with rice and beans and tamales, but it's also used as a marinade for beef, pork, and chicken.

vegetable-chickpea chili with fried almonds

SERVES 4

- 3 Tbs. extra-virgin olive oil
- 3 medium cloves garlic, minced
- 1 large red onion, finely chopped

  Kosher salt
- 1 to 2 Tbs. hot paprika
- 1 Tbs. chili powder
- 1 Tbs. ground cumin
- 1 28-oz. can whole peeled tomatoes
- 2 15-oz. cans chickpeas, drained and rinsed
- 2 cups fresh (or frozen) corn kernels (from about 4 medium ears)
- 1 medium red bell pepper, quartered, cored, and thinly sliced crosswise
- 1 medium jalapeño, thinly sliced crosswise into rounds
- ½ cup sliced or slivered almonds
- ¼ cup small basil leaves
- 6 scallions (white and light green parts only), thinly sliced; more for garnish

  Sour cream, for serving (optional)

Make this quick vegetarian chili for a weeknight meal, then enjoy the leftovers later in the week; the chili tastes even better after it's mellowed in the refrigerator for a day or so. Almonds fried in olive oil until golden brown are a creative and crunchy garnish for this chili. Serve with basmati rice.

1. Heat 2 Tbs. of the oil in a 5- to 6-quart heavy-duty pot over medium-high heat until shimmering hot, about 2 minutes. Add the garlic and onion, season with 1 tsp. salt, and cook, stirring occasionally, until the onion begins to soften, 3 to 5 minutes. Stir in the paprika, chili powder, and cumin, cook for 1 minute, and then add the tomatoes and their juice. Stir, smashing the tomatoes against the side of the pot to break them up slightly. Add 2 cups water and bring to a simmer. Stir in the chickpeas, corn, bell pepper, jalapeño, and 1 Tbs. salt and cook until the peppers have lost their raw crunch, 8 to 12 minutes (at this point, if the chili looks too thick, add an additional 1 cup of water).

2. While the vegetables cook, heat the remaining 1 Tbs. olive oil in a 10-inch skillet over medium-high heat. Add the almonds and cook, stirring constantly, until golden brown, 2 to 3 minutes. Using a slotted spoon, transfer them to a plate lined with paper towels and immediately season them with ½ tsp. salt.

3. Stir the basil and scallions into the chili. Serve the chili with a dollop of sour cream (if using), more scallions, and the almonds.
—*Alexandra Guarnaschelli*

PER SERVING: 510 CALORIES | 19G PROTEIN | 65G CARB | 22G TOTAL FAT | 2G SAT FAT | 13G MONO FAT | 5G POLY FAT | 0MG CHOL | 1,900MG SODIUM | 17G FIBER

Make Ahead

You can make the chili up to 4 days ahead; store it in an airtight container in the refrigerator. Reheat gently to serve.

wild mushroom and arugula risotto

SERVES 4

- **1½ cups (1 oz.) dried mushrooms, rehydrated (see p. 62) and chopped, plus ¾ cup soaking liquid**
- **5 cups lower-salt chicken broth**
- **2 oz. (4 Tbs.) unsalted butter**
- **1 medium yellow onion, finely diced (about 1 cup)**
- **½ tsp. kosher salt**
- **1½ cups carnaroli or arborio rice**
- **½ cup dry sherry**
- **3 oz. baby arugula (4 cups, loosely packed)**
- **1 cup freshly grated Parmigiano-Reggiano or Grana Padano**
- **⅓ cup sliced chives**
- **Freshly ground black pepper**

Bulk dried mushrooms typically include more exotic types like oyster, shiitake, and morel. This satisfying risotto makes a meal on its own when accompanied by a green salad.

1. Heat the mushroom soaking liquid with the chicken broth in a 3-quart saucepan over medium heat. Meanwhile, in a large (4-quart) pot, melt 2 Tbs. butter over medium-high heat. Add the onion and sprinkle with the salt. Cook the onion, stirring, until it softens and turns a light brown, about 3 minutes. Add the rice and mushrooms and cook, stirring, for 1 minute. Add the sherry; raise the heat to high, and cook, stirring, until it almost completely reduces, about 1 minute.

2. Reduce the heat to medium; add ¾ cup of the broth to the rice, and cook, stirring often, until the rice absorbs the broth, 2 to 3 minutes. Add another ¾ cup of broth and cook until absorbed. Continue adding broth in this manner until the rice is creamy and tender, about 20 minutes total—you may or may not need all of the broth. Stir in the arugula, Parmigiano, all but a couple tablespoons of the chives, and the remaining 2 Tbs. butter and continue stirring until the arugula is just wilted, about 1 minute. Serve immediately in individual bowls, sprinkled with a few grinds of black pepper and the remaining chives.
—*Tony Rosenfeld*

baked eggplant "parmesan"

2 medium globe eggplant (about 2 lb.), cut crosswise into ¼-inch-thick rounds

Kosher salt

1 cup unbleached all-purpose flour

4 large eggs, beaten

3 cups dry fine breadcrumbs

2 tsp. chopped fresh thyme

Canola oil for frying (about 2 cups)

3 cups marinara sauce, warmed

16 basil leaves, torn into large pieces

10 oz. fresh mozzarella, thinly sliced (about 2 cups)

1½ cups freshly grated Grana Padano

Serve this hearty dish with a portion of pasta or between two slices of toasted Italian bread for a delicious sandwich.

1. Line a large plate with paper towels. Put down a layer of eggplant slices, and sprinkle generously with salt; add another layer of paper towels and another layer of eggplant and salt; repeat until you've layered the rest of the eggplant. Let sit for 20 minutes.

2. Put the flour and eggs in separate wide, shallow bowls. In another wide bowl, toss the breadcrumbs with the thyme and ½ tsp. salt. Line a baking sheet with paper towels. Dredge the eggplant slices in the flour, dip in the egg, and then coat with the breadcrumbs, pressing down to pat the crumbs onto the eggplant, and put on the baking sheet.

3. Line another baking sheet with fresh paper towels. Pour enough oil into a large (12-inch) skillet or frying pan to measure about ½ inch deep and heat over medium heat until hot (if you dip a piece of eggplant into the oil, it will sizzle immediately). Working in batches, add as much eggplant as will fit in a single layer and fry, flipping once, until golden brown, 1 to 2 minutes per side. Transfer to the baking sheet. Repeat, frying the remaining eggplant and layering it between sheets of paper towel.

4. Position a rack in the center of the oven and heat the oven to 425°F. Arrange a layer of eggplant in a 9x13-inch baking dish. Top with 1 cup of the marinara and then cover with a third of the basil, mozzarella, and Grana Padano. Repeat with two more layers of the remaining eggplant, marinara, basil, mozzarella, and Grana Padano.

5. Bake until the cheese melts and browns and the sauce bubbles around the edges, 25 to 30 minutes (cover with foil if the top browns too quickly). Let cool for a couple of minutes and serve.
—*Tony Rosenfeld*

To store Grana Padano, simply wrap it in a few layers of parchment, waxed paper, or foil and put it in the crisper drawer of the refrigerator. It will keep for about 3 weeks; if any mold develops on the surface of the cheese, shave off the moldy parts and surrounding area. The rest of the cheese is still good.

grilled halloumi with rosemary-grape-walnut relish and garlic bread

SERVES 2

- **1** medium red onion, cut into 3 to 4 thick slices
- **2** Tbs. plus 4 tsp. extra-virgin olive oil

  Kosher salt and freshly ground black pepper
- **12** oz. halloumi, cut into ⅜-inch-thick slabs (or aged provolone, cut into ½-inch-thick slices)
- **2** large cloves garlic, minced
- **1** small loaf ciabatta (about 8 oz.), cut into ½-inch-thick slices
- **½** cup walnuts
- **1** tsp. minced fresh rosemary
- **1** large bunch seedless black or red grapes (about 1¼ lb.)
- **2** to 3 tsp. balsamic vinegar

Halloumi, a goat and sheep's milk cheese from Cyprus, is perfect for grilling: It softens over the heat but doesn't melt. Complete with grilled grapes and rustic bread, this is a nice light meal, but add a green salad for a little more substance.

1. Prepare a high gas or charcoal grill fire.

2. Drizzle the onion slices with 2 tsp. of the oil and lightly season them with salt and pepper. Pat the cheese dry and drizzle with 2 tsp. of the oil. In a small bowl, mix the remaining 2 Tbs. of oil, the garlic, and a pinch each of salt and pepper; brush the mixture evenly over one side of the bread slices.

3. Meanwhile, toast the walnuts in a small skillet over medium heat, stirring frequently, until golden brown, 4 to 5 minutes. Coarsely chop the walnuts while still hot and transfer them to a medium bowl. Mix in the rosemary.

4. Put the onion slices and bunch of grapes on the grill grate. Cover and grill, turning once, until the grapes are bursting and the onion is grill marked, about 10 minutes. Transfer the grapes to the bowl with the walnuts and the onion to a cutting board. Use tongs to simultaneously pull the grapes from their stems and crush them, dropping them into the bowl. Chop the grilled onion and add to the bowl. Season to taste with the vinegar, salt, and pepper.

5. Clean and oil the grill grate. Put the bread and cheese on the grate and grill uncovered, turning once, until marked on both sides, 4 to 5 minutes (about 1 minute if using provolone).

6. Divide the cheese, bread, and relish among 4 plates and serve immediately. —*Pam Anderson*

PER SERVING: 700 CALORIES | 27G PROTEIN | 60G CARB | 41G TOTAL FAT | 18G SAT FAT | 9G MONO FAT | 7G POLY FAT | 60MG CHOL | 1,290MG SODIUM | 4G FIBER

thai yellow curry with vegetables and tofu

SERVES 4

- 1 (13.5- to 14-oz.) can coconut milk
- ¼ cup yellow curry paste
- 1 cup lower-salt chicken broth, or homemade chicken or vegetable broth
- 2 Tbs. light brown sugar or light brown palm sugar; more as needed
- 1 tsp. fish sauce; more as needed
- ¾ cup bite-size green bean pieces
- ¾ cup sliced onions (½-inch-thick slices)
- 3 stalks fresh lemongrass, trimmed, bruised, and cut into 3- to 4-inch pieces
- 6 whole fresh or thawed frozen wild lime leaves (or substitute 1 tsp. finely grated lime zest)
- 14 oz. extra-firm tofu, drained and cut into bite-size pieces
- ¾ cup diced bell peppers (red, orange, or yellow)
- ¾ cup oyster mushrooms, pulled apart into bite-size pieces
- ¾ cup loosely packed fresh Italian or Thai basil leaves

  Lime wedges, for garnish

This meatless curry is bursting with a rainbow of colorful vegetables and a range of textures, from crunchy bell peppers to soft tofu.

1. Shake the can of coconut milk or stir it well (this creates a consistent thickness, since the fat often solidifies at the top of the can).

2. In a 3- to 4-quart saucepan or wok over medium heat, simmer ½ cup of the coconut milk, stirring occasionally, until reduced by about half, 3 to 5 minutes. It will get very thick and shiny and may or may not separate; either is fine.

3. Add the curry paste, whisk well, and cook, continuing to whisk, for 1 minute. Whisk in the broth, sugar, fish sauce, and remaining coconut milk. Bring to a simmer over medium-high heat.

4. Add the green beans, onion, lemongrass, and lime leaves and continue to simmer, adjusting the heat as necessary.

5. After 2 minutes, add the tofu, bell pepper, and oyster mushrooms and continue to simmer until everything is tender and cooked through, about 3 more minutes.

6. Remove the curry from the heat. Season to taste with more sugar and fish sauce and stir in the basil. Transfer to a serving bowl (or serve right out of the pot). Remove the lemongrass and lime leaves or tell your guests to eat around them. Garnish with the lime wedges.
—*Robert Danhi*

PER SERVING: 420 CALORIES | 21G PROTEIN | 25G CARB | 30G TOTAL FAT | 20G SAT FAT | 3G MONO FAT | 5G POLY FAT | 0MG CHOL | 1,120MG SODIUM | 7G FIBER

winter vegetable soup
with coconut milk and pear
(recipe on p. 192)

soups, stews & chilis

tortellini soup with carrots, peas & leeks

SERVES 4

- 2 **medium leeks (12 oz. untrimmed)**
- 1 **Tbs. unsalted butter**
- 3 **cloves garlic, finely chopped (about 1 Tbs.)**
- ½ **medium carrot, peeled and finely diced (2 Tbs.)**

  Kosher salt

  Freshly ground black pepper

- 5 **cups lower-salt canned chicken broth**
- 8 **oz. frozen cheese tortellini**
- 1 **cup frozen peas**
- ¼ **cup freshly grated Parmigiano-Reggiano or Grana Padano**

You can make most of the soup ahead, but don't add the tortellini until you're ready to eat or they'll become mushy.

1. Trim the roots and dark green leaves from the leeks. Slice the white and light green part in half lengthwise and then slice the halves thinly crosswise. Rinse well and drain.

2. Melt the butter in a 4-quart saucepan over medium heat. Add the garlic, leeks, and carrot. Season with a couple pinches of salt and cook, stirring occasionally, until tender, 5 to 7 minutes. (It's fine if the vegetables brown lightly.) Stir in ¼ tsp. pepper and cook for about 20 seconds, then add the chicken broth and bring to a boil. Add the tortellini and cook for 3 minutes. Reduce the heat to a simmer and add the peas. Continue to simmer until the tortellini are cooked, 3 to 5 minutes.

3. Season to taste with salt and pepper. Portion the soup into warm bowls, top each with some of the cheese, and serve.
—Joanne McAllister Smart

PER SERVING: 310 CALORIES | 17G PROTEIN | 43G CARB | 9G TOTAL FAT | 4.5G SAT FAT | 2.5G MONO FAT | 1G POLY FAT | 35MG CHOL | 540MG SODIUM | 4G FIBER

summer bouillabaisse with smoky rouille

SERVES 4

3   **Tbs. extra-virgin olive oil; more for the sauce**

1½ **Tbs. chopped garlic, plus ½ tsp. finely grated or minced garlic**

2   **lb. ripe tomatoes, cored and large diced (about 4½ cups)**

1   **cup dry white wine**

1   **tsp. sweet smoked paprika (Spanish pimentón)**

¼   **cup mayonnaise**

   Kosher salt

1   **14-oz. can lower-salt chicken broth (1¾ cups)**

1   **large pinch saffron**

1   **lb. halibut, cod, or other firm white fish, cut into 1-inch chunks**

2   **cups fresh corn kernels (from 4 medium ears)**

   Freshly ground black pepper

1   **to 2 Tbs. chopped fresh flat-leaf parsley, for garnish (optional)**

This recipe relies on really fresh ripe corn and tomatoes, so only make this dish when they're in season.

1. In a 5- to 6-quart soup pot or Dutch oven, heat the oil over medium heat. Add the 1½ Tbs. chopped garlic and cook until fragrant, about 30 seconds. Add the tomatoes and wine, increase the heat to medium high (if necessary), and simmer vigorously until the tomatoes are broken down and the mixture is slightly soupy, about 15 minutes.

2. While the tomatoes are cooking, whisk the ½ tsp. grated garlic, paprika, and mayonnaise in a small bowl. Whisk in a little olive oil and enough cool water to make a creamy, pourable sauce. Taste and add salt if you like.

3. Add the broth and saffron to the tomato mixture and simmer to slightly reduce the broth and concentrate the flavors, 5 minutes. Add the fish and simmer until it's opaque throughout, 3 to 5 minutes more. Stir in the corn. Season to taste with salt and black pepper. Serve in large bowls with a big drizzle of the sauce on top and a generous sprinkle of parsley, if using. —*Martha Holmberg*

PER SERVING: 490 CALORIES | 30G PROTEIN | 29G CARB | 25G TOTAL FAT | 3.5G SAT FAT | 9G MONO FAT | 2.5G POLY FAT | 40MG CHOL | 480MG SODIUM | 5G FIBER

> To dress this up for entertaining, add ½ lb. peeled medium or large shrimp and ½ lb. Manila clams or mussels. Wash the shellfish well before adding and use only the tightly closed shells. Simmer until the shells open.

curried carrot soup with cilantro

SERVES 4

- 2 Tbs. vegetable oil
- 1½ lb. carrots, cut into 1-inch chunks (about 4 cups)
- 1 large yellow onion, cut into 1-inch chunks
- 3 large cloves garlic, thinly sliced
- 1 tsp. curry powder
- 3 cups lower-salt chicken broth

  Kosher salt

- 1½ cups carrot juice; more as needed
- ¼ cup packed fresh cilantro leaves

  Freshly ground black pepper

  Chopped peanuts, for garnish (optional)

This warming soup is perfect in cooler weather and is a good substitution for creamy tomato soup.

1. Heat the oil in a 10- or 11-inch, straight-sided sauté pan over medium-high heat until hot. Add the carrots and then the onion. Cook, stirring very little at first and more frequently toward the end, until the vegetables are golden brown, 6 to 8 minutes.

2. Add the garlic and curry and cook, stirring, for about 30 seconds. Add the broth and ½ tsp. salt and bring to a simmer over medium-high heat. Reduce the heat to low, cover, and simmer until the vegetables are very tender, 10 to 15 minutes. Add the carrot juice and cilantro.

3. Purée the soup in a blender, working in two batches and making sure to vent the blender by removing the pop-up center or lifting one edge of the top (drape a towel over the top to keep the soup from leaking).

4. Return the soup to the pan, heat through, and season to taste with salt and pepper. If necessary, add more carrot juice to thin to your liking. Ladle into bowls and serve, sprinkled with the peanuts, if using.
—*Pam Anderson*

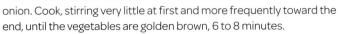

PER SERVING: 140 CALORIES | 4G PROTEIN | 21G CARB | 6G TOTAL FAT | 1G SAT FAT | 2.5G MONO FAT | 2.5G POLY FAT | 0MG CHOL | 230MG SODIUM | 4G FIBER

curried lentil soup

YIELDS ABOUT 1 QUART;
SERVES 4

- **1 large clove garlic**
- **1 piece (⅓ inch long) peeled fresh ginger**
- **½ small bulb fennel, cored and cut into large chunks, or 1 small rib celery, cut into large chunks**
- **1 small carrot, peeled and cut into large chunks**
- **1 small parsnip, peeled and cut into large chunks**
- **1 large shallot, cut in half**
- **3 Tbs. unsalted butter**
- **2 tsp. curry powder**
- **1 cup brown lentils, picked over and rinsed**
- **1 quart homemade or lower-salt canned chicken or vegetable broth**
- **Kosher salt**
- **Freshly ground black pepper**

Garnish with a dollop of plain whole-milk yogurt and chopped fresh mint or cilantro, or both.

1. Pulse the garlic and ginger in a food processor until chopped. Add the fennel or celery, carrot, parsnip, and shallot and pulse until coarsely chopped.

2. Melt 2 Tbs. of the butter in a 4-quart saucepan over medium-high heat. Add the chopped vegetables and cook, stirring, until softened, about 3 minutes. Add the curry powder and cook, stirring, until the curry powder is fragrant, about 30 seconds. Add the lentils, broth, ¼ tsp. salt, and ¼ tsp. pepper. Bring the soup to a boil over high heat, reduce the heat to maintain a brisk simmer, cover, and cook until the lentils are tender, 25 to 30 minutes.

3. Transfer 1½ cups of the soup to a blender or a food processor and purée until smooth. Stir the purée back into the soup along with the remaining 1 Tbs. butter. Season to taste with salt and pepper, and adjust the consistency with water, if you like. *—Allison Ehri Kreitler*

PER SERVING: 330 CALORIES | 19G PROTEIN | 43G CARB | 11G TOTAL FAT | 6G SAT FAT | 3G MONO FAT | 1G POLY FAT | 25MG CHOL | 320MG SODIUM | 14G FIBER

winter vegetable soup with coconut milk and pear

YIELDS ABOUT 8 CUPS;
SERVES 6

Tossing pears into the mix of vegetables adds another layer of flavor and a wonderful texture.

3	Tbs. unsalted butter
1½	cups thinly sliced onion
1	cup medium-diced carrot
1	cup medium-diced parsnip
1	cup medium-diced turnip
1	cup medium-diced parsley root or celery root
½	cup finely chopped inner celery stalks with leaves
1	cup thinly sliced Savoy cabbage
1	Tbs. peeled, minced fresh ginger
1	tsp. fresh thyme leaves; more leaves lightly chopped for garnish
1	medium clove garlic, finely chopped
	Kosher salt and freshly ground black pepper
1	13½- or 14-oz. can coconut milk (do not shake)
2	cups lower-salt chicken broth; more as needed
3½	cups ½-inch-diced butternut squash (from a 2-lb. squash)
2	medium firm-ripe Bosc pears, peeled, cored, and cut into ½-inch pieces (1¼ cups)

1. Melt the butter in a 5- to 6-quart Dutch oven over medium heat. Stir in the onion, carrot, parsnip, turnip, parsley or celery root, and celery and cook, stirring occasionally, until the vegetables begin to soften, about 8 minutes. Stir in the cabbage, ginger, thyme, garlic, ¾ tsp. salt, and ¼ tsp. pepper and cook, stirring occasionally, until the cabbage begins to soften, about 3 minutes.

2. Scoop ¼ cup of coconut cream from the top of the can and set it aside in a small bowl at room temperature. Add the remaining coconut milk, broth, squash, and pears to the vegetables. Bring the mixture just to a boil over medium heat, stirring to scrape up any browned bits. Reduce the heat to low, cover, and cook at a bare simmer, stirring occasionally, until the squash is very soft, 20 minutes.

3. Purée with an immersion blender in the Dutch oven or in batches in a regular blender. Pour the soup through a large coarse strainer set over a large glass measure or bowl. If the soup is too thick, add more chicken broth until thinned to your liking. Season to taste with salt and pepper.

4. If necessary, reheat the soup in a clean pot. Ladle the soup into bowls, drizzle with the reserved coconut cream, and sprinkle with the lightly chopped thyme. —*Lori Longbotham*

PER SERVING: 220 CALORIES | 4G PROTEIN | 23G CARB | 15G TOTAL FAT | 12G SAT FAT | 1.5G MONO FAT | 0.4G POLY FAT | 10MG CHOL | 310MG SODIUM | 6G FIBER

What's the Difference between Coconut Water, Coconut Milk & Coconut Cream?

At 4 months old, the young coconut (also called a jelly or green coconut) contains a delicate, clear, slightly sweet liquid called coconut water. Coconut milk, however, is white and thick and is made by blending grated mature coconut with hot water and then straining the liquid. (Reduced-fat, or "lite," coconut milk is just regular canned coconut milk with water added.) Coconut cream is the thick substance that floats to the top of the coconut milk and may be spooned off.

noodle soup with kale and white beans

SERVES 6

- 2 Tbs. extra-virgin olive oil
- 3 medium carrots, peeled and chopped
- 1 medium red onion, chopped
- 1 cup broken (2- to 3-inch pieces) dried capellini pasta
- 2 quarts lower-salt chicken broth
- 1 small bunch kale, ribs removed, leaves roughly chopped (about 6 cups)
- 1 15-oz. can cannellini beans, rinsed and drained
- 3 Tbs. fresh lime juice; more to taste

  Kosher salt and freshly ground black pepper
- ¼ cup coarsely chopped fresh cilantro

If you can find fideo noodles in the Latin section of your supermarket, try them in place of the capellini.

1. Heat 1 Tbs. of the oil in a large pot over medium-high heat. Add the carrots and onion and cook, stirring occasionally, until the onion is soft and just golden brown, about 10 minutes. With a rubber spatula, scrape the vegetables into a medium bowl and set aside. If necessary, wipe the pot clean.

2. Heat the remaining 1 Tbs. oil in the pot over medium-high heat. Add the pasta and cook, stirring often, until dark golden brown, 3 to 4 minutes. Add the broth and stir, scraping the bottom of the pot to release any stuck-on pasta. Add the carrots and onion, kale, beans, lime juice, ½ tsp. salt, and ¼ tsp. pepper and bring to a boil. Reduce the heat to medium low and simmer until the kale, carrots, and pasta are tender, 8 to 10 minutes.

3. Remove the pot from the heat, stir in the cilantro, and season to taste with lime juice, salt, and pepper before serving. —*Liz Pearson*

PER SERVING: 200 CALORIES | 11G PROTEIN | 29G CARB | 6G TOTAL FAT | 1G SAT FAT | 3G MONO FAT | 1G POLY FAT | 0MG CHOL | 230MG SODIUM | 4G FIBER

spicy sausage, escarole & white bean stew

SERVES 4

- **1** Tbs. extra-virgin olive oil
- **1** medium yellow onion, chopped
- **¾** lb. hot Italian sausage, casings removed
- **2** medium cloves garlic, minced
- **2** 15-oz. cans cannellini beans, rinsed and drained
- **1** small head escarole, chopped into 1- to 2-inch pieces, washed, and lightly dried
- **1** cup lower-salt canned chicken broth
- **1½** tsp. red-wine vinegar; more to taste
  Kosher salt
- **¼** cup freshly grated Parmigiano-Reggiano

Toasted bread rubbed with garlic and drizzled with olive oil makes a nice accompaniment.

1. Heat the oil in a heavy 5- to 6-quart Dutch oven over medium heat. Add the onion and cook, stirring occasionally, until tender, 5 to 6 minutes. Add the sausage, raise the heat to medium high, and cook, stirring and breaking up the sausage with a wooden spoon or spatula until lightly browned and broken into small (1-inch) pieces, 5 to 6 minutes. Add the garlic and cook for 1 minute, then stir in the beans. Add the escarole to the pot in batches; using tongs, toss with the sausage mixture to wilt the escarole and make room for more.

2. When all the escarole is in, add the chicken broth, cover the pot, and cook until the beans are heated through and the escarole is tender, about 8 minutes. Season to taste with the vinegar and salt. Transfer to bowls and sprinkle each portion with some of the Parmigiano.
—*Joanne McAllister Smart*

PER SERVING: 390 CALORIES | 20G PROTEIN | 40G CARB | 17G TOTAL FAT | 5G SAT FAT | 8G MONO FAT | 3G POLY FAT | 25MG CHOL | 1,070MG SODIUM | 13G FIBER

black bean soup with sherry

SERVES 4

- 3   Tbs. extra-virgin olive oil
- 1   large yellow onion, finely chopped
- 1   medium green bell pepper, stemmed, seeded, and finely chopped
- 3   medium cloves garlic, finely chopped
- 2   cups lower-salt chicken broth
- 2   15½-oz. cans black beans, including liquid
- 1   tsp. ground cumin
- 1   tsp. dried oregano
- 1   Tbs. tomato paste
- ¼   cup dry sherry, preferably fino

    Kosher salt and freshly ground black pepper

Dry sherry gives this soup an extra boost of flavor. A garnish of queso fresco and chopped tomatoes adds color.

1. Heat the oil in a 4- to 5-quart heavy-duty pot over medium heat. Add the onion, green pepper, and garlic and cook, stirring occasionally, until tender, about 5 minutes.

2. Meanwhile, purée the chicken broth with one can of black beans and bean liquid in a blender.

3. Add the cumin and oregano to the pot and cook, stirring, for 1 minute. Add the tomato paste and cook, stirring, for 1 minute more. Stir in the black bean purée and the remaining whole beans with their liquid; bring to a boil over high heat. Reduce the heat to low, partially cover the pot, and simmer, stirring frequently, until the flavors are melded, about 10 minutes. Stir in the sherry and season to taste with salt and pepper. —*Shelley Wiseman*

PER SERVING: 310 CALORIES | 13G PROTEIN | 40G CARB | 11G TOTAL FAT | 1.5G SAT FAT | 8G MONO FAT | 1.5G POLY FAT | 0MG CHOL | 440MG SODIUM | 10G FIBER

chicken soup with lime and hominy

SERVES 4

- 12 oz. boneless, skinless chicken breasts
- 1 Tbs. vegetable oil
- 1 small white onion (8 oz.), chopped
- 4 medium cloves garlic, minced
- 1 small jalapeño, minced
- 1 quart lower-salt chicken broth
- 1 15-oz. can hominy, drained
- 1 tsp. dried Mexican oregano, crumbled if the leaves are large
- 4 to 5 Tbs. fresh lime juice
- Kosher salt and freshly ground black pepper
- 2½ oz. Cotija or feta, cut into ¼-inch cubes (½ cup)

This is a quick and easy version of sopa de lima, a comforting yet refreshing Yucatan chicken soup made tangy with fresh lime juice. Tasty garnishes include fried tortilla strips (or tortilla chips), diced avocado, and fresh cilantro.

1. Cut each chicken breast crosswise into 1½-inch-wide pieces.

2. Heat the oil in a 6-quart pot over medium-high heat until shimmering. Add the onion and cook, stirring often, until softened, about 5 minutes. Stir in the garlic and jalapeño and cook, stirring often, until fragrant, about 45 seconds. Add the broth, hominy, oregano, and chicken. Raise the heat to high and bring to a boil. Reduce the heat to medium, cover, and simmer gently, stirring occasionally and adjusting the heat as needed to maintain a simmer, until the chicken is cooked through, about 10 minutes.

3. Transfer the chicken to a plate. Using two forks, shred the meat into bite-size pieces and return to the pot. Bring the soup back to a simmer over medium heat, stir in the lime juice, and season to taste with salt and pepper. Ladle into bowls, top with the cheese, and serve immediately. *—Dawn Yanagihara*

PER SERVING: 680 CALORIES | 29G PROTEIN | 27G CARB | 12G TOTAL FAT | 4G SAT FAT | 4G MONO FAT | 3G POLY FAT | 65MG CHOL | 680MG SODIUM | 4G FIBER

summer corn chowder with scallions, bacon & potatoes

**YIELDS ABOUT 5½ CUPS;
SERVES 6**

- **5   ears fresh corn**
- **7   oz. scallions
    (about 20 medium)**
- **3   slices bacon, cut into
    ½-inch pieces**
- **1   Tbs. unsalted butter**
- **1   jalapeño, cored, seeded,
    and finely diced**
- **Kosher salt**
- **Freshly ground black pepper**
- **3½   cups lower-salt chicken
    broth**
- **1   large Yukon Gold potato
    (8 to 9 oz.), peeled and
    cut into ½-inch dice
    (about 1½ cups)**
- **1½   tsp. chopped fresh thyme**
- **2   Tbs. heavy cream**

This quick, satisfying soup uses the cobs to infuse even more corn flavor into the broth.

1. Husk the corn and cut off the kernels. Reserve two of the corn cobs and discard the others. Trim and thinly slice the scallions, keeping the dark green parts separate from the white and light green parts.

2. Cook the bacon in a 3- or 4-quart saucepan over medium heat until browned and crisp, about 5 minutes. With a slotted spoon, transfer the bacon to a paper-towel-lined plate. Pour off and discard all but about 1 Tbs. of the bacon fat. Return the pan to medium heat and add the butter. When the butter is melted, add the white and light green scallions and the jalapeño, 1 tsp. salt, and a few grinds of black pepper. Cook, stirring, until the scallions are very soft, about 3 minutes.

3. Add the broth, corn, corn cobs, potatoes, and thyme and bring to a boil over medium-high heat. Reduce the heat to medium low and simmer until the potatoes are completely tender, about 15 minutes. Discard the corn cobs.

4. Transfer 1 cup of the broth and vegetables to a blender and purée. Return the purée to the pot and stir in the cream and all but ⅓ cup of the scallion greens. Simmer, stirring occasionally, for a couple of minutes to wilt the scallions and blend the flavors. Season to taste with salt and pepper and serve sprinkled with the bacon and reserved scallions.   —*Tony Rosenfeld*

PER SERVING: 180 CALORIES | 8G PROTEIN | 25G CARB | 7G TOTAL FAT | 3G SAT FAT | 2.5G MONO FAT | 1G POLY FAT | 15MG CHOL | 320MG SODIUM | 3G FIBER

how to cut corn off the cob

Removing corn kernels from the cob can be messy—they like to bounce off the cutting board and end up scattered all over the counter and floor. To keep those kernels in their place, insert the tip of the ear of corn into the center hole of a bundt pan. Cut the kernels away from the cob in long downward strokes, letting them fall into the pan.

More about Sweet Corn

There are four types of sweet corn: standard sweet, sugar-enhanced, supersweet, and synergistic. You won't see these agricultural terms used at grocery stores or even at farmers' markets, but they help to explain the differences among them in terms of sweetness, tenderness, and how well they store.

If you really want to know what type of corn you're buying, ask the farmer. Just be prepared to try something new each time. The corn variety you saw on your last visit is probably not the same one you're going to find on your next. In general, the more sugary varieties of corn take longer to grow and appear later at the market.

TYPES OF SWEET CORN
Standard sweet
Common varieties include Butter and Sugar, with white and yellow kernels, and Silver Queen, with white kernels. This type of corn has a traditional corn flavor and texture, although sweetness varies among varieties. Its sugars are quicker to convert to starch, so it doesn't keep long after harvest.

Sugar-enhanced
Delectable, Kandy Korn, and Seneca Dancer are three popular varieties. Known for having a more tender texture than the standard type, sugar-enhanced corn is widely popular. Its degree of sweetness changes with the variety, but the conversion of sugar to starch is slower than that of standard sweet corn, so it holds up better.

Supersweet
Varieties include Sun & Stars and Xtra-Sweet. The most sugary of all, this type of corn has less true corn flavor and a firmer, almost crunchy texture, because the skin on the kernels is tougher. It holds its sweetness longer than any other type of corn, which is why you'll often see it in supermarkets, where the corn isn't typically freshly picked.

Synergistic
A popular variety is Serendipity. This type has both the tenderness of sugar-enhanced corn and the more pronounced sweetness of supersweet. It requires more time to mature than sugar-enhanced corn and can be watery if harvested too soon.

CHOOSING CORN
Farmers' markets and roadside stands are your best bet for finding fresh and delicious corn. Look for plump, green ears that have fresh-looking cuts at their stems and slightly sticky brown silk at the top. If the supermarket is your only option, adopt a more hands-on approach: Pull back the husks and inspect the kernels. They should be firm and shiny. When buying corn, there's only one absolute rule: Never buy shucked corn. This trick hides the evidence of old corn.

STORING CORN
If you're not going to cook your corn the day you buy it, stow the ears in the refrigerator, loosely wrapped in a dry plastic bag. Don't shuck it until you're ready to use it.

beef and black bean chili with chipotle and avocado

SERVES 4

- **3** 15-oz. cans black beans, rinsed and drained
- **1** 14½-oz. can diced tomatoes
- **1** medium chipotle plus 2 Tbs. adobo sauce (from a can of chipotles in adobo sauce)
- **2** Tbs. extra-virgin olive oil
- **1** lb. 85% lean ground beef
- Kosher salt
- **1** large red onion, finely diced
- **1½** Tbs. chili powder
- **2** tsp. ground cumin
- **1** lime, juiced
- **½** cup chopped fresh cilantro
- Freshly ground black pepper
- **1** ripe avocado, cut into medium dice

Coarsely crumble about 3 handfuls of tortilla chips in a zip-top bag and use them as an additional chili topping.

1. Put one-third of the beans into the bowl of a food processor, along with the tomatoes and their juices, chipotle, and adobo sauce. Process until smooth and set aside.

2. Heat the oil in a 5- to 6-quart Dutch oven or similar heavy-duty pot over medium-high heat until it's shimmering hot, about 2 minutes. Add the beef, season with ½ tsp. salt, and cook, using a wooden spoon to break up the meat, until it loses its raw color, about 3 minutes. Transfer the beef to a large plate using a slotted spoon. Add half of the onion and ¼ tsp. salt, and cook, stirring, until it begins to brown and soften, about 3 minutes. Reduce the heat to medium. Add the chili powder and cumin and cook for 20 seconds. Add the remaining black beans, the puréed bean mixture, and the beef to the pot and simmer for 10 minutes, stirring frequently. Add half of the lime juice, half of the cilantro, and salt and pepper to taste. If the chili is thicker than you like, thin it with water.

3. Meanwhile, in a small bowl, mix the remaining lime juice and onion with the avocado. Season generously with salt and pepper. Serve the chili topped with the avocado mixture and remaining cilantro.
—*Tony Rosenfeld*

PER SERVING: 670 CALORIES | 42G PROTEIN | 64G CARB | 29G TOTAL FAT | 7G SAT FAT | 17G MONO FAT | 2.5G POLY FAT | 85MG CHOL | 1,070MG SODIUM | 18G FIBER

sausage and white bean stew with tomatoes, thyme & crisp breadcrumbs

SERVES 6

1½   Tbs. unsalted butter

1½   cups fresh breadcrumbs

2   Tbs. coarsely chopped
     fresh thyme leaves

9   sweet Italian sausages

2   Tbs. extra-virgin olive oil

1   medium onion, cut into
     medium dice

3   cloves garlic, minced

1½   cups dry white wine,
     like Sauvignon Blanc

1   14.5-oz. can petite-diced
     tomatoes

3   15.5-oz. cans cannellini
     beans, drained and rinsed

1   cup lower-salt chicken broth

     Kosher salt and freshly
     ground black pepper

You can substitute any type of raw sausage for the Italian sausage; lamb sausage is especially nice.

1. In a 12-inch skillet, melt the butter over medium heat. Add the breadcrumbs and 1 Tbs. of the thyme and cook, stirring frequently, until the breadcrumbs are golden, about 3 minutes. Transfer to a bowl to cool. Wipe out the skillet.

2. Using a small, sharp knife, pierce each sausage in 3 or 4 places. Heat 1 Tbs. of the oil in the skillet over medium heat. Add the sausages and cook, turning occasionally, until cooked through and golden brown on all sides, 15 to 20 minutes. Transfer the sausages to a cutting board and tent with foil to keep warm.

3. While the sausages cook, heat the remaining 1 Tbs. oil in a deep, 10- to 11-inch-wide pot over medium heat. Add the onion and cook, stirring, until softened, about 5 minutes. Add the garlic and the remaining 1 Tbs. thyme and cook, stirring, until fragrant, about 1 minute. Add the wine, raise the heat to high, and simmer until reduced by half, about 7 minutes. Add the tomatoes with their juices and cook until very soft and about a quarter of the liquid has evaporated, about 5 minutes. Add the beans and broth.

4. Bring to a simmer and cook, uncovered, for about 10 minutes to blend the flavors. Using a potato masher, gently crush some of the stew with 4 to 5 strokes, or just enough to thicken it a bit. Season to taste with salt and pepper.

5. Cut the sausages in half on the diagonal. Ladle the stew into wide, deep bowls, arrange the sausages on the stew, and top with the breadcrumbs. *—Pam Anderson*

PER SERVING: 530 CALORIES | 31G PROTEIN | 46G CARB | 19G TOTAL FAT | 7G SAT FAT | 9G MONO FAT | 2.5G POLY FAT | 2.5MG CHOL | 1,490MG SODIUM | 9G FIBER

shrimp stew with coconut milk, tomatoes & cilantro

- **3** lb. jumbo (21 to 25 per lb.) shrimp, peeled and deveined

  Kosher salt

- **2** Tbs. extra-virgin olive oil

- **1** large red bell pepper, sliced into very thin 1½-inch-long strips

- **4** scallions, thinly sliced (white and green parts kept separate)

- **½** cup chopped fresh cilantro

- **4** large cloves garlic, finely chopped

- **½** to 1 tsp. crushed red pepper flakes

- **1** 14.5-oz. can petite-diced tomatoes, drained

- **1** 13.5- or 14-oz. can coconut milk

- **2** Tbs. fresh lime juice

The full teaspoon of red pepper flakes will give this stew a little kick. Start with ½ tsp. and taste before adding the full amount.

1. In a large bowl, sprinkle the shrimp with 1 tsp. salt; toss to coat, and set aside.

2. Heat the oil in a 5- to 6-quart Dutch oven over medium-high heat. Add the bell pepper and cook, stirring, until almost tender, about 4 minutes. Add the scallion whites, ¼ cup of the cilantro, the garlic, and the pepper flakes. Continue to cook, stirring, until fragrant, 30 to 60 seconds.

3. Add the tomatoes and coconut milk and bring to a simmer. Reduce the heat to medium and simmer to blend the flavors and thicken the sauce slightly, about 5 minutes.

4. Add the shrimp and continue to cook, partially covered and stirring frequently, until the shrimp are just cooked through, about 5 minutes more. Add the lime juice and season to taste with salt. Serve sprinkled with the scallion greens and remaining ¼ cup cilantro.

—Pam Anderson

PER SERVING: 270 CALORIES | 29G PROTEIN | 6G CARB | 15G TOTAL FAT | 10G SAT FAT | 3G MONO FAT | 1G POLY FAT | 250MG CHOL | 580MG SODIUM | 1G FIBER

quick chicken chili

SERVES 6 TO 8

- 2 Tbs. vegetable oil
- 1 large onion, cut into medium dice
- 2 Tbs. ground cumin
- 2 tsp. dried oregano
- 3 medium cloves garlic, minced
- 1 3½- to 4-lb. store-bought rotisserie chicken, meat removed and chopped
- 1 jar or can (about 4 oz.) diced mild green chiles, drained
- 1 quart lower-salt chicken broth
- 2 15.5-oz. cans white beans, drained
- 1 cup frozen corn

Store-bought rotisserie chicken makes this tasty chili come together fast (perfect for busy weeknights). You can also substitute leftover roasted chicken if you have it.

1. Heat the oil over medium-high heat in a 5- to 6-quart Dutch oven. Add the onion and cook, stirring, until tender, 4 to 5 minutes. Add the cumin, oregano, and garlic and cook until fragrant, about 1 minute longer. Stir in the chicken and chiles and then add the broth and 1 can of beans. Bring to a simmer. Reduce the heat to low and simmer, partially covered and stirring occasionally, until the flavors blend, about 20 minutes.

2. Meanwhile, purée the remaining can of beans in a food processor. Stir the puréed beans into the chicken mixture along with the corn. Continue to simmer to blend the flavors, about 5 minutes longer. Ladle into bowls and serve. *—Pam Anderson*

PER SERVING: 590 CALORIES | 69G PROTEIN | 32G CARB | 20G TOTAL FAT | 5G SAT FAT | 7G MONO FAT | 5G POLY FAT | 175MG CHOL | 270MG SODIUM | 7G FIBER

> Serve the chili with any combination of the following: tortilla or corn chips, shredded sharp cheese, thinly sliced scallions, cilantro leaves, sliced pickled jalapeño chiles, red or green hot sauce, sour cream, guacamole, red or green salsa, and lime wedges.

shrimp salad rolls with
tarragon and chives
(recipe on p. 213)

burgers, sandwiches & more

salmon burgers with herb aïoli

SERVES 4

2 small cloves garlic

Kosher salt

1½ cups mayonnaise

⅓ cup finely chopped fresh chives

2 Tbs. finely chopped fresh dill

½ Tbs. Dijon mustard

1 Tbs. fresh lemon juice

⅛ tsp. cayenne

Freshly ground black pepper

5 brioche or hamburger buns, 1 cut into large cubes, the other 4 split

1 lb. skinless salmon fillets, preferably wild, pin bones removed, cut into 1-inch pieces (about 2 cups)

2 oz. (4 Tbs.) unsalted butter

Ask your fishmonger to remove the pin bones from the salmon, or do it yourself with a pair of small tweezers or pliers. Ripe tomato slices sprinkled with salt and pepper would be a colorful addition to these burgers.

1. Chop the garlic. Using the flat side of a chef's knife, mash the garlic to a paste with a pinch of salt. Transfer the garlic paste to a small bowl and stir in the mayonnaise, chives, dill, mustard, lemon juice, cayenne, ¼ tsp. pepper, and salt to taste. Set the aïoli aside.

2. In a food processor, pulse the cubed bun into crumbs. Set aside ½ cup of the crumbs and save the rest for another use. Pulse the salmon until coarsely chopped, about 5 pulses. Transfer the salmon to a medium bowl and stir in ¾ cup of the aïoli, the reserved breadcrumbs, ¼ tsp. salt, and ⅛ tsp. pepper. Shape into four 1-inch-thick patties.

3. Heat 2 Tbs. of the butter in a 12-inch nonstick skillet over medium-high heat. When melted and hot (but not smoking or brown), add the patties and cook until they are firm and each side is crisp and golden brown, 3 to 5 minutes per side.

4. Meanwhile, position a rack 6 inches from the broiler and heat the broiler on high. Melt the remaining 2 Tbs. butter in a microwave or on the stovetop. Brush it on the insides of the split buns. Put the buns on a baking sheet, butter side up, and toast under the broiler until light golden brown, 1 to 2 minutes.

5. Serve the burgers on the buns, spread with the remaining aïoli.
—*Dina Cheney*

PER SERVING: 870 CALORIES | 35G PROTEIN | 55G CARB | 53G TOTAL FAT | 22G SAT FAT | 8G MONO FAT | 12G POLY FAT | 265MG CHOL | 1,140MG SODIUM | 1G FIBER

grilled mozzarella and spinach blts

SERVES 4

- **12** slices thick-cut bacon
- **1** medium clove garlic, finely chopped
- **3** cups lightly packed baby spinach

  Kosher salt and freshly ground black pepper
- **8** slices country-style white bread
- **8** oz. fresh mozzarella, sliced
- **1** large tomato (about 8 oz.), cored and thinly sliced
- **1** Tbs. extra-virgin olive oil

Creamy mozzarella is a good foil for the salty, smoky bacon in this grilled version of a BLT. Before cooking, remove any tough stems from the spinach.

1. Working in batches, cook the bacon in a 12-inch skillet over medium heat until crisp, about 8 minutes per batch. Transfer to a paper-towel-lined plate and drain off all but 1 Tbs. of the fat. Return the pan to medium heat, add the garlic, and cook until fragrant, about 30 seconds. Stir in the spinach and cook until just wilted, about 30 seconds longer. Season to taste with salt and pepper.

2. Heat a panini or sandwich press according to the manufacturer's instructions. (Alternatively, heat a nonstick grill pan over medium-high heat.)

3. While the press is heating, arrange the spinach on 4 pieces of the bread. Top each with some bacon, mozzarella, and tomato, sprinkle lightly with salt, and complete each sandwich with a slice of the remaining bread. Brush both sides of the sandwiches with the oil.

4. Put the sandwiches on the press, pull the top down, and cook until browned and crisp and the cheese is melted, 3 to 6 minutes, depending on how hot your machine is. (If using a grill pan, put a heavy pan on top of the sandwiches and cook, turning the sandwiches over once.) Carefully remove from the press and serve. —*Lauren Chattman*

PER SERVING: 570 CALORIES | 29G PROTEIN | 46G CARB | 29G TOTAL FAT | 12G SAT FAT | 11G MONO FAT | 2G POLY FAT | 70MG CHOL | 1,510MG SODIUM | 5G FIBER

bison burgers with thousand island barbecue dressing

SERVES 4

- ¼ **cup mayonnaise**
- 1 **Tbs. chili sauce, such as Heinz®**
- 4 **tsp. smoky barbecue sauce**
- 1 **tsp. sweet pickle relish**
- ¼ **tsp. Worcestershire sauce**
- 1½ **lb. ground bison**
- 1¼ **tsp. kosher salt**
- ¾ **tsp. freshly ground black pepper**
   Oil for the grill
- 4 **rolls or hamburger buns, split**
- 4 **leaves iceberg lettuce**
- 1 **large vine-ripened tomato, preferably heirloom, sliced**

Bison (buffalo) meat is a great substitute for beef—it's just as flavorful but much leaner.

1. Prepare a medium-high gas or charcoal grill fire.

2. Mix the mayonnaise, chili sauce, 2 tsp. of the barbecue sauce, sweet pickle relish, and Worcestershire sauce in a small bowl. Set aside.

3. In a medium bowl, use your hands to gently mix the bison with the remaining 2 tsp. barbecue sauce, the salt and pepper. Form into four ½- to ¾-inch-thick patties.

4. Lightly oil the grill grate and place the patties on the grate. Cover and grill for 4 to 5 minutes. Flip the burgers, cover, and cook to desired doneness, about 5 minutes for medium (130°F to 135°F on an instant-read thermometer).

5. While the burgers cook, toast the rolls on the grill. Spread some of the dressing on each half of the roll and arrange a lettuce leaf and a slice or two of tomato on the top halves. When the burgers are done, put them on the bottom halves. Assemble the sandwiches, cut in half if you like, and serve.   —*Bruce Aidells*

PER SERVING: 570 CALORIES | 30G PROTEIN | 36G CARB | 34G TOTAL FAT | 11G SAT FAT | 11G MONO FAT | 8G POLY FAT | 95MG CHOL | 940MG SODIUM | 2G FIBER

More about Buffalo Meat

The meat of the iconic animal of the American West, no-longer-endangered bison has become a leaner beef alternative for health-conscious cooks.

Since bison tends to be raised on grass-based feed more than grain-based feed, it has many of the qualities of grass-fed beef: a deeper red color, a stronger "meaty" flavor, and lower fat content (2.42 grams of fat in a 3.5-oz. serving of bison compared to 18.54 grams in choice beef).

Bison is available in many specialty and natural-foods stores. You may see it sold as steaks or ground.

As with grass-fed beef, take care not to overcook bison. Because it is leaner than regular beef, it can quickly become dry if overcooked.

chicken burgers with red cabbage and apple slaw

SERVES 4

- 1 lb. ground chicken (not chicken breast)
- 1½ cups small-diced peeled Granny Smith apple (about 1 large)
- ½ cup small-diced red onion (about ½ medium)
- ¼ cup small-diced celery (about ½ stalk)
- 5 Tbs. mayonnaise
- 2 tsp. Dijon mustard
- 2 tsp. minced garlic
- ⅛ tsp. kosher salt
- ⅛ tsp. freshly ground black pepper
- 2 Tbs. vegetable oil
- 1 tsp. fresh lime juice; more as needed
- 1½ cups packed thinly sliced red cabbage
- 4 challah rolls or hamburger buns, split and toasted

> Mixing mayonnaise with the chicken makes these burgers juicy. To keep them from getting tough, be gentle when shaping the patties.

For a fresh take on a burger, give these chicken patties a try. Apples and celery mixed into the ground chicken give the burgers a subtly sweet, aromatic note, while the bright, creamy slaw provides great crunch.

1. In a medium bowl, combine the chicken with ½ cup of the apple, the onion, celery, 2 Tbs. of the mayonnaise, 1 tsp. of the mustard, the garlic, ½ tsp. salt, and ¼ tsp. pepper. Gently mix with your hands and form four ½-inch-thick patties. Make an indentation in the center of each one with your thumb.

2. In a 12-inch nonstick skillet, heat the vegetable oil over medium heat until shimmering hot. Cook the burgers until golden brown on one side, about 5 minutes. Flip, and continue cooking until the internal temperature reaches 165°F on an instant-read thermometer, 5 to 9 minutes more.

3. Meanwhile, in a medium bowl, mix the remaining 3 Tbs. mayonnaise and 1 tsp. mustard with the lime juice. Add the remaining apple, the cabbage, salt, and pepper; toss to combine. Season to taste with more lime juice, salt, and pepper.

4. Serve the burgers in the rolls, topped with the slaw. *—Dina Cheney*

PER SERVING: 560 CALORIES | 27G PROTEIN | 38G CARB | 34G TOTAL FAT | 6G SAT FAT | 12G MONO FAT | 13G POLY FAT | 190MG CHOL | 650MG SODIUM | 1G FIBER

middle eastern turkey burgers

1½ lb. ground turkey, preferably including some dark meat (93% lean)

2 medium cloves garlic

1½ tsp. kosher salt

¼ cup lightly packed chopped fresh mint

¼ cup lightly packed chopped fresh parsley

2 Tbs. olive oil

2 tsp. sweet paprika

1 tsp. ground cumin

½ tsp. ground coriander

¼ tsp. cayenne

Cucumber and Yogurt Sauce (recipe on the facing page)

Forget the buns and instead pick up some pita bread to serve with these burgers.

1. Gently break the meat into large pieces in a large bowl. Mince the garlic, sprinkle with the salt, and using the flat side of a chef's knife, smear and mash to a paste. Gently mix the garlic paste, mint, parsley, olive oil, paprika, cumin, coriander, and cayenne into the turkey. Shape the meat into 4 equal 1-inch-thick patties. Refrigerate, uncovered, for at least 20 minutes and up to 4 hours.

2. Prepare a medium charcoal or gas grill fire. Grill the burgers, covered with vents open, until nicely marked and just cooked through (an instant-read thermometer inserted in a burger should read 165°F), 4 to 6 minutes per side.

3. Serve with the Cucumber and Yogurt Sauce. *—John Ash*

PER SERVING: 400 CALORIES | 36G PROTEIN | 4G CARB | 26G TOTAL FAT | 7G SAT FAT | 11G MONO FAT | 5G POLY FAT | 130MG CHOL | 840MG SODIUM | 1G FIBER

More about paprika

Paprika is a spice made from dried ground chiles. All paprikas are made from the same family of peppers. Different varieties within this family account for the unique flavors and degrees of spicy heat found in different paprikas. Where and how it was made also add to the nuances of flavor. Most paprikas come from Hungary or Spain.

Hungarian paprika is available in several heat levels and grinds, including special, mild, delikatess, semisweet, sweet, and hot, but only the latter two are commonly found in the United States. Hungarian paprika is especially good in rich dishes with sour cream, potatoes, egg noodles, cabbage, or meat. It can be used generously—think tablespoons.

Spanish paprika, or pimentón, differs from Hungarian paprika in that the chiles are dried over smoldering oak logs, giving them a smoky flavor. It comes in three heat levels: dulce, agridulce, and picante (sweet, bittersweet, and hot). It's delicious wherever you'd like a smoky flavor, but remember that smokiness can easily overwhelm a dish, so start experimenting by using only ¼ to ½ teaspoon.

Both Spanish and Hungarian paprika are generally better than the generic paprika found in supermarkets. Spanish smoked paprika (preferably pimentón de la Vera) is mostly available in specialty groceries, but you should have no trouble finding Hungarian paprika in many supermarkets.

cucumber and yogurt sauce

YIELDS ABOUT 1 CUP

½ cup peeled, seeded, and finely diced English cucumber

2 Tbs. finely chopped red onion

Kosher salt

½ cup plain whole-milk or low-fat yogurt, preferably Greek

2 Tbs. finely chopped fresh cilantro

Pinch of sugar

Pinch of cayenne or Aleppo pepper; more to taste

This sauce can be made several hours ahead and stored in the refrigerator.

Combine the cucumber, onion, and 1 tsp. salt in a bowl. Let sit at room temperature for at least 20 minutes. Drain off the liquid and rinse to remove excess salt. Drain well and taste a few pieces; if it's too salty, rinse and drain again. In a small bowl, combine the cucumber and onion with the yogurt, cilantro, sugar, and cayenne or Aleppo pepper. Let sit for 30 minutes for the flavors to develop. Season to taste with salt and cayenne.

grilled lamb burgers with marinated red onions, dill & sliced feta

SERVES 4

- 1¼ lb. ground lamb
- 2 tsp. sweet paprika
- 2 tsp. dried oregano
- 1 small clove garlic, minced and mashed to a paste
- 1½ tsp. kosher salt
- 6 oz. feta, cut into ¼-inch-thick slices (about 8)
- 2 Tbs. extra-virgin olive oil
- 2 Tbs. chopped fresh dill
- ½ small red onion, thinly sliced
- 3 Tbs. red-wine vinegar
- 1 tsp. granulated sugar
- 4 whole-wheat pita bread, warmed
- 4 thin slices tomato
- 8 thin slices English cucumber

When you tire of the basic burger, this Mediterranean-inspired version is just the ticket. The quick-pickled red onions add dimension and are a great addition to cucumber, tomato, and pasta salads. To keep with the Greek theme, serve the burgers in warm pita bread, though whole-wheat hamburger buns would work, too.

1. Prepare a medium charcoal or gas grill fire. Clean and oil the grill grates. Gently mix the lamb with the paprika, oregano, garlic, and 1 tsp. salt. Form into four ½-inch-thick patties.

2. On a large plate, lay out the slices of feta and sprinkle with the olive oil and 1 Tbs. of the dill. In a small bowl, toss the onion with the vinegar, sugar, ½ tsp. salt, and the remaining 1 Tbs. dill, and let sit for 10 to 15 minutes at room temperature.

3. Grill the burgers on one side until they have good grill marks, about 5 minutes. Flip and cook the other side until it has good grill marks, too, and the burgers are just light pink inside (make a nick with a paring knife), about 5 minutes for medium doneness.

4. Serve the burgers in the warmed pita with the feta, tomato, cucumber, and a heaping teaspoon of pickled onions. —*Tony Rosenfeld*

Feta is best stored in the salty brine it is sometimes packed in. Once opened, it will keep in the refrigerator for at least a week. If the cheese is not in brine, mix 1 cup water with ¼ cup kosher salt to make a quick brine, and refrigerate in an airtight container.

shrimp salad rolls with tarragon and chives

SERVES 6

Kosher salt

2 lb. large shrimp (31 to 40 per lb.), preferably easy-peel

¾ cup finely chopped celery with leaves

½ cup mayonnaise

¼ cup thinly sliced fresh chives

1 Tbs. finely chopped fresh tarragon

1 Tbs. fresh lemon juice; more to taste

Freshly ground black pepper

6 hot dog rolls, preferably New England-style split-top rolls

Full of bright flavors, the shrimp salad is delicious without a roll, too. If you're really in a hurry, you can use precooked shrimp.

1. Bring a large pot of well-salted water to a boil over high heat. Add the shrimp and cook, stirring, until bright pink and cooked through, about 2 minutes—the water needn't return to a boil. Drain in a colander and run under cold water to stop the cooking. Shell the shrimp, devein if necessary, and cut into ½- to ¾-inch pieces.

2. In a large bowl, stir the celery, mayonnaise, chives, tarragon, lemon juice, ¼ tsp. salt, and ¼ tsp. pepper. Stir in the shrimp and season to taste with more lemon, salt, and pepper.

3. Position a rack 6 inches from the broiler element and heat the broiler to high. Toast both outside surfaces of the rolls under the broiler, about 1 minute per side. Spoon the shrimp salad into the rolls, using about ⅔ cup per roll, and serve. *—Lori Longbotham*

PER SERVING: 390 CALORIES | 29G PROTEIN | 25G CARB | 18G TOTAL FAT | 3.5G SAT FAT | 1G MONO FAT | 1G POLY FAT | 230MG CHOL | 800MG SODIUM | 1G FIBER

Make Ahead

The shrimp salad will keep for up to 2 days, covered, in the refrigerator.

To make this a lobster roll, substitute 1½ lb. (4 cups) cooked lobster meat for the cooked shrimp.

salade aux lardons pizza

SERVES 4

- **3** Tbs. extra-virgin olive oil; more for the baking sheet

  Flour for shaping the dough

- **¾** lb. pizza dough, at room temperature

- **¼** cup Dijon mustard

- **8** oz. Jarlsberg, grated (2 cups)

- **6** oz. center-cut bacon, cut into 1-inch pieces (2 cups)

- **1** medium shallot, halved lengthwise and thinly sliced crosswise

- **2** cups packed arugula

- **2** cups packed frisée

- **1** Tbs. white-wine vinegar

- **½** tsp. kosher salt

- **½** tsp. freshly ground black pepper

This salad pizza replicates the flavors of a French bistro salad, complete with a shortcut version of lardons (diced bacon that's been blanched and fried). Here, the bacon is simply sautéed and then baked on the pizza.

1. Position a rack in the center of the oven and heat the oven to 475°F.

2. Lightly oil a large rimmed baking sheet. On a lightly floured surface, shape the dough into a 10x14-inch oval, using your fingers or a rolling pin. If the dough resists, let it rest for a few minutes before continuing. Transfer the dough to the baking sheet. Spread the mustard evenly over the crust, leaving a ½-inch border. Top with the cheese and bake until the cheese begins to melt, about 10 minutes.

3. Meanwhile, cook the bacon in a 12-inch nonstick skillet over medium heat until browned and just starting to crisp, about 5 minutes. With a slotted spoon, sprinkle the bacon evenly over the pizza and continue to bake until the pizza is crisp and browned, about 10 minutes.

4. In the same skillet used to cook the bacon, cook the shallot in the bacon fat over medium heat until soft, 2 minutes. With a slotted spoon, transfer to a large bowl and add the arugula and frisée. (Discard the fat.)

5. In a small bowl, whisk the oil, vinegar, salt, and pepper. Pour the dressing over the greens and shallots and toss well.

6. Using a wide spatula, transfer the pizza from the baking sheet to a cutting board. Mound the salad on top, cut into squares or wedges, and serve.   *—Bruce Weinstein and Mark Scarbrough*

PER SERVING: 590 CALORIES | 27G PROTEIN | 49G CARB | 33G TOTAL FAT | 12G SAT FAT | 10G MONO FAT | 2G POLY FAT | 50MG CHOL | 1,710MG SODIUM | 2G FIBER

falafel with tomato-cucumber salad

SERVES 4

- 1 15-oz. can chickpeas, rinsed and drained
- 7 Tbs. extra-virgin olive oil
- 1 tsp. ground cumin
- ½ tsp. ground coriander
- Kosher salt
- ½ tsp. freshly ground black pepper
- 1 medium yellow onion, diced
- ½ cup plain, fine dry bread-crumbs; more as needed
- 1½ cups cherry tomatoes, quartered
- 1 medium pickling cucumber or ⅓ English cucumber, halved and sliced ¼ inch thick
- 1 Tbs. fresh lemon juice
- 4 pitas, warmed

Falafel are usually deep-fried, but pan-searing these chickpea fritters is healthier (and not as messy). Serve them in pita bread, topped with thick yogurt or tahini sauce, if you like.

1. Heat the oven to 425°F.

2. In a food processor, pulse the chickpeas, 2 Tbs. of the oil, the cumin, coriander, 1 tsp. salt, and ½ tsp. black pepper into a chunky paste. Add the onion and breadcrumbs and pulse until the mixture tightens up. You should be able to easily form it into a patty—add more bread-crumbs as needed. Gently form the chickpea mixture into twelve ½-inch-thick patties.

3. Heat 2 Tbs. of the oil in a 10-inch nonstick skillet over medium heat until shimmering hot. Add 6 of the patties and cook until nicely browned, about 2 minutes. Flip and cook the other sides until browned, 1 to 2 minutes more. Transfer the patties to a baking sheet. Repeat with 2 Tbs. more oil and the remaining 6 patties. Bake the patties until heated through, about 5 minutes.

4. Meanwhile, toss the tomatoes and cucumber with the lemon juice, the remaining 1 Tbs. oil, and salt to taste.

5. Split the pitas and stuff them with the falafel and tomato-cucumber salad. —*Tony Rosenfeld*

PER SERVING: 640 CALORIES | 18G PROTEIN | 80G CARB | 28G TOTAL FAT | 4G SAT FAT | 18G MONO FAT | 4.5G POLY FAT | 0MG CHOL | 920MG SODIUM | 12G FIBER

grilled portobello and goat cheese sandwiches with green olive pesto

SERVES 4

- **1 cup tightly packed fresh basil leaves**
- **½ cup pitted green olives, such as manzanilla, coarsely chopped**
- **1 Tbs. walnuts or pine nuts**
- **1 small clove garlic, coarsely chopped**
- **½ cup plus 2 tsp. extra-virgin olive oil**
- **Kosher salt and freshly ground black pepper**
- **8 small to medium portobello mushrooms, stemmed, gills removed, and wiped clean**
- **4 soft round rolls, such as Portuguese or kaiser, split in half**
- **4 oz. fresh goat cheese, crumbled**

The earthy flavor of the portobellos goes well with the mild, tangy goat cheese and salty olive pesto.

1. Heat a panini or sandwich press according to the manufacturer's instructions. (Alternatively, heat a nonstick grill pan over medium-high heat.)

2. While the press is heating, put the basil, olives, nuts, and garlic in a food processor and process until finely chopped. With the motor running, add 6 Tbs. of the olive oil in a slow, steady stream through the feed tube and continue to process until thick and smooth. Season to taste with salt and pepper.

3. Brush the mushrooms with 2 Tbs. of the olive oil and sprinkle with salt and pepper. Put them on the press, pull the top down, and cook until softened and browned, 3 to 5 minutes (or cook in the grill pan, flipping once). Transfer to a plate and let cool slightly.

4. Spread the pesto on the bottom halves of the rolls. Put 2 mushrooms on each and then some cheese. Top the sandwiches with the other halves of the rolls. Brush both sides of the sandwiches with the remaining 2 tsp. oil.

5. Put the sandwiches on the press pesto side up, pull the top down, and cook until browned and crisp and the cheese is melted, 5 to 7 minutes, depending on how hot your machine is. (If using a grill pan, put a heavy pan on top of the sandwiches and cook, turning the sandwiches over once.) Carefully remove from the press and serve.
—*Lauren Chattman*

PER SERVING: 590 CALORIES | 15G PROTEIN | 40G CARB | 42G TOTAL FAT | 9G SAT FAT | 26G MONO FAT | 6G POLY FAT | 15MG CHOL | 1,010MG SODIUM | 4G FIBER

More about Portobello Mushrooms

The word portobello originated as a way to help glamorize and sell mature cremini mushrooms. But if all of this sounds more like Marketing 101 than cooking, know this: Creminis have more flavor than white mushrooms, and portobellos have more flavor still.

The portobello was "discovered," probably by accident, when cremini caps were left to grow, open up, and develop gills. Creminis take about seven weeks to grow to the size at which they're picked. Those that are not picked then mature to become portobellos within 3 to 5 days, often growing to 6 inches across in size. During this growth spurt, the mushroom's gills become fully exposed, causing it to lose moisture. The loss of moisture concentrates the mushroom's flavor and gives it the dense, meaty texture for which it's renowned.

Choosing
Choose firm, plump portobellos with a pleasant, earthy smell. Avoid any that appear limp or dried out. The mushrooms should not be shriveled or slippery, which suggests decomposition.

Prepping
Though you can eat portobellos raw, cooking them makes them tender and intensifies their flavor. These large mushrooms take especially well to searing, grilling, roasting, and braising.

Though most people are concerned only with the meaty caps, you can use all parts of a portobello. The stems, once trimmed and wiped cleaned, can be chopped up to use as you would the stems of cultivated mushrooms. The gills, however, will turn anything you cook dark grayish brown, so it's best to scrape them off. You can also scrape out the gills to make a little more room if you're stuffing the mushrooms. But if you don't want to waste the gills, add these flavorful scrapings to stocks or dark sauces.

soft-shell crab sandwiches with spicy tartar sauce

SERVES 4

FOR THE TARTAR SAUCE

- ½ **cup mayonnaise**
- 1 **Tbs. minced red onion**
- 1 **Tbs. finely chopped dill pickle**
- 1 **Tbs. rinsed and finely chopped capers**
- 1 **Tbs. thinly sliced fresh chives**
- 1½ **tsp. Old Bay® Seasoning**
- 1 **tsp. fresh lemon juice**
- ¼ **tsp. hot pepper sauce, such as Tabasco**

FOR THE CRABS

- ¼ **cup unbleached all-purpose flour**
- ¼ **cup medium-grind yellow cornmeal**
- ½ **tsp. kosher salt**
- ¼ **tsp. freshly ground black pepper**
- 4 **jumbo soft-shell crabs, cleaned (bodies about 5 inches across; 3 to 3½ oz. each after cleaning)**
- 2 **Tbs. canola or vegetable oil**
- 1 **Tbs. unsalted butter**

TO ASSEMBLE

- 8 **slices white sandwich bread, toasted**
- 4 **large leaves bibb lettuce**
- 4 **to 8 slices ripe tomato**

Soft-shell crabs cook in minutes, are easier to eat than hard-shell crabs, and their sweet, briny flavor and crunchy-soft juicy texture can't be beat. Soft-shells are usually eaten whole, and they make for a killer sandwich.

MAKE THE SAUCE

In a small bowl, combine the mayonnaise, onion, pickle, capers, chives, Old Bay, lemon juice, and hot pepper sauce. Set aside.

COOK THE CRABS

1. In a wide, shallow bowl, combine the flour, cornmeal, salt, and pepper. Dredge the crabs to coat on both sides (if the top shells are thicker than a piece of paper, pull them off before dredging).

2. Heat the oil in a 12-inch skillet (preferably cast iron) over medium-high heat until shimmering hot. Add the butter to the skillet and swirl the pan to melt it. Add the crabs top side down and cook, shaking the pan once or twice, until crisp and browned, about 3 minutes. The crabs may pop and splatter, so be careful. Flip the crabs and cook until crisp and just cooked through (an instant-read thermometer inserted in the center of the crab should read 145°F), about 3 minutes more. Transfer the crabs to a large paper-towel-lined plate.

ASSEMBLE THE SANDWICHES

Spread the tartar sauce on the 8 slices of toast. Top 4 of the toast slices, sauce side up, with a piece of lettuce and 1 or 2 slices of tomato. Put one crab on each sandwich, top with the remaining toast, sauce side down, and serve. —*Denise Mickelsen*

PER SERVING: 600 CALORIES | 34G PROTEIN | 35G CARB | 35G TOTAL FAT | 6G SAT FAT | 11G MONO FAT | 15G POLY FAT | 115MG CHOL | 1,380MG SODIUM | 2G FIBER

how to clean a soft-shell crab

Whenever possible, soft-shell crabs should be purchased alive so they're at their freshest. Store live soft-shells uncovered in the fridge on ice for no more than 1 day.

Rinse the crab under cold running water.

Using a pair of poultry shears, quickly cut off the front of the crab about ¼ inch behind the eyes. This kills the crab.

Lift up the tapered points on each side of the top shell to reveal the gills. Pull out and discard them.

Turn the crab over and pull off the bottom part of the shell, called the apron.

chopped steak sandwiches

SERVES 4

- 2 Tbs. ketchup
- 1 Tbs. Dijon mustard
- 1 jarred hot cherry pepper, stemmed, seeded, and chopped
- 1 tsp. red-wine vinegar
- 1 lb. beef sirloin tips (flap meat), cut into 1-inch pieces
- 1 tsp. kosher salt
- ½ tsp. freshly ground black pepper
- 3 Tbs. olive oil
- 1 small yellow onion, halved and thinly sliced
- 6 oz. sliced white mushrooms (2 cups)
- 1½ cups shredded sharp Cheddar
- 4 long rolls, split and lightly toasted
- 1½ oz. baby arugula

The steak is "chopped" by pulsing it quickly in a food processor into tender little pieces.

1. Mix the ketchup, mustard, cherry pepper, and vinegar in a small bowl and set aside.

2. In a food processor, pulse half of the beef until just coarsely chopped. Transfer to a bowl. Repeat with the remaining beef. Toss the beef with ½ tsp. salt and the pepper.

3. Heat 1½ Tbs. of the oil in a 12-inch, heavy skillet over medium-high heat until shimmering hot. Add the beef and cook, stirring occasionally, until it loses most of its raw color, about 3 minutes. Transfer to a plate. Heat the remaining 1½ Tbs. oil in the pan. Add the onion and ¼ tsp. salt; cook, stirring often, until beginning to soften and brown, about 4 minutes. Add the mushrooms and ¼ tsp. salt; cook, stirring often, until they soften and begin to release their juice, about 2 minutes. Add the ketchup mixture and beef and any accumulated juices. Cook, stirring often, until heated through, about 2 minutes. Stir in the cheese until melted, about 1 minute more.

4. Split the rolls almost through lengthwise and pile on the steak and arugula. Cut the sandwiches in half and serve. *—Tony Rosenfeld*

PER SERVING: 830 CALORIES | 47G PROTEIN | 75G CARB | 37G TOTAL FAT | 14G SAT FAT | 17G MONO FAT | 3G POLY FAT | 100MG CHOL | 1,610MG SODIUM | 5G FIBER

crispy catfish po' boys

SERVES 4

- 3 cups coleslaw mix
- ¼ cup mayonnaise
- 1 Tbs. cider vinegar
- 2 tsp. granulated sugar
- 1 tsp. celery seed
- 2 large eggs
- ¾ cup yellow cornmeal
- 1¼ tsp. kosher salt
- ½ tsp. freshly ground black pepper
- 4 4- to 5-oz. catfish fillets
- 4 long soft-crust Italian rolls, split
- 1¾ cups canola oil
- 8 sandwich-style dill pickle slices

Topped with creamy coleslaw and pickles, this rendition of the classic New Orleans sandwich makes a satisfying dinner.

1. Position a rack 6 inches from the broiler and heat the broiler on high.

2. Combine the coleslaw mix, mayonnaise, vinegar, sugar, and celery seed in a medium bowl; set aside.

3. Beat the eggs in a wide shallow bowl until well mixed. In another wide shallow bowl, combine the cornmeal, ¾ tsp. salt, and ¼ tsp. pepper. Season the fish all over with ½ tsp. salt and ¼ tsp. pepper. Dip a fillet in the egg to coat, shake off the excess, and then dredge it in the cornmeal mixture, again shaking off the excess. Repeat with remaining fillets.

4. Arrange the rolls cut sides up on a baking sheet and toast until golden brown, 30 seconds. Remove from the oven and turn off the broiler.

5. Heat the oil in a 10-inch skillet over medium heat. Working in batches if necessary, cook the fillets, turning once, until the coating is golden and crisp and the fish is cooked through, 4 to 5 minutes per side. Transfer the fillets to a clean baking sheet lined with paper towels and keep warm in the oven.

6. To assemble, arrange 2 pickle slices on the bottom half of each roll. Top each with a fillet, a quarter of the coleslaw, and the other half of the roll. Cut the po' boys in half and serve. *—David Bonom*

PER SERVING: 810 CALORIES | 35G PROTEIN | 86G CARB | 36G TOTAL FAT | 5G SAT FAT | 17G MONO FAT | 12G POLY FAT | 110MG CHOL | 1,360MG SODIUM | 6G FIBER

smoky grilled meatball subs

SERVES 4

- 5 6-inch soft sub rolls
- 1 lb. ground pork
- 1 large egg, lightly beaten
- 2 large cloves garlic, minced
- 2 tsp. finely grated lemon zest
- 2 tsp. chopped fresh thyme
- 1 tsp. smoked sweet paprika
- 1¼ tsp. kosher salt
- ½ tsp. freshly ground black pepper
- 2 Tbs. extra-virgin olive oil; more for the grill
- 1 medium tomato (8 oz.), halved crosswise
- 2 jarred piquillo peppers
- ½ tsp. crushed red pepper flakes
- 1 oz. finely grated manchego (about 1 cup)

The pork meatballs in these saucy sandwiches get a double dose of smoky flavor: first from smoked paprika and then from the grill. Sweet, fire-roasted chiles and grilled tomatoes form the base for a delicious sauce.

1. Prepare a medium-high gas or charcoal grill fire.

2. Tear half of one roll into ¼-inch pieces and put in a small bowl. Add ¼ cup water and let sit until the bread has absorbed the water, about 5 minutes. Gently squeeze the bread to remove excess water and finely chop the soaked bread (you should have about ¼ cup).

3. In a large bowl, break up the pork with your hands. Add the soaked bread, egg, garlic, lemon zest, thyme, smoked paprika, salt, and pepper. Use your hands to gently combine the mixture. Shape into 16 meatballs (each about 1½ inches).

4. Split the remaining rolls, but don't cut them completely in half. Brush the insides of the rolls with 1 Tbs. of the olive oil. Brush the cut side of the tomato and the meatballs with the remaining olive oil.

5. Oil the grill grate and grill the tomato until softened and lightly browned, turning once, 4 to 6 minutes. Grill the bread split side down until golden and lightly charred on the edges, 1 to 3 minutes. Grill the meatballs until they're just cooked through, turning once, about 8 minutes. Remove each item as it finishes cooking and set aside.

6. In a food processor, purée the grilled tomato, piquillo peppers, and red pepper flakes. Season to taste with salt.

7. Put 4 meatballs in each roll and top with one-quarter of the sauce and one-quarter of the cheese. Serve hot. —*Samantha Seneviratne*

PER SERVING: 500 CALORIES | 34G PROTEIN | 40G CARB | 24G TOTAL FAT | 8G SAT FAT | 11G MONO FAT | 2.5G POLY FAT | 135MG CHOL | 930MG SODIUM | 2G FIBER

Piquillo peppers are fire-roasted sweet chiles from northern Spain. Look for them in the grocery store near the roasted red peppers. If unavailable, use one large, jarred roasted red pepper instead.

turkey and corn quesadillas with guacamole

SERVES 4

- 2 medium ripe avocados
- ¼ cup finely chopped red onion
- 1 medium lime, one half juiced and the other cut into wedges
- 1 serrano chile, seeded and minced
-   Kosher salt
- ½ tsp. freshly ground black pepper
- 4 cups shredded roast turkey or chicken
- 2 cups fresh corn kernels, blanched, or frozen corn, cooked according to package directions and drained
- ½ cup packed coarsely chopped fresh cilantro
- 8 7-inch flour tortillas
- 2 cups (5 oz.) grated pepper jack cheese
- 2 Tbs. canola oil

These quesadillas make great use of leftover turkey. Serve them with a mango and jícama salad.

1. Position a rack in the center of the oven and heat the oven to 200°F.

2. Halve and pit the avocados. Scoop the flesh into a medium bowl and mash with a potato masher. Stir in the onion, 1 Tbs. of the lime juice, the chile, ½ tsp. salt, and the pepper. Season to taste with more salt and lime juice. Put a piece of plastic wrap directly on the surface of the guacamole to prevent browning.

3. In a large bowl, toss the turkey, corn, and cilantro with 1 tsp. salt. Top half of each tortilla with one-eighth of the filling mixture and ¼ cup of the cheese. Fold the uncovered half of each tortilla over the filling.

4. Heat 1½ tsp. of the oil in a large nonstick skillet over medium heat. Add 2 of the quesadillas to the pan and weigh down with a lid. Cook until golden brown and a bit crisp, 2 to 3 minutes. With a spatula, carefully flip each quesadilla and cook until golden brown and the cheese has melted, about 2 minutes more. Transfer the quesadillas to a baking sheet and put in the oven.

5. Wipe out the pan. Repeat, cooking the remaining quesadillas in 3 more batches, using 1½ tsp. oil for each batch.

6. Cut the quesadillas into wedges and serve with the guacamole and lime wedges on the side. —*Dina Cheney*

PER SERVING: 510 CALORIES | 30G PROTEIN | 39G CARB | 27G TOTAL FAT | 7G SAT FAT | 11G MONO FAT | 4.5G POLY FAT | 75MG CHOL | 600MG SODIUM | 6G FIBER

garlic-rubbed grilled cheese with prosciutto and tomatoes

SERVES 4

- **3 oz. grated aged Gruyère (1¼ cups)**
- **3 oz. grated Fontina (about 1 cup)**
- **2 Tbs. finely grated Parmigiano-Reggiano**
- **¼ tsp. crushed red pepper flakes (or to taste)**
- **8 ½-inch-thick slices rustic Italian bread**
- **4 very thin slices prosciutto, halved crosswise**
- **2 medium ripe tomatoes, cut into ¼-inch-thick slices**
- **Kosher salt**
- **1 oz. (2 Tbs.) salted butter, at room temperature**
- **1 to 2 large cloves garlic, halved and peeled for rubbing**

> Rubbing grilled or toasted bread with the cut side of a raw garlic clove is an easy way to add a hint of garlic flavor.

Three kinds of cheese, salty prosciutto, fresh tomatoes, and a touch of spice make this anything but your everyday grilled cheese sandwich. Serve with a lightly dressed green salad.

1. Lightly toss the cheeses and red pepper flakes in a small bowl. Put 4 slices of the bread on a work surface and evenly distribute half of the cheese mixture on top. Put 2 pieces of prosciutto (1 full slice) on each sandwich and top with 2 to 3 slices of tomato—enough to cover the cheese and prosciutto in a single layer. Season the tomatoes with salt and sprinkle the remaining cheese on top. Lightly butter one side of the remaining bread slices and place them butter side up on the sandwiches.

2. Heat a griddle or a large skillet over medium-low heat. Arrange the sandwiches butter side down on the griddle and cook until the bread is toasted and golden brown, about 2 minutes. Meanwhile, spread an even layer of butter on the top slice of bread.

3. Using a spatula, flip the sandwiches and cook until golden brown on the other side, gently pressing the sandwiches with the back of the spatula to compress, about 2 minutes. Remove the sandwiches from the griddle and lightly rub both sides of each with the cut side of the garlic. Using a serrated knife, slice the sandwiches in half and serve immediately. *—Tasha DeSerio*

PER SERVING: 380 CALORIES | 20G PROTEIN | 23G CARB | 23G TOTAL FAT | 13G SAT FAT | 7G MONO FAT | 1.5G POLY FAT | 80MG CHOL | 1,140MG SODIUM | 2G FIBER

More about Prosciutto

Prosciutto is a hindquarter cut of pork that's cured, dried, and aged. The best ones are slightly sweet with just the right degree of saltiness and a silken texture. Traditionally the best prosciutto is from Italy; if the prosciutto is to be cooked, consider using a lesser grade.

Thin-sliced jambon from Spain or other hams can make a good substitution, especially in cooked dishes. Just watch for salt content as good prosciutto is not overly salty.

When sliced, prosciutto is layered between pieces of butcher paper; store it that way, too, in the refrigerator, where it will keep for a week or more. Cryovaced prosciutto, unopened, will last longer.

lamb and sweet onion pitas with orange-cucumber salad

SERVES 4

2½   Tbs. extra-virgin olive oil

1   medium sweet onion, halved lengthwise and sliced ¼ inch thick

Kosher salt and freshly ground black pepper

1   lb. ground lamb

½   tsp. ground cinnamon

2   large oranges

1   small English cucumber, halved lengthwise and thinly sliced

2   Tbs. red-wine vinegar

1   Tbs. coarsely chopped fresh mint

2   pitas, halved and very lightly toasted

⅓   cup plain Greek yogurt

Ground lamb is often a bargain buy. Here, it's put to delicious use in an all-in-one meal of stuffed pita sandwiches and a bright, citrusy salad.

1. Heat 1½ Tbs. of the oil in a 12-inch skillet over medium heat. Add about three-quarters of the onion, ½ tsp. salt, and ⅛ tsp. pepper and cook, stirring occasionally, until golden brown, 8 to 10 minutes. With a slotted spoon, transfer the onion to a small bowl; set aside.

2. Cook the lamb, cinnamon, ¾ tsp. salt, and ¼ tsp. pepper in the skillet over medium-high heat, stirring occasionally and breaking up the meat, until cooked through, 5 to 7 minutes; drain well.

3. Meanwhile, finely chop the remaining raw onion and transfer to a large bowl. Cut the peels and pith from the oranges. Working over a bowl to collect the juice, cut the orange segments free from the membranes. Cut the segments into chunks. Add the oranges, orange juice, cucumber, vinegar, mint, and the remaining 1 Tbs. oil to the chopped raw onion; toss to combine. Season to taste with salt and pepper.

4. Fill the pitas with the lamb and cooked onion. Add some of the orange-cucumber salad and a dollop of yogurt. Serve the remaining salad on the side.   —*Liz Pearson*

PER SERVING: 470 CALORIES | 25G PROTEIN | 33G CARB | 26G TOTAL FAT | 9G SAT FAT | 13G MONO FAT | 2G POLY FAT | 80MG CHOL | 580MG SODIUM | 4G FIBER

niçoise tuna melts

SERVES 2

- **1** **5-oz. can water-packed tuna, well drained**
- **¼** **cup small-diced tomato**
- **2** **Tbs. minced red onion**
- **1** **Tbs. chopped Kalamata olives**
- **1** **Tbs. chopped fresh dill**
- **1½** **tsp. red-wine vinegar**
- **1** **tsp. extra-virgin olive oil**
- **1** **small anchovy, minced (about ½ tsp.)**
- **¼** **tsp. kosher salt**
- **Freshly ground black pepper**
- **2** **slices artisanal boule-type bread (about 5x3 inches, ½ inch thick)**
- **3** **oz. (1 cup) finely grated Comté, Emmentaler, or Gruyère**

This open-face sandwich is an inspired cross between a classic tuna melt and a Niçoise salad. A boule—a round loaf of crusty white bread—makes a sturdy base for the sandwich. Don't skip the anchovy; it adds a subtle depth of flavor.

1. Position a rack 4 inches from the broiler element and heat the broiler on high.

2. In a medium bowl, combine the tuna, tomato, red onion, olives, dill, vinegar, olive oil, anchovy, ¼ tsp. salt, and a few grinds of pepper.

3. Put the bread on a rimmed baking sheet and broil until nicely toasted, 30 seconds to 1 minute. Remove the pan from the broiler, flip the bread over, and spread the tuna mixture evenly over each slice. Sprinkle the cheese evenly over the tuna and continue to broil until the cheese is melted and beginning to brown, 1 to 2 minutes. Serve.
—Dabney Gough

PER SERVING: 470 CALORIES | 40G PROTEIN | 23G CARB | 23G TOTAL FAT | 10G SAT FAT | 8G MONO FAT | 2.5G POLY FAT | 95MG CHOL | 1,660MG SODIUM | 3G FIBER

open-face grilled eggplant sandwiches with olive-walnut relish

SERVES 4

- 3 Tbs. extra-virgin olive oil; more for brushing
- 2 Tbs. minced fresh mint, plus small leaves for garnish
- 2 Tbs. minced shallot
- 1 Tbs. balsamic vinegar
- ⅓ cup pitted Kalamata olives, finely chopped
- 2 Tbs. toasted walnuts, finely chopped
- 1 to 1¼ lb. globe eggplant (2 small or 1 slender large), peeled if you like, trimmed, and cut into ½-inch-thick rounds
- 4 ½- to ¾-inch-thick slices crusty, artisan-style white bread

  Kosher salt and freshly ground black pepper
- 1 oz. mixed baby greens
- 1 8-oz. package burrata (or fresh mozzarella), drained

The succulent texture and nutty flavor of grilled eggplant is complemented here by burrata, a rich cream-filled mozzarella that's a must-try.

1. Prepare a medium-high gas or charcoal grill fire.

2. In a small bowl, combine the oil, mint, shallot, and vinegar. In another small bowl, combine the olives and walnuts. Beat the vinaigrette with a fork to blend, and then mix 2 tsp. into the olive mixture.

3. Arrange the eggplant and bread on a rimmed baking sheet. Brush the eggplant on both sides with olive oil and sprinkle with salt and pepper. Brush the bread slices on one side with oil, and sprinkle with salt and pepper.

4. Grill the eggplant, covered, until tender, about 3 minutes per side. Transfer to a plate. Grill the bread, covered, until toasted, 1 to 2 minutes per side.

5. Arrange the grilled bread on a cutting board, oiled side up. Top each slice with some of the mixed greens. Arrange the eggplant rounds atop the greens. Beat the vinaigrette with a fork to blend, and then spoon about 1 tsp. over each round. Slice the burrata about ½ inch thick and arrange over the eggplant. Sprinkle lightly with salt and spoon about 1 tsp. of the olive relish over each burrata slice. Cut the sandwiches in half and transfer to plates. Garnish with small mint leaves and serve. —*Kristine Kidd*

PER SERVING: 380 CALORIES | 5G PROTEIN | 28G CARB | 23G TOTAL FAT | 9G SAT FAT | 10G MONO FAT | 2G POLY FAT | 45MG CHOL | 440MG SODIUM | 6G FIBER

METRIC EQUIVALENTS

LIQUID/DRY MEASURES	
U.S.	METRIC
¼ teaspoon	1.25 milliliters
½ teaspoon	2.5 milliliters
1 teaspoon	5 milliliters
1 tablespoon (3 teaspoons)	15 milliliters
1 fluid ounce (2 tablespoons)	30 milliliters
¼ cup	60 milliliters
⅓ cup	80 milliliters
½ cup	120 milliliters
1 cup	240 milliliters
1 pint (2 cups)	480 milliliters
1 quart (4 cups; 32 ounces)	960 milliliters
1 gallon (4 quarts)	3.84 liters
1 ounce (by weight)	28 grams
1 pound	454 grams
2.2 pounds	1 kilogram

OVEN TEMPERATURES		
°F	GAS MARK	°C
250	½	120
275	1	140
300	2	150
325	3	165
350	4	180
375	5	190
400	6	200
425	7	220
450	8	230
475	9	240
500	10	260
550	Broil	290

CONTRIBUTORS

Bruce Aidells is the author of 10 cookbooks, including *The Complete Meat Cookbook*.

Pam Anderson is a contributing editor to *Fine Cooking* and the author several books, including *Perfect One-Dish Dinners*. She blogs about food and life with daughters Maggy and Sharon on their website, www.threemanycooks.com.

Jennifer Armentrout is editor in chief of *Fine Cooking*.

John Ash is the founder and chef of John Ash & Co., in Santa Rosa, California. He teaches at the Culinary Institute of America at Greystone and is an award-winning cookbook author. His latest, *John Ash: Cooking One on One*, won a James Beard award.

Jessica Bard is a food stylist, food writer, and recipe tester who teaches cooking classes at Warren Kitchen and Cutlery in Rhinebeck, New York.

David Bonom is a food writer in New Jersey.

Lauren Chattman has written 12 cookbooks. Her latest are *Simply Great Breads* and *Cookie Swap*.

Dina Cheney is the author of *Tasting Club, Williams-Sonoma: New Flavors for Salads*, and a forthcoming slow cooker cookbook. She has been the "Taste Test" columnist for *Everyday with Rachael Ray* for over two years.

Robert Danhi runs Chef Danhi & Co., a food consulting firm based in Los Angeles. He is the author of *Southeast Asian Flavors*.

Tasha DeSerio is a caterer, cooking teacher, and food writer. Her latest book is *Salad for Dinner*.

Tom Douglas has been featured by the media as the Seattle chef who has helped to define the Northwest Style. He was awarded the James Beard Award for Best Northwest Chef in 1994.

Maryellen Driscoll is a *Fine Cooking* contributing editor. She and her husband own Free Bird Farm in upstate New York.

Melissa Gaman is a recipe developer and food stylist in the New York City area.

Dabney Gough is a frequent contributor to FineCooking.com and a former recipe tester for the magazine.

Julianna Grimes is a recipe developer and food writer.

Alex Guarnaschelli is a New York chef and the host of Food Network's "Alex's Day Off" and "The Cooking Loft."

Martha Holmberg is the former editor in chief of *Fine Cooking* and a food writer and cookbook author.

Jill Silverman Hough is a cookbook author, food writer, recipe developer, and culinary instructor from Napa, California. Her first cookbook is *100 Perfect Pairings: Small Plates to Enjoy with Wines You Love*.

Sara Jenkins is co-author of *Olives and Oranges: Recipes and Flavor Secrets from Italy, Spain, Cyprus, and Beyond*. She is the owner of Porchetta, a takeout restaurant in New York City.

Elizabeth Karmel is a nationally known grilling and barbecue expert and cookbook author and teacher. Her latest book is *Soaked, Slathered, and Seasoned*.

Jeanne Kelley is a food writer, recipe developer, and food stylist based in Los Angeles, California. She is also the author of *Blue Eggs and Yellow Tomatoes*.

Kristine Kidd is a food writer, culinary educator, and former food editor for *Bon Appétit* magazine. She is the author of *Weeknight Fresh & Fast*.

Allison Ehri Kreitler is a *Fine Cooking* contributing editor. She has also worked as a freelance food stylist, recipe tester and developer, and writer for several national food magazines and the Food Network.

Lori Longbotham is a recipe developer and cookbook author whose books include *Luscious Coconut Desserts* and *Luscious Creamy Desserts*.

Ivy Manning is a cooking teacher, food writer, and cookbook author; her most recent book is *The Farm to Table Cookbook*.

Domenica Marchetti is a food writer and cooking instructor who focuses on contemporary Italian home cooking. She is the author of *The Glorious Soups and Stews of Italy* and *Big Night In*.

Perla Meyers teaches cooking at workshops around the country and has cooked in restaurants throughout Italy, France, and Spain.

Denise Mickelsen is a senior editor of *Fine Cooking*.

Susie Middleton is the former editor and current editor at large for *Fine Cooking*. She is also consulting editor, writer, and photographer for *Edible Vineyard* magazine, as well as a cookbook author.

Liz Pearson is a food writer and recipe developer based in Austin, Texas.

Melissa Pellegrino is a former assistant food editor at *Fine Cooking* and author of *The Italian Farmer's Table*.

Laraine Perri is a writer based in New York City.

Joanna Pruess is a food and travel writer and a consultant to the food industry. She is the author of nine cookbooks including *Seduced by Bacon* and most recently *Griswold & WagnerWare Cast-Iron Cookbook*.

Adam Ried is a cooking columnist, cookbook author, recipe developer, and tester of all things kitchen-related. His latest book, *Thoroughly Modern Milkshakes*, came out in the summer of 2009.

Julissa Roberts is assistant food editor for *Fine Cooking* magazine.

Tony Rosenfeld, a *Fine Cooking* contributing editor, is also a food writer and restaurant owner in the Boston area. His second cookbook, *Sear, Sauce, and Serve*, was published in spring 2011.

Samantha Seneviratne is a former associate food editor and food stylist at *Fine Cooking*.

Maria Helm Sinskey is a noted chef, cookbook author, and culinary director at her family's winery, Robert Sinskey Vineyards, in Napa Valley, California. Her most recent book, *Family Meals,* was a 2010 IACP Cookbook Award winner.

Joanne McAllister Smart has co-authored two Italian cookbooks with Scott Conant and *Bistro Cooking at Home* with Gordon Hamersley.

Adeena Sussman is a food writer, recipe developer, chef, and cooking instructor based in New York City.

Anna Thomas is a food writer and author of *The Vegetarian Epicure*. Her cookbook *Love Soup,* won the James Beard Foundation Book of the Year, Healthy Focus award in 2010.

Sue Torres is the chef at Suenos and Los Dados, both in New York City.

Annie Wayte is the former executive chef of Nicole's and 202 in New York City. Her first cookbook is *Keep It Seasonal: Soups, Salads, and Sandwiches*.

Bruce Weinstein and **Mark Scarbrough** are the award-winning authors of 19 cookbooks, contributing editors to *Eating Well,* and columnists for www.weight watchers.com.

Jay Weinstein is a New York City–based food writer and former chef. His latest book is *The Ethical Gourmet*.

Shelley Wiseman is a senior food editor of *Fine Cooking* as well as a chef and author of *Just Tacos*. She co-authored *The Mexican Gourmet*, which was nominated for a Julia Child cookbook award.

Dawn Yanagihara is a former editor at *Cook's Illustrated*.

INDEX

Numbers in **bold** indicate pages with photographs

If you like this cookbook then you'll love everything about *Fine Cooking* magazine

Fine Cooking magazine is the choice for people who love to cook. And there's even more beyond our award-winning pages: With our apps, e-newsletters, interactive web tools, and online recipe search, we're ready to help you cook great food every day.

Discover all that *Fine Cooking* has to offer.

Subscribe today at
FineCooking.com/more